T0323855

The Origins of Capitalism as a Social System

Economists, historians and social scientists have offered a variety of conflicting answers to the issue of the beginnings of capitalism, and these deviating answers imply different conceptualizations of what capitalism actually is. This book provides a simultaneous inquiry into the origins of capitalism as well as provides a theoretical treatise on capitalism.

The Origins of Capitalism as a Social System explores the line between what is and is not capitalism, (re)producing a theory of capitalism as a system of class domination and exploitation. Part I focuses on the monetary theory of value and capital developed by Karl Marx, while at the same time critically reviews an array of economic and historical literature, both Marxist and non-Marxist. Following this, Part II expounds the first emergence of capitalism in Venice. It highlights the historical contingencies that made capitalism in the Venetian society possible, as well as the structural elements of the capitalist system and their interconnectedness. Finally, Part III discusses the capitalist character of the Venetian social formation from the end of the fourteenth century until the fall of the republic to Napoleon in 1797. As part of this, the author investigates the significance of forms of governmentality beyond national cohesion and territorialization.

Of great interest to economists, historians and both undergraduate and postgraduate students, this book gives special emphasis to a critical evaluation of the tensions and controversies among historians, economists and other social scientists with regard to the character and role that money and trade played in societies and economies.

John Milios is Professor of Political Economy and the History of Economic Thought at the National Technical University of Athens (NTUA), Greece. He is also Director of the quarterly journal of economic and political theory, *Theseis* (published since 1982 in Greek).

In this grand style reconstruction of the genesis of capitalism, Milios brings together Marx, Braudel, Weber, Lenin, and his own analysis of 'money-begetting' modes of production, under the aegis of the Althusserian 'aleatory encounter' of social forces. In a path-breaking concrete analysis, he invents the Venetian Paradigm of *decalage* between financialization and proletarianization. It is impressive, convincing, and surprisingly actual.

Etienne Balibar,
co-author of *Reading Capital*

The publication of this book is a rather significant moment in the history of reflections on capitalism, and moreover a turning point in the history of the transformative present. Raising yet once again the question of what capitalism as a system actually is, John Milios reassembles his subject of study, traversing centuries and places in history so as to identify and discern heterogeneous practices being objectivised – or not – in the name of capitalism, ultimately establishing a genealogy of a 'capitalist state, beyond national territorialisation'. This book, or shall we dare say this 'machine-book', offers the bizarre completeness one might feel when reading an important book: full and empty at the same time.

Marios Emmanouilidis,
Independent researcher

A fascinating book that provides us with an exciting new perspective on the origins of capitalism. John Milios asks more precisely than usual what distinguishes capitalism *as a social system* from precapitalist societies. Taking seriously that the origin of capitalism is a singular process, he avoids any deterministic approach to analyzing history. The – historically surprising – ascent of Venice as a leading commercial and colonial power during the 13th and 14th centuries, with its rather special form of original accumulation towards the end of the 14th century, is demonstrated to be a capitalist social formation which practically introduced capitalism to Western Europe. This book really provides us with a fundamental and exciting new turn in the long-lasting discussion about the origins of capitalism.

Michael Heinrich,
Author of *An Introduction to the three Volumes of Karl Marx's* Capital

Routledge Frontiers of Political Economy

The Origins of Capitalism as a Social System

as a Social System

The Prevalence of an Aleatory Encounter

John Milios

Routledge
Taylor & Francis Group

LONDON AND NEW YORK

First published 2018 by Routledge

2 Park Square, Milton Park, Abingdon, Oxfordshire OX14 4RN
52 Vanderbilt Avenue, New York, NY 10017

Routledge is an imprint of the Taylor & Francis Group, an informa business

First issued in paperback 2019

British Library Cataloguing-in-Publication Data
A catalogue record for this book is available from the British Library

Library of Congress Cataloging-in-Publication Data
A catalog record has been requested for this book

ISBN: 978-1-138-03670-3 (hbk)
ISBN: 978-0-367-89467-2 (pbk)

Typeset in Bembo
by codeMantra

Contents

Acknowledgements

I would like to thank Paul Auerbach (Kingston University, London), Dimitri Dimoulis (Escola de direito de São Paulo da Fundação Getúlio Vargas, Brazil), Vassilis Droucopoulos (University of Athens), George Economakis (University of Patras), Marios Emmanouilidis (Independent Researcher, Thessaloniki), Dimitris Kyrtatas (University of Thessaly) and Dimitris P. Sotiropoulos (The Open University, UK) for having read drafts of the book and providing me with valuable observations that helped me to improve the quality of my work.

I am also indebted to several people at the international conference "150 Years ~ Karl Marx's *Capital*: Reflections for the 21st Century" (Athens, 14–15 January 2017) who, during discussions of my theses on Marx's notion of 'original accumulation' and the pre-capitalist money-owner, raised questions that assisted in the development of my arguments while the book was still in the making.

A special mention is also owed to Barbara Santos for her valuable suggestions and for having improved the style of the manuscript.

Introduction

When did capitalism start? Economists, historians and social scientists have provided a wide variety of conflicting answers to this simple question. Let me mention only a few examples.

According to the leading twentieth-century economist John Maynard Keynes (1883–1946), capitalism was born in ancient Babylonia and thereafter was adopted by, or adapted to, ancient Greece and Rome, only to be later inherited by Western Europe (Keynes 2013). Prominent academic historians like Lujo Brentano (1844–1931), member of the so-called 'German Historical School', or Patricia Crone, of Princeton University (1945–2015), shared similar views (see Chapter 6).

According to Max Weber (1864–1920), who is often referred to as a 'founding father' of sociology and responsible for the Weberian theoretical tradition that followed, *modern* capitalism emerged from and was shaped in accordance with a spirit of abstinence introduced in Western societies by Calvinism, following the Reformation, which henceforth functioned as the 'spirit of capitalism' (Weber 2001; see also Chapter 6).

According to an enduring Marxist tradition, introduced shortly after the Second World War by the distinguished British economist Maurice Dobb (1900–1974) of Cambridge University, capitalism was first born in the agrarian sector of England in the late sixteenth and seventeenth centuries through the transformation of existing production assets from the feudal to the capitalist ownership form (see Chapter 5).

However, there have been totally divergent Marxist views as to whether agriculture was the focal point of capitalism's rise.

Karl Kautsky (1854–1938), probably the most influential Marxist at the turn of the nineteenth to the twentieth century, wrote in *The Agrarian Question* (first published in 1899), a book celebrated by V. I. Lenin as "the most important event in present-day economic literature since the third volume of *Capital*" (Lenin 1977, Vol. 4: 94), that capitalism, even if it succeeds in conquering the countryside (which was not the case in most capitalist countries), does so only after it has been established in the city: "capitalist agriculture only began to become significant once urban capital, and hence the credit system, had become well developed" (Kautsky 1988: 88; see also Chapter 4).

More recently, Oliver Cromwell Cox (1901–1974), a distinguished social scientist from Lincoln University of Missouri and inspired by Marxist theory, argued that it was not England, but "Venice, which nurtured the first capitalist society" (Cox 1964: xi) centuries before it conquered England. The eminent Marxist economist Ernest Mandel (1923–1995) also stressed the significance of "the accumulation of money capital by the Italian merchants who dominated European economic life from the eleventh to the fifteenth centuries" (Mandel 1968: 103) as a factor in the emergence of capitalism.

The famous French historian Fernand Braudel (1902–1985), a leading figure of the second generation of the 'Annales School', reached similar conclusions in regard to the origins of capitalism. He argued that capitalism first emerged as early as the thirteenth century, when "both Genoa and Venice" were "merchant and colonial powers (and the *colonial* tells us that they had already reached an advanced stage of capitalism)" (Braudel 1984: 118; see Chapter 11).

How can one explain such divergence of views as to when (and how) capitalism was born? How is it that theoreticians belonging to the same school of thought, as, for example, Marxism, reach totally conflicting conclusions?

This question, which has bothered me for quite some time as both a social scientist and a Marxist, seems easier to answer if one contemplates the issue of origins, or genesis, as follows: What was it that actually originated or was born? In other words, what is capitalism, whose genesis can be traced as a social process in history? Obviously, capitalism is a specific social structure, or equivalently, a social system, a historically unique configuration of social relations, which, according to the Marxist point of view, is built upon specific forms of class domination and exploitation.

At first glance, capitalism is a completely comprehensible term for Marxists (a system of exploitation of wage labour by capital), but to a great extent also for non-Marxists (the 'free market' economic system). However, what seems obvious at first glance is not at all obvious if one penetrates deeper into the constituent elements of the system under investigation and their forms of interconnectedness. Analyses on the 'beginning' or 'birth' of capitalism bring to the fore the divergent understandings of what features and social relations constitute the sine qua non of the capitalist system, with issues of money, trade and finance always dividing Marxist (and non-Marxist) social scientists, economists and historians.

It becomes clear that the differing approaches to the issue of the beginnings of capitalism denote, or rather imply, different conceptualizations of what capitalism actually is. This is because the theory of a system (or a structure) is the indispensable presupposition for one to comprehend when and how (i.e. through which processes) this system (or structure) was first formed – as a unique social system (structure) possessing specific differences from the systems that preceded or coexisted with it.

We may therefore conclude that (i) we need a theory of capitalism as a social system in order to be able to understand when and how capitalism *emerged* and that (ii) the broad divergence of opinions regarding the origins of capitalism reveals an equally broad divergence of opinions as to what capitalism as a system actually *is*.

Besides, what came to be was not *destined* to be. *First*, as Marcus Rediker of the University of Pittsburgh remarked nearly thirty years ago, "capitalism 'arrived in some parts of the production process much earlier than in others'" (Rediker 1989: 341). In other words, the emergence of capitalism was initially a singular historical process that subsequently played a catalytic role in the spread of capitalist social relations in other territories. If one does not accept the singularity of the process of the genesis of capitalism, then it is assumed as if he/she accepts "that modes of production burst upon the historical scene Minerva-like, fully-formed" (Rediker op.cit.). *Second*, a singular process is always bound to a set of contingencies, i.e. it is by definition an aleatory process. According to Marxist theory, which provides *the* scientific investigation of social evolution, opposing trends and tendencies towards alternative paths of evolution can be traced to nearly all conjunctures of historic significance, reflecting in each and every case the dynamics of a particular balance of class forces. An assortment of eventualities of historical evolution is therefore repeatedly formed, and is not an 'iron necessity' of a predestined path of historical continuity or change. A scientific study of history refers precisely to the uncovering of these potentials and eventualities, and the understanding of the *specific conditions* that favoured the ultimate prevalence of a specific trend, which then materialized as a 'historical event'.

The two epistemological premises stated above imply that the study of the first traces of capitalism, or of its later dissemination in a social formation or territory, presupposes, on the one hand, a theory of capitalism as a system, and, on the other, a concrete analysis of the concrete situation under investigation; as György Lukács wrote, *"the concrete analysis of the concrete situation [...] is the culmination of all genuine theory,* its consummation" (Lukács 2009: 41–42).

The present book, being an inquiry into the origins of capitalism, is simultaneously a theoretical treatise on capitalism. The whole analysis has Karl Marx's theory as a point of departure, especially as developed in *Capital* and his other mature texts in the period between 1857 and 1881. As already stated, by endeavouring an investigation of the origins of capitalism, my analysis focuses on the demarcation line between what is and what is not capitalism, and in this sense presupposes, but also (re)produces, a theory of capitalism as a system of class domination and exploitation, and its structural characteristics.

The book contains three parts.

Part I focuses on the monetary theory of value and capital developed by Marx, at the same time critically reviewing an array of economic and historical literature, Marxist and non-Marxist. On this basis, it also illuminates historical forms of pre-capitalist money-begetting production and finance, which are often confused with capitalism. The book thus investigates the extent to which these money-begetting production forms facilitated the emergence of capitalism or coexisted with it. Part I comprises seven chapters.

Chapter 1 highlights the fundamental characteristics that, in their inter-connectedness, distinguish capitalism from all other social systems: (i) wage labour, (ii) monetization of the whole economy (money-begetting money), (iii) concentration of the means of production and dissociation of the capi-talist from the labour process as such, (iv) free competition and the fusion of individual capitals into aggregate-social capital, (v) the financial mode of existence of capital and (vi) the formation of a specific juridical–political–ideological structure and a corresponding state form.

Chapter 2 deals with Marx's own contradictions in regard to the genesis of capitalism. Furthermore, the controversies and polemics among Marxists around the two, albeit contradictory, theoretical schemes that Marx himself formulated in his writings are discussed: on the one hand, the 'production forces – relations of production dialectic' and on the other, the 'so-called original accumulation' or the coming "face to face and into contact" (Marx 1887: 507) of the owners of money with the propertyless proletarians.

In Chapter 3, Lenin's contribution to Marxist theory concerning preindus-trial capitalist economic forms is discussed. Lenin's analysis of the develop-ment of capitalism in Russia in the late nineteenth century is rendered useful in exploring arguments about the genesis of capitalism insofar as it sheds light on forms of the formal subordination of labour to (commercial) capital, and elucidates as capitalist, production processes that later Marxist theoreticians would consider to be feudal or 'pre-capitalist'.

In Chapter 4, Karl Kautsky's analysis on the 'agrarian question' is presented and critically assessed. According to Kautsky, capitalism first develops not in the countryside, but in the non-agrarian sectors of a country's economy, and especially in trade and finance. Following the dissolution of feudal social relations, the agricultural sector in a capitalist society is characterized by the tendency towards the creation and preservation of small- and medium-scale commercialized family farms. This form of simple commodity production complements industrial capitalism, as it itself is embedded in the overall pro-cess of capitalist reproduction: it provides agrarian commodities at relatively low prices, as these prices do not contain absolute rent and profit, and at best suffice for the subsistence of the farmer's family.

Chapter 5 critically presents (on the basis of theses and arguments devel-oped in Chapters 1–4) post-Second World War debates among Marxist schol-ars on the 'transition from feudalism to capitalism': first, the debate initiated by Paul Sweezy's critique of Maurice Dobb's book *Studies in the Development of Capitalism* and the so-called 'Brenner debate'. Subsequently, it discusses al-ternative Marxist approaches on the rise of capitalism, such as the 'world cap-italism' tradition and the 'aleatory encounter' between the money-owner and the proletarian approach, the latter initially introduced by Étienne Balibar in 1965, and later elaborated upon by Gilles Deleuze and Felix Guattari, and by Louis Althusser. The chapter culminates with an inquiry into an issue that constitutes one of the most disputed subjects in Marxist literature: the question of the productive or non-productive character of merchant capital, a subject about which Marx himself is sometimes ambiguous.

In Chapter 6, I start by critically delineating the main arguments of the 'German Historical' debate on the origins of capitalism during the period 1902–1935, as it may serve to lay the groundwork for reflections on the monetary, 'entrepreneurial' and ideological–cultural origins of capitalism. The starting point of this debate was Werner Sombart's *Modern Capitalism*, a treatise first published in 1902, in which the notion of 'the spirit of capitalism' was coined as *the* indispensable pre-existing premise that made the emergence of capitalism possible. Soon after the publication of Sombart's book, the debate was fuelled, on the one hand, by its criticisms, and, on the other, by Max Weber's fully reshaping Sombart's concept, which was now comprehended in connection with the ideological climate allegedly brought to the fore by the Reformation. The chapter continues by commenting on more recent non-Marxist approaches to capitalism, which, like those of the 'German Historical' debate, substantially underestimate the structural role of wage labour in the formation of capitalism. Finally, Fernand Braudel's fruitful distinction between market economy and capitalism is discussed in connection with the lack of emphasis on class domination and exploitation, which characterizes the distinguished historian's oeuvre.

Concluding Part I, Chapter 7 utilizes the Marxist notion of the mode of production to exploit the critical conclusions of all previous chapters in an effort to provide the concept of the historical figure, which Marx describes as the pre-capitalist money-owner. In this context, two notions are introduced: (i) the *money-begetting slave mode of production*, existing since antiquity and clearly distinguishing itself from the classical (or "patriarchal", as Marx names it) slave mode of production and (ii) the *contractual money-begetting mode of production* that emerged in the Middle Ages in relation to financial schemes based on partnerships or associations. The 'contract' between the money-owner and the labourer, who in the latter case was free from all forms of personal servitude or bondage, entailed a complex form of exploitation. The labourer was in part a wage earner, but also had (limited) access to the ownership of the means of production (of 'capital') through both 'profit sharing' and the right to trade merchandise on voyages. In other words, he was not a proletarian, even if part of his income came from wage payment. The taskmaster of each of these two pre-capitalist modes of production is thus a pre-capitalist money-owner; his latter coming "face to face and into contact" with the labourer who has become a proletarian, that is, the emergence of capitalism, is discussed mainly in Part II.

Part II comprises three chapters and focuses on the emergence of capitalism in the city states on the Italian peninsula and more precisely in Venice, which until the end of the fifteenth century prevailed as a political, economic and colonial power in the broader Mediterranean area and beyond, and which also remained an independent state for more than eight centuries. My point of departure is not only existing historical research pointing to Venice's primacy as a money-begetting commercial and manufactural social formation, but also Marx's notion that "in Italy, where capitalistic production developed earliest, [...] [the] free proletarian [...] found his master ready waiting for him in the towns" (Marx 1887: 508–509).

What differentiates my analysis from other approaches that stress the early development of capitalism in Venice and other city states on the Italian peninsula is my distinction between capitalist and non-capitalist forms of money-begetting 'entrepreneurial' activities. The most pronounced difference between capitalist and non-capitalist money-begetting activities is the 'taking hold' of the wage relationship as the *main form* of remuneration of labourers subjected to the rule of money-owners, or, in other words, the final incorporation of personal coercion into the economic relation as such.

In Chapter 8, I focus on the first phase of the history of Venice, up to 1204, outlining the main historical events that allowed her to be transformed from a former Byzantine province into an independent social formation, from an ally of the Byzantine Empire to the conqueror of Constantinople and from a provincial commercial town in the Adriatic into a major colonial power across the Mediterranean. Despite the fact that the whole process was linked to manifold historical contingencies – a concatenation of accidental circumstances and incidental causes – an explanation for this extraordinary ascent is equally sought in the social character, or the internal structure and cohesiveness, of Venetian society and the thereof derived strength of the Venetian state.

In Chapter 9, I analyze the historically unique class relations of power in the Venetian social formation, which functioned as pre-requisites to her success. The economic upswing of Venice never had as its 'prime mover' the 'private initiative' of certain ingenious merchants or any other 'self-made' and 'risk-taking' individuals. The 'instigator' of Venice's economic rise was the collectivity of a patrician class, having organized itself from the onset of the eleventh century as a militarized naval state that functioned as both coordinator and main undertaker of a multiplicity of money-begetting 'ventures': trade, piracy, plunder, slave trade, war, etc. Venice remained a pre-capitalist economy and society under the economic, political and social rule of a class of pre-capitalist merchants, ship-owners and directors of state-owned enterprises until the fourteenth century. The money-begetting activities of the Venetian ruling class constituted an *unsettled process* of *original accumulation*, in Marx's context of the term. One pole of the process, the Venetian money-owners and their state, had already attained the clearly defined characteristics of a spurious bourgeoisie. The other pole, however, the *propertyless* proletarian, had not yet emerged, and this is precisely why the bourgeoisie remained *spurious*. The wage-remunerated poor still participated in the ownership of the means of production through forms of 'association' mediated by the very fact of their being wage earners.

In Chapter 10, I investigate the historical contingencies chiefly related to economic antagonisms, the Venetian–Genoese wars beginning in the thirteenth century, the crises in the Venetian colonial system and the plague, all of which ultimately led to the prevalence of the capitalist mode of production in the second half of the fourteenth century in the Venetian social formation. These conditions led to the formation, in the late fourteenth century, of huge, state-owned manufactures organized on the basis of the capital – wage labour relation. It is clear that the encounter of the propertyless proletarian with the collective money-owner of the Venetian Commune clearly took hold in these manufactures. In parallel, all non-salaried sources of income of the majority of seamen were drastically restricted, creating a proletariat of wage-earning mariners. In this case as well, money-owners auctioning off state-owned fleets, and ship-owners commanding private ships became capitalists, as their coming "face to face and into contact" with the emerging proletariat took hold. In all instances where a lack of 'free labour' existed, forms of coerced labour, and above all the money-begetting slave mode of production, reappeared as a 'necessary' manifestation of 'entrepreneurship'. Finally, in order to support the wars, a huge internal public debt was created, which nurtured both advanced budgetary management and fiscal policies, and greatly expanded capitalist finance. By the end of the fourteenth century, Venice emerged as a capitalist social formation, practically introducing capitalism in Europe.

Part III expounds the capitalist character of the Venetian social formation from the end of the fourteenth century until the final subjugation of the republic to Napoleon in 1797. It comprises two chapters.

Chapter 11 mainly focuses on the economic restructuring and changing geopolitical role of Venice after the spread of capitalism in Western Europe, the expansion of the Ottoman Empire and the consolidation of large European territorial states. It also reviews various historiographical treatises and Marxist perspectives on the character of Venetian society. Venice remained a capitalist social formation until the last days of her existence, despite the fact that her prominence in European economy and politics had been receding since the sixteenth century, as capitalist social relations spread throughout Western Europe and new economic and military powers emerged. From the late sixteenth century, as Venetian commercial supremacy was challenged by new competitors, a restructuring of the Venetian economy took place based on the rapid growth of the manufacturing and financial spheres. Furthermore, Venice succeeded in becoming a significant colonial power in the Mediterranean with its colonial territory extending out into the eastern Mediterranean and Aegean Seas, in Dalmatia and Istria (the *Stato da Màr*), and on the Italian mainland (the *Domini di Terraferma*). Despite Ottoman expansion, which had been gradually chipping away at Venice's eastern colonies since the sixteenth century, both colonial dominions were sustained until the republic's demise, being shaped as hybrid sovereignties, somewhere between a colonial realm and a confederation of dominions.

Finally, Chapter 12 focuses on the Venetian state, highlighting its capitalist features. At the same time, it criticizes certain views claiming that Venice (and other city states on the Italian peninsula) 'failed' to become actual capitalist social formations because they could not develop a 'national political entity'.

The capitalist state 'condenses' the overall rule of capital in a social formation, at the same time presenting it as being in the 'common interest' of society. In other words, the capitalist state must always homogenize every community within its political territory into an *indigenous population* supposedly possessing *common interests* and distinguish it from the 'other' (the populations of other states or territories). This means that the strategic interests of the capitalist class that are being 'condensed' by the state always entail a compromise with the subaltern classes. Modern nation-building and nationalism have played an important role in the homogenization of a capitalist state's indigenous populations: the nation constitutes the historically shaped and specifically capitalist unity (cohesion) of the antagonistic classes of a social formation, tending to unify the 'internal' and demarcate and distinguish it from the 'external', i.e. the 'non-national'. The process of nation-building, however, was initiated in Europe centuries after capitalism had established its rule in many social formations and parts of the continent. Nationalism and national identity emerged in the late eighteenth and nineteenth centuries, roughly in the wake of the French Revolution.

The Venetian state had acquired two basic characteristics of a capitalist type of state as early as the fourteenth century: the impersonal functioning of state apparatuses based on the 'rule of law' and 'equal justice' for all inhabitants of Venetian territory, regardless of their special status (patricians, citizens by birth, 'popolari', immigrants, servants or slaves) and the 'relative autonomy' of the state and its political and economic functions or interventions from all fractions of the ruling class, so as to establish the strategic interests of the Venetian bourgeoisie as being 'common interests' of the republic. Both elements played a decisive role in creating consensus for political power by the subaltern classes, and also by colonial populations and immigrants settling in Venice from other parts of the Mediterranean and the Italian peninsula.

Being not just a city state but a colonial empire, Venice developed institutions and techniques through which heterogeneous populations were dealt with on collective and statistical – on impersonal – terms. The Venetian capitalist state, without being a national state, successfully created forms of economic and social interaction, coercion, republican representation and loyalty to authorities, which facilitated the expanded reproduction of capitalist relations of exploitation and domination, while simultaneously preserving a multicultural society.

From this point of view, the lack of a national – Italian – identity (the disastrous Venetian–Genoese wars never contained an element of civil war) seems to me to be less an element of archaism and more a return to the future.

Part I

Capitalism and its origins

The theoretical context

1 Marx's notion of capitalism

A synoptic account

The terms 'capital', 'capitalist' and 'capitalism' were coined many centuries ago. Outside Western Europe, the word 'capital' (*kefalaion*) appeared in *Ecloga*, the compilation of laws formulated during the reign of the Byzantine Emperor Leo III, 717–741. Later, the word 'capital' (*al-māl*) appeared in the works of the Muslim jurist al-Shāfiʿī (727–820) in the year 820 (Udovitch 1970: 81; Pryor 1977: 25; Banaji 2010: 262. See also Chapter 7).

According to Fernand Braudel,

> Capitale (a late Latin word based on caput = head) emerged in the twelfth to thirteenth centuries in the sense of funds, stock of merchandise, sum of money, or money carrying interest. […] Italy, the forerunner of modernity in this respect, was at the centre […]. It was here that the word was first coined, made familiar and to some extent matured. It appears incontestably in 1211 and is found from 1283 in the sense of the capital assets of a trading firm.
>
> (Braudel 1982: 232)

It was the analysis of Karl Marx, however, that coloured the term 'capital' with its contemporary notional contents and distinguished it from the conventional definition of 'property that is expected to yield an income', or the neoclassical conception of capital as a 'factor of production' along with 'labour' and natural resources.

As Marxist historian R. H. Hilton noted in 1952,

> 'The subject of capitalism', wrote Professor M. M. Postan, 'owes its present place in political and scientific discussion to the work of Marx and the Marxians.' Many historians substantially follow him. Mr. E. Lipson in his *Economic History of England* on the whole adopts Marx's definition of capitalism. He agrees that its essential feature is the division of classes between propertyless wage-earners and entrepreneurs who own capital, in contrast to the characteristic medieval organisation of industry and agriculture on the basis of the small producer who owned his own means of production.
>
> (Hilton 1952: 32)[1]

Marx's theory of capitalism as a social system is, of course, more complex and more often expounded than the definitions just mentioned. In his major work, *Capital*, he highlights six fundamental characteristics which, in their interconnectedness, distinguish capitalism from all other social systems: (i) wage labour; (ii) monetization of the whole economy (money-begetting money); (iii) concentration of the means of production and dissociation of the capitalist from the labour process as such; (iv) free competition and the fusion of individual capitals into aggregate-social capital; (v) the financial mode of existence of capital; (vi) the formation of a specific juridical–political–ideological structure and a corresponding state form.

The *prevalence* of wage labour differentiates capitalism from previous social systems. It is a relation between the owner of the means of production (the capitalist) and the worker who has been freed from all personal forms of servitude, but who is also deprived of any direct access to the means of production, except through selling his/her labour power to the capitalist on the basis of a wage contract. The worker is unable to produce without subsuming himself/herself under capital, labouring under the command of the capitalist, who has full control of the production process.

The *wage relation* is therefore *the first fundamental characteristic of capitalism*.

Labour power becomes a commodity in a fully commercialized economy; generalized commodity ownership and commodity production are the discernible features of capitalism: the market economy. The first volume of Marx's *Capital* begins with the following phrase:

> The wealth of those societies in which the capitalist mode of production prevails, presents itself as an 'immense accumulation of commodities'.
>
> (Marx 1887: 27)

A commodity is not simply a useful thing (a 'use value'); it is a (useful) thing for exchange, a thing carrying a price and produced as a price-carrying thing and a thing that aims at expressing itself in monetary units on the market; it is an exchange value. Generalized commodity production is at the same time generalized money circulation. Capitalist production expresses itself as a money circuit.

The capitalist appears in the market as the owner of money (M) buying commodities (C), which consist of means of production (Mp) and labour power (Lp). In the process of production (P), these commodities (C) are productively used up (consumed) so as to generate an output of other commodities, a product (C′) whose value exceeds that of (C). Finally, he/she sells that output to recover a sum of money (M′), which is higher than (M).

A comprehensive introductory definition of capital could, therefore, be the following: a historically specific social relation that expresses itself (i), on the one hand, in free labour (the labourer as wage earner), and (ii) as 'money as an end in itself' or 'money that creates more money', on the other. Capital appears as self-valorizing money, in accordance with the formula M-C-M′.

Marx has shown that this formula of money circulation can actually be regarded as an expression of capitalist economic and social relations, incorporating as it does the process of direct production, which now becomes production-for-exchange and production-for-profit. A historically specific form of exploitation then emerges: capitalist exploitation of the labouring classes. Money has now become the most general form of appearance of value, and thus of capital. "Capital is not a thing, but a social relation between persons, established by the instrumentality of things" (Marx 1887: 543).

In the context of capitalist economic and social relations, the movement of money as capital binds the production process *to* the circulation process: commodity production becomes a phase or moment (and indeed, for the whole valorization process, the *decisive* moment) of the circuit of social capital:

$$M - C\left[= Lp + Mp\right]...P...C' - M'\left[= M + \Delta M\right]$$

In Marx's own words:

> Capital is money: Capital is commodities. In truth, however, value is here the active factor in a process, in which, while constantly assuming the form in turn of money and commodities, it at the same time changes in magnitude, [...] expands spontaneously. [...] *The circulation of money as capital* [...] *is an end in itself. The circulation of capital has therefore no limits.*
> (Marx 1887: 107, emphasis added)

The *full monetization of the economy (money-begetting money)* is therefore the *second fundamental characteristic of capitalism,* according to Marx's analysis.

However, a capitalist, as the personification of capital, is not every entrepreneur or owner of the means of production. For the owner of the means of production to be 'capital', the *scale of production* and the number of wage earners employed by the entrepreneur must be such that *the capitalist is disengaged from actual labour*, and thereby focused on the supervision and direction of the production process. The capitalist's income (i.e. profit) depends on the magnitude of the capital advanced, and not on their labour. This precondition differentiates the capitalist class from the class of small entrepreneurs, who employ wage labour, and whom we refer to as the 'middle bourgeoisie' (see Milios and Economakis 2011).

> Capitalist production only then really begins [...] when each individual capital employs simultaneously a comparatively large number of labourers [...] A certain stage of capitalist production necessitates that the capitalist be able to devote the whole of the time during which he functions as a capitalist, i.e. as personified capital, to the appropriation and therefore the control of the labour of others, and to the selling of the products of this labour.
> (Marx 1887: 227, 216)

The *concentration of the means of production* and the *dissociation of the capitalist from the labour process as such* thus constitute the *third fundamental characteristic of capitalism,* according to Marx's analysis.

Each individual capital, motivated by the sole driving force of "appropriation of ever more and more wealth in the abstract" (Marx 1887: 107), competes with other individual capitals, also motivated by the same driving force. Through free competition, they all become constituent elements of aggregate-social capital (Gesamtkapital).

In Marx's conception, free competition ensures the reciprocal engagement, peculiar to the capitalist system, of institutionally independent production units, imposing the laws of capitalist production on the respective capitals. Through their structural interdependence, that is to say their organization as aggregate-social capital, the individual capitals proclaim themselves a *social class*: they function as a uniform social force counter-posing themselves against, and dominating, labour.

As individual capitals, enterprises are supposed to maximize their profit. However, this tendency, through free competition, is subject to the laws inherent in the concept of aggregate-social capital, and more specifically to the process of equalization of the rate of profit: convergence of their profit rate towards the average profit rate. The tendency towards equalization of the rate of profit is thus *a structural characteristic of the capitalist relation as such.*

This tendency is related to two processes:

a   Competition *within each branch* or sector of production, which in principle ensures for each commodity the "establishment of a uniform market value and market price" (Marx 1991: 281). Competition within each branch of production therefore tends in every instance to impose on all individual capitals more productive manufacturing techniques and in this way tends to equalize the rate of profit within each branch.

b   Competition *at the level of overall capitalist production*, which ensures such sufficient mobility of capital from one branch to another that a uniform rate of profit tends to emerge for the entire capitalist economy (the general rate of profit). The shaping of the uniform general rate of profit is achieved on the basis of *production prices*. These are, in other words, precisely those prices for the product of each individual capital that guarantee it a rate of profit (= ratio of the total profit for a certain period of production to the total capital advanced) equal to (tending towards equality with) the general rate of profit in the economy.

The freedom of capital, its concentration and centralization and its capacity to move from one sphere of production to another, serves to secure the predominance of this tendency towards equalization of the rate of profit. As Marx puts it:

> *Free competition* is the relation of capital to itself as another capital, i.e. the real conduct of capital as capital. The inner laws of capital – which

appear merely as tendencies in the preliminary historic stages of its development – are for the first time posited as laws; production founded on capital for the first time posits itself in the forms adequate to it only in so far as and to the extent that free competition develops, for it is the free development of the mode of production founded on capital.

(Marx 1993: 650–651)

Free competition and the *'fusion'* of individual capitals into *'aggregate-social capital'* is thus the *fourth fundamental characteristic of capitalism,* according to Marx's theory.

Marx's notion of capital is not derived from an analysis of the actions of the capitalist. It is not a response to the striving, the decisions or the actions of a *subject.* On the contrary, it is the movement of total-social capital (often mentioned by Marx as the 'laws of capital') that imparts 'consciousness' to the individual capitalist. The power of capital is impersonal; in reality, it is the power of money as such (Balibar 1984; Marx 1887: 107–108).

Proceeding to a more concrete level of analysis, Marx acknowledges that the place of capital is occupied by two distinct albeit complementary roles: a *money capitalist* and a *functioning capitalist.* This means that a detailed description of capitalism cannot ignore the circulation of interest-bearing capital, which depicts the structure of the financial system. Marx's argumentation might be represented in the following schema (Sotiropoulos et al. 2013: 52 ff.) (Figure 1.1).

In the course of the lending process, money capitalist A becomes the recipient and proprietor of a *security* S, that is to say a written *promise* of payment from functioning capitalist B. This promise certifies that A remains *owner* of money capital M. He does not transfer his capital to B but cedes to him the right to make use of it for a specified period. Two general types of securities enter into this process: *bonds* S_B and *shares* S_S. In the case of the former, the enterprise undertakes to return fixed and prearranged sums of money irrespective of the profitability of its own operations. In the latter case, it secures loan capital by selling a part of its property, thereby committing itself to paying dividends proportional to its profits. If the company enters the stock

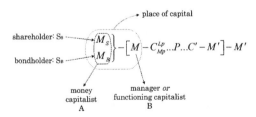

Figure 1.1 The place of capital.

Source: Sotiropoulos, Dimitris P., John Milios, and Spyros Lapatsioras (2013) *A Political Economy of Contemporary Capitalism and its Crisis: Demystifying Finance,* London and New York: Routledge, p. 52.

exchange and what is involved is share issue, then capitalist B corresponds to the managers, and capitalist A to the legal owner.

In the hands of B, the sum M functions as capital. Money taken as the independent expression of the value of commodities enables active capitalist B to purchase the necessary means of production Mp and labour power Lp for organizing the production process. The latter takes place under a regime of specific *relations of production* (comprising a specific historical form of relations of exploitation), and in this way is transformed into a process for producing surplus value. The money reserve that B now has at his/her disposal is the material expression of his/her *social power* to set in motion the productive process and to control it.

In Marx's view, the place of capital (the incarnation of the powers stemming from the structure of the relations of production) is occupied by both the money capitalist and the functioning capitalist. In other words, the place of capital is occupied by agents that are both internal to the enterprise (managers) and external to it (security holders). Marx's general conception abolishes the basic distinction drawn by Keynes between the productive classes within the enterprise and the parasitical class of external rentiers. The contradictions that develop between managers and big investors certainly do exist, but they evidently pertain to secondary aspects of the capital relation:

> In the production process, the functioning capitalist represents capital against the wage-labourers as the property of others, and the money capitalist participates in the exploitation of labour as represented by the functioning capitalist.
>
> (Marx 1991: 504)

Capital takes on a Janus-faced existence, as both a means of production and as financial securities. In the circuit of money capital, credit becomes the prevalent money form. As a consequence,

> [the] social character of capital is mediated and completely realised only by the full development of the credit and banking system.
>
> (Marx 1991: 742)

The pure form of legal ownership over capital is *financial security*, corresponding, that is, to "imaginary money wealth" (Marx 1991: 609). The ownership title is a paper duplicate, either of the money capital ceded in the case of the bond S_B, or of the 'material' capital in the case of the share S_S. Nevertheless, the *price* of security does not emerge either from the value of the money made available or from the value of the 'real' capital. Ownership titles are priced on the basis of the (future) income they will yield for the person who owns them (capitalization in accordance with the current interest rate that embodies the risk), which of course is part of the surplus value produced. In this sense, they are *sui generis commodities*, plotting a course that is their very own (see Marx 1991: 597–598, 607–609).

The *financial mode of existence of capital*, functioning as a promise and at the same time a forward-looking claim, is therefore the *fifth fundamental characteristic of capitalism*, according to Marx's theory.

Finally, capitalism as a social system implies the formation of a specific state form and specific forms of concealment of class domination and exploitative relations (ruling ideology):

> It is in each case the direct relationship of the owners of the conditions of production to the immediate producers [...] in which we find the innermost secret, the hidden basis of the entire social edifice, and hence also the political form of the relationship of sovereignty and dependence.
> (Marx 1991: 927)

The capitalist class possesses not only economic, but also *political power*, and not because capitalists man the highest political offices in the state, but because the structure of politics in capitalist societies, and above all the capitalist state (its hierarchical–bureaucratic organization, its classless functioning on the basis of the rule of law, etc.), corresponds to capitalist class domination, which ensures its overall preservation and reproduction.

It is similarly evident that the dominant bourgeois *ideology* (the ideology of freedom and equality, of individual rights, of the common interest, etc.) favours the perpetuation and reproduction of the capitalist social order and in general the long-term interests of the capitalist class. These ideological forms are inherent in capitalist domination, and they reproduce self-generating consequences of concealment of the exploitative and coercive character of capitalist social relations. As Marx puts it, this spontaneously produced ideology

> forms the basis of all the juridical notions of both labourer and capitalist, of all the mystifications of the capitalistic mode of production, of all its illusions as to liberty, of all the apologetic shifts of the vulgar economists.
> (Marx 1887: 381)

The political and ideological power of the capitalist state must be thus approached in terms of the objective (political) interests of the capitalist class. Within this framework, the state plays a *central organizational role*, representing and organizing the long-term political interests of the bourgeois class, politically unifying its various fractions, all of which occupy positions – albeit unequal ones – in the terrain of political domination over the ruled–exploited classes of society.

> [E]very form of production creates its own legal relations, form of government, etc. In bringing things which are organically related into an accidental relation, into a merely reflective connection, they [the bourgeois economists] display their crudity and lack of conceptual understanding.
> (Marx 1993: 88)

The *specifically capitalist state form and juridical–ideological structure* is thus the *sixth fundamental characteristic of capitalism* as a social system, according to Marx's analysis.

Marx uses the notion of *capitalist mode of production* to codify this historically specific social order, the *causal nucleus* of capitalist social relations. It is this notion that allows one to grasp "the specific characteristics which distinguish capital from all other forms of wealth – or modes in which (social) production develops" (Marx 1993: 449). The same notion therefore enables the conceptualization of 'forms, which precede capitalist production', i.e. the different pre-capitalist or non-capitalist modes of production. I will further elaborate on the concept of the capitalist and non-capitalist modes of production in Chapter 7.

At this point, a crucial question arises: historically, how did this complex social structure of capitalism come into existence? And thence a second question: did certain social forms, or even fundamental characteristics of capitalism, pre-exist its emergence? More specifically, how can one assess the fact that the function of 'money as an end in itself', which characterizes capitalism, has made an appearance in various social formations since antiquity?

These questions are not only of mere historical interest; responding to them means understanding the nature of capitalism. I will commence by critically investigating Marx's own (divergent) approaches to the riddle of the emergence of capitalism.

Note

1 As Pellicani (1994: 13) aptly notes: "All theories developed to explain the formation of modern market society have been seen as either alternatives to the Marxian account or parts of it".

2 Marx's two approaches to the genesis of capitalism

The 'productive forces – relations of production dialectic' vs. 'so-called original accumulation'[1]

2.1 A note on the status of Marx's theoretical oeuvre

Marx's writings are not parts of a Holy Gospel, in which every phrase supposedly reflects 'the truth'. They are facets of a theoretical revolution that developed through successive breaks with the dominant bourgeois theoretical schemes, a revolution that has remained open and unfinished, and which has also been characterized by internal contradictions and even regressions towards the theoretical ground that Marx challenged with his new system.

Marx first challenged theoretical–philosophical humanism and essentialism, that is, all theoretical approaches that derive the form and evolutionary patterns of societies from an axiomatically assessed 'human nature'. Beginning with his (1845) *Theses on Feuerbach*, Marx pictures history as a process driven by class antagonisms, i.e. a process whose *motive force* is class struggle. He writes:

> Feuerbach resolves the essence of religion into the essence of man. But the essence of man is no abstraction inherent in each single individual. In its reality it is the ensemble of the social relations.
>
> (6th Thesis on Feuerbach, in Marx and Engels 1998: 570)

> The history of all hitherto existing society is the history of class struggles.
>
> (Marx and Engels 1985: 79)

Marx's second great theoretical achievement is his 'Critique of Political Economy', which is substantiated in *Capital*.

Capital constitutes a major theoretical rupture in the history of the social sciences. It establishes a new theoretical system of concepts that aims at deciphering the economic and social structures of capitalism in its diverse forms, and not just that of nineteenth-century England, where Marx lived. This is because the object of *Capital* is, as Marx aptly stresses, the 'ideal average'[2] of the capitalist system, the causal relationships that operate beneath the surface of each and every capitalist society.

Capital is not just a book; in essence, it is a research project, a project that Marx started without completing, and that is basically ongoing. The following concise review of Marx's texts, which he labelled (as the title or subtitle) 'Critique of Political Economy', may suffice for the moment.

Marx began his research work in 1857. In 1858, he had completed his first manuscript, which was published posthumously under the title *Grundrisse: Foundations of the Critique of Political Economy* (Marx 1993). In 1859, he published *For a Critique of Political Economy* (*Zur Kritik der Politischen Ökonomie*, translated as *A Contribution to the Critique of Political Economy*, Marx 1987). By 1867, he had written manuscripts of several thousand pages published in German in nine volumes (MEGA II/3.1–3.6, MEGA II/4.1–4.3), among which were the drafts of the three volumes of *Capital*. In 1867, he published the first volume of *Capital*, which he revised for the second edition (1872) and for the French version (1872–1875). At the time of his death in 1883, Marx had not completed the other two volumes of *Capital* (edited and published by Engels in 1885 – Vol. 2 – and in 1894 – Vol. 3; Marx 1887, 1991). However, throughout the period of 1876–1881, he worked intensively on the second volume of *Capital*, leaving behind four additional manuscripts (V–VIII manuscripts of Vol. 2: MEGA II/12). In the German Complete Edition (MEGA) of Marx's works and drafts, his writings related to *Capital* (MEGA II) comprise twenty-three volumes!

From this brief description of Marx's work, we can see that he had in fact initiated a theoretical research project that has remained open for future Marxist theoreticians.

Moreover, the fact that Marx's project constituted a radical break with the entire previous theoretical framework (and first and foremost with classical political economy), as with the banalities of the dominant ideology, lends it a clear, confrontational character. Within the enormous amount of published work and drafts, ambiguities, or even regressions towards classical political economy, seem to be inevitable. The duty of Marxist researchers to preserve and further develop Marx's theoretical legacy thus becomes more challenging.

As will be evident in what follows, the multiple divergent Marxist approaches as regards to the nature and origins of capitalism have their roots partly in Marx's own theoretical ambiguities.

2.2 A 'philosophy of history' and a 'general law of human development'?

In Marx's text, one finds two different approaches to the problem of 'transition' from one historical form of society to another.

According to Marx's initial approach, which we also find in the 'Introduction' to the *A Contribution to the Critique of Political Economy* of 1859, "the development of the productive forces" comes "in conflict with the existing relations of production which turn into their fetters", a situation that ultimately results in "revolutionary change" of production relations. Here, we have the dialectics of a single contradiction between Productive Forces (PF) and Relations of Production (RP); the independent variable is the PF, the progress (development) of which determines the evolution of the dependent variable, the RP. Marx writes:

> At a certain stage of development, the material productive forces of society come into conflict with the existing relations of production or [...] with the property relations within the framework of which they have operated hitherto. From forms of development of the productive forces these relations turn into their fetters. Then begins an era of social revolution. [...] *No social order is ever destroyed before all the productive forces for which it is sufficient have been developed*, and new superior relations of production never replace older ones before the material conditions for their existence have matured within the framework of the old society.
>
> (Marx 1987: 263–264, emphasis added)

This approach is a 'philosophy of history', at the base of which lies a 'general law of human development'. The 'independent variable', i.e. development of the PF, and more specifically of the production technique, determines the course of history and opens the path to historical progress towards a 'telos' of history, as 'the prehistory of human society' paves the way to human emancipation, i.e. to socialism and communism. It became the 'quintessence' of 'Marxist dialectics' according to Soviet Marxist theory, especially during the Stalinist era. As Stalin himself puts it:

> First the productive forces of society change and develop, and then, *depending* on these changes and *in conformity with them*, men's relations of production, their economic relations, change.
>
> (Stalin 1975: 26)[3]

It is evident from the above quotation that PF are considered to be the driving force of history (since they determine the evolution of RP – of class domination and subordination relations). Consequently, class struggle becomes a mere 'reflection' of the development of PF and of technique (see, for example, the theory of 'scientific–technical revolution'), and Marxism degenerates into teleological evolutionary dogma.

This progressivist-teleological approach is, however, alien to the main tenets of Marx's theoretical analysis as developed in *Capital* and his other mature 'economic' writings. Besides, it hardly comes to grips with the issue of the origins of capitalism, as several authors have pointed out.[4]

The first politically influential critique to the approach under discussion was formulated by Mao Tse-tung and the theoreticians of the Communist Party of China in the 1960s.

In a text written between 1961 and 1962, Mao reverses the causality between PF and PR. He writes:

First the production relations have to be changed, then and only then the productive forces can be broadly developed. This rule is universal.

After the old production relations had been destroyed new ones were created, and these cleared the way for the development of new social productive forces.

The bourgeoisie first changed the superstructure [...]. When the production relations had been taken care of and they were on the right track they then opened the way for the development of the productive forces.

(Mao Tsetung 1977: 93, 51, 66)

This 'reversal' by Mao of the causality arrow between PF and RP (the latter now regarded as the independent variable) is consistent with Marx's main analyses in his mature economic writing. Marx repeatedly argues that the prevalence of capitalism results in a tendency of growth of the PF, peculiar to the specific system of RP, which is only temporarily inhibited by economic crises:

Capital [...] constantly revolutionizes it, *tearing down all the barriers which hem in the development of the forces of production*, the expansion of needs, the all-sided development of production, and the exploitation and exchange of natural and mental forces.

(Marx 1993: 410; emphasis added)[5]

The PF–RP debate is closely connected with the 'transition to socialism' controversies. Can a less developed country overthrow capitalism and build socialism before the capitalist PF have been adequately developed? The answer of Chinese Marxists in the 1960s was affirmative, and it was documented on the basis of a radical critique of all approaches perceiving historical development as a by-product of the 'development of PF'. In Issue No. 38 (19 September 1969) of the official Chinese news magazine *Peking Review*, celebrating the Twentieth Anniversary of the founding of the People's Republic of China, two polemic articles were published against the 'theory of productive forces', as it was called, giving priority to the development of PF. In Kao Hund's article, entitled 'From Bernstein to Liu Shao-chi', we read: "The 'theory of productive forces' is an international revisionist trend of thought".[6]

It is worth reminding the reader at this point that V. I. Lenin was confronted with a similar problematique shortly before the Russian October Revolution of 1917. According to Lenin, the February Russian Revolution, as a specific moment of historical significance, was not the result of a single cause or prime mover (such as the development of the PF, or the contradiction between labour and capital – which had always existed – or the peculiarity of Russian capitalism or the cruelty of the tsarist regime), but the outcome of a fusion of the totality of social and economic contradictions at a *specific conjuncture*, which 'overdetermined' (Althusser 1990: 87–128) the capital–labour relation. Lenin specifically argued that in the first phase of the

Russian Revolution, the intervention of imperialism, namely of the superpowers of England and France, significantly strengthened the attempt of the bourgeoisie to advance a new power bloc in order to impose a new regime of political hegemony. Evidently, such a strengthening could have no chance if the suitable political forces needed to pave the way for imperialist intervention did not already exist. In the end, they proved altogether incapable of influencing the political outcome and averting the coming revolution.

> That the revolution succeeded so quickly and – seemingly, at the first superficial glance – so radically, is only due to the fact that, as a result of an extremely unique historical situation, *absolutely dissimilar currents, absolutely heterogeneous* class interests, *absolutely contrary* political and social strivings have *merged*, and in a strikingly 'harmonious' manner.
>
> (Lenin 1917)

In Western Europe, the approach giving priority to PF was thoroughly criticized by Ernest Mandel, Charles Bettelheim and Louis Althusser and his disciples.[7]

Mandel, discussing the "Asiatic Mode of Production and the Pre-Conditions for the Rise of Capital" (Mandel 1971: 116–139), strongly criticizes

> [...] the mechanistic and anti-Marxist straitjacket of the 'four stages' which all mankind was supposed to have necessarily passed through: primitive communism, slaveowning society, feudalism, capitalism. This straitjacket had compelled writers who claimed to be Marxists but who wanted to be accepted as 'orthodox' by the Communist parties to assemble under the heading 'feudal society' a most variegated collection of socioeconomic formations.
>
> (Mandel 1971: 119)

Bettelheim, writing on the transition between capitalism and socialism, stresses:

> [...] the system of productive forces only [exists] as an articulation within a system of relations of production which both *dominates* it and gives it its form.
>
> (Bettelheim: 1975: 53–54)

In a later publication on the Chinese Cultural Revolution, Bettelheim further clarifies this issue:

> In the combination productive forces/production relations, the latter play the dominant role by imposing the conditions under which the productive forces are reproduced. Conversely, the development of the productive forces never directly determines the transformation of the production

relations; this transformation is always the focus of intervention by the contending classes – that is, of class struggle.

(Bettelheim 1974: 91–92)

Louis Althusser regarded the PF problematique as an expression of 'economism', that is, one of hard-core forms of the dominant bourgeois ideology.[8] In an article first published in 1972, he claims:

> The economism/humanism pair, when it is introduced into Marxism, does not really change in form, even if it is forced to make some changes (only some) in its vocabulary. [...] Economism remains economism: for example, in the exaltation of the development of the Productive Forces, of their 'socialization' (what kind of socialization?), of the 'scientific and technical revolution', of 'productivity', etc. Can we make a comparison? Yes, we can. And we discover the factor which permits us to identify the ideological pair *economism/humanism* and its practices as bourgeois: it is the elimination of something which never figures in economism or humanism, *the elimination of the relations of production and of the class struggle.*
>
> (Althusser 1984a: 87–88)

Following this critical presentation of the 'PF–RP dialectic', which, as we have seen, culminates in a 'general law of human development' (or a 'philosophy of history'), I have come to the conclusion that this approach, already rejected by certain Marxist streams of thought, is hardly compatible with Marx's main theoretical thesis "of class struggle as the immediate driving force of history".[9] I regard this approach, to the extent that it appears in Marx's writings, as a regression towards the (bourgeois) theoretical terrain from which Marx had broken away since 1845, albeit in a contradictory, at certain points, way.

In the next section, I will examine Marx's notion of 'original accumulation', which constitutes an analysis radically differing from the 'PF–RP dialectic' on the question of the 'transition to capitalism'.

2.3 'So-called original[10] accumulation'

2.3.1 Marx's problematique in Capital and the Grundrisse

In *Capital*, a new approach to the genesis of capitalism is introduced. Capital was born as a result of the coming "face to face and into contact" of two social forms that *pre-existed capitalism*: the money-owner and the propertyless proletarian. The capital relation was formed only when these forms were bound to one another.

Marx here speaks about an *original accumulation* of money and means (of production and subsistence) that are *transformed into capital* only after their 'contact' with 'free' labour ('free' from personal relations of servitude, but also from production means – the condition of 'double freedom'). The two poles of this contact, the money-owner and the proletarian, were the outcome of historical processes more or less independent of one another, through which the capital relation was shaped.

> In themselves money and commodities are no more capital than are the means of production and of subsistence. They want transforming into capital. But this transformation itself can only take place under certain circumstances that centre in this, viz., that two very different kinds of commodity-possessors must *come face to face and into contact*; on the one hand, the owners of money, means of production, means of subsistence, who are eager to increase the sum of values they possess, by buying other people's labour power; on the other hand, free labourers, the sellers of their own labour power, and therefore the sellers of labour. Free labourers, in the double sense that neither they themselves form part and parcel of the means of production, as in the case of slaves, bondsmen, &c., nor do the means of production belong to them, as in the case of peasant proprietors [...]. The process, therefore, that clears the way for the capitalist system, can be none other than the process which takes away from the labourer the possession of his means of production.
>
> (Marx 1887: 507–508, emphasis added)

I have cited this lengthy passage from *Capital* in order to be able to discuss the inner interconnections in Marx's analysis:

a   The money-owner pre-existed capitalism; he/she became capitalist when he/she *confronted* the free (in the double sense) individual and established a wage labour relation with him/her.
b   The free individual emerged out of multiple processes that Marx describes, focusing mainly on England and Scotland, in a *concise* historical account covering several centuries (roughly from the fourteenth to nineteenth centuries).

The double freedom of the proletarian refers to two processes: (i) emancipation from all forms of direct personal dependence or servitude; (ii) an expropriation process of the worker from his/her means of production. However, even the emancipation process, i.e. freedom (ownership of oneself) and equality (equal rights or even citizenship), constitutes the form of a specific relation of class domination and exploitation: of capitalism.

> Equality and freedom are thus not only respected in exchange based on exchange values but, also, the exchange of exchange values is the productive, real basis of all equality and freedom. As pure ideas they are merely the idealised expressions of this basis; as developed in juridical, political, social relations they are merely this basis to a higher power.
>
> (Marx 1993: 245)[11]

In parallel, Marx focuses on the methods and policies that render possible the process of separation of the labourer from the means of production and from all 'masters' in the pre-capitalist sense.

> Colonial system, public debts, heavy taxes, protection, commercial wars, &c., these children of the true manufacturing period, increase gigantically during the infancy of Modem Industry. The birth of the latter is heralded by a great slaughter of the innocents. Like the royal navy, the factories were recruited by means of the press-gang.
>
> (Marx 1887: 537)

2.3.2 A 'circular argument'?

Nearly all methods of engendering the creation of the proletariat described by Marx in the context of his original accumulation approach (e.g. the bloody legislation against the expropriated, the forcing down of wages by acts of parliament, the violent expropriation of pre-capitalist forms of ownership – enclosures, etc., plunder and the colonial system), methods that violently promoted the capital relation, presupposed an *already existing capitalist class interest and a capitalist strategy*, aiming at the consolidation of wage labour, of capitalist social relations and of capitalist exploitation.

For instance, when Marx discusses the laws for 'the compulsory extension of the working day' (Marx 1887, Chapter 28), he clearly illustrates a well-defined state policy existing in England since the fourteenth century, which controls wage labour in order to safeguard surplus-value extraction:

> The first 'Statute of Labourers' ([...] 1349) found its immediate pretext (not its cause, for legislation of this kind lasts centuries after the pretext for it has disappeared) in the great plague that decimated the people, so that, as a Tory writer says, 'The difficulty of getting men to work on reasonable terms (i.e., at a price that left their employers a reasonable quantity of surplus labour) grew to such a height as to be quite intolerable.' Reasonable wages were, therefore, fixed by law as well as the limits of the working day.
>
> (Marx 1887: 181–182)

The very fact, according to Marx's own account, that 'original accumulation' had been implemented by state policies and social strategies deliberately promoting capitalist interests, allowed certain critics of Marx to claim that his whole analysis was based on circular reasoning: "the birth of capitalism presupposes capitalism itself" (Pellicani 1994: 17).

This argument may be justified only if one forgets Marx's emphasis on the coming "face to face and into contact" (Marx 1887: 507) of the *money-owner* with the *propertyless proletarian* that *pre-existed capitalism*. In other words, we have to bear in mind that Marx described original accumulation as two distinct historical processes: (i) on the one hand, the process of *genesis of the capital relation as such* (coming "face to face and into contact" ...) and (ii) on the other, the state-driven processes that paved the way for the *broadening and deepening of the (already-born) capital relation.*

Processes of expropriation of peasants or other subsistence producers from their means of production *follow* (both logically and historically) the original coming "face to face and into contact" of the money-owner with the proletarian. Commenting on the colonial system, Marx stresses in the third volume of *Capital*:

> The sudden expansion of the world market, the multiplication of commodities in circulation, the competition among the European nations for the seizure of Asiatic products and American treasures, the colonial system, all made a fundamental contribution towards shattering the feudal barriers to production. And yet the modem mode of production in its first period, that of manufacture, *developed only where the conditions for it had been created in the Middle Ages.* [...] the defeat of the old mode of production and the rise of the capitalist mode, [...] *happened in reverse on the basis of the capitalist mode of production, once it had been created.*
> (Marx 1991: 450–451, emphasis added)

Focusing, therefore, on the birth of capitalism, the decisive element is the coming "face to face and into contact" of the money-owner with the propertyless individual. Marx himself poses the crucial question: given that the peasants were initially subjected not to money-owners, but to landlords, who was the *money-owner,* and out of whom, in a later historical era, did the capitalist emerge?

> whence came the capitalists originally? For the expropriation of the agricultural population creates, directly, none but the greatest landed proprietors.
> (Marx 1887: 528)

To this question, Marx responds in *Capital* pointing to two social figures who were external to the landlord–peasant relationship:

> But the Middle Ages had handed down two distinct forms of capital, which mature *in the most different economic and social formations,* and which *before the era of the capitalist mode of production,* are considered as capital [...] usurer's capital and merchant's capital.
> (Marx 1887: 533, emphasis added)

And in the second part of Volume 1, when he introduces the notion of capital, Marx stresses:

> As a matter of history, capital, as opposed to landed property, invariably takes the form at first of money; it appears as moneyed wealth, as *the capital of the merchant and of the usurer.*
> (Marx 1887: 104, emphasis added)

This whole problematique is exposed in more detail in the *Grundrisse*:

> The monetary wealth which becomes transformed into capital in the proper sense, into industrial capital, is rather the *mobile wealth piled up through usury* – especially that practised *against landed property* – *and through mercantile profits*. [...] they appear *not as themselves forms of capital*, but as *earlier forms of wealth*, as presuppositions for capital [...]. *The formation of capital thus does not emerge from landed prop*erty [...] but rather from merchant's and usurer's wealth.
>
> (Marx 1993: 504–505, emphasis added)

The money-owner, who was transformed into a capitalist after his coming "face to face and into contact" with the proletarian, did not belong to the realm of pre-capitalist dominant class relations of power and exploitation, which were rooted in landed property; he is a historical figure that existed prior to the processes of proletarianization, the emergence of the proletariat:

> But the *mere presence of monetary wealth*, and even the achievement of a kind of supremacy on its part, is in no way sufficient for this *dissolution into capital* to happen. Or else ancient Rome, Byzantium etc. would have ended their history with free labour and capital, or rather begun a new history. There, too, *the dissolution of the old property relations was bound up with development of monetary wealth* – *of trade* etc. But instead of leading to industry, this dissolution led in fact to the supremacy of the countryside over the city. [...] Capital does not create the objective conditions of labour.
>
> (Marx 1993: 506–507, emphasis added)

Marx's approach does not base itself therefore on any kind of circular argument in the form of 'the genesis of capitalism is rendered possible by strategies aiming at the genesis of capitalism'. However, a critique for circular reasoning may be justified concerning many post-Second World War Marxist approaches to the genesis of capitalism, as they fully disregard the coming "face to face and into contact" of monetary "wealth piled up through usury and through mercantile profits" (Marx) with the proletarian and restrict the notion of original accumulation to capitalist *strategies* of shaping the proletariat (see Chapter 5).

I will commence my study on the issue of the money-owner in pre-capitalist societies and the historical process of his/her coming "face to face and into contact" with the proletarian in Chapter 7. In the subsequent chapters of this book, I will continue my investigation of Marxist and non-Marxist approaches to the notion of capitalism and its origins, beginning with a vivid debate among Russian Marxists at the turn of the nineteenth to the twentieth century, on the question of 'what is capitalism?' and the perspectives of capitalist development in the Russian social formation of the time.

Notes

1 'Die sogenannte ursprüngliche Akkumulation': the term 'ursprüngliche Akkumulation' has been literally translated into English as 'primitive accumulation'. As Paul Sweezy correctly comments,

> This [translation] is likely to be misleading, however, since the point is not that the process is primitive in the usual sense of the term [...], but that it is not preceded by previous acts of accumulation. Hence 'original' or 'primary' is a better rendering of *ursprünglich* in this context.
>
> (Sweezy 2006: 52)

The term is translated as 'original accumulation' by Martin Nicolaus in Marx 1993 (*Grundrisse*).

2 "We are only out to present the internal organization of the capitalist mode of production, its ideal average, as it were" (Marx 1991: 970). See also Heinrich 2012: 31.

3 Of course it was not Stalin or third International Marxists who systemized the PF approach. The 'theory' of the primacy of the PF was common ground in the second International as well:

> The character of the 'economic structure' and the direction in which that character changes depend, not upon human will but on the *state of the productive forces and on the specific changes* in production relations which take place and become necessary to society *as a result of the further development of those forces.*
>
> (Plekhanov 1898)

4 See, e.g., Sayers 1980, Suchting 1982, and the discussion that follows in the text below.

5 See also in the *Results of the Immediate Process of Production*:

> The *productivity of labour* in general = the *maximum of product* with the *minimum of labour*, hence the greatest possible cheapening of the commodities. This becomes a *law* in the capitalist mode of production, independently of the will of the individual capitalist.
>
> (Marx 1864 [§480])

6 In the second paper, by Hung Hsueh-ping, entitled 'The Essence of the "Theory of Productive Forces" is to Oppose Proletarian Revolution', we read: "The renegade, hidden traitor and scab Liu Shao-chi consistently advocated the reactionary theory of productive forces". Both papers can be found in *Peking Review* 1969. See also Sayers 1980.

7 Other critical approaches to the 'PF–RP dialectic' include Richards 1986 and Katz 1993.

8 An ideology that

> is born spontaneously, that is to say necessarily, of the bourgeois practices of production and exploitation, *and at the same time* of the legal practices of bourgeois law and its ideology, which provide a sanction for the capitalist relations of production and exploitation and their reproduction.
>
> (Althusser 1984a: 86)

9 "For nearly 40 years we have raised to prominence the idea of the class struggle as the immediate driving force of history'" (Marx-Engels 1989, MECW Vol. 24: 269).

10 See Endnote 2.

11 Freedom and equality, as the *specific forms of capitalist political and ideological domination*, are explicitly analyzed by Marx in *Capital*:

This sphere that we are deserting, within whose boundaries the sale and purchase of labour-power goes on, is in fact a very Eden of the innate rights of man. There alone rule Freedom, Equality, Property and Bentham. Freedom, because both buyer and seller of a commodity, say of labour power, are constrained only by their own free will. They contract as free agents, and the agreement they come to, is but the form in which they give legal expression to their common will. Equality, because each enters into relation with the other, as with a simple owner of commodities, and they exchange equivalent for equivalent. Property, because each disposes only of what is his own. And Bentham, because each looks only to himself.

(Marx 1887: 123)

See also Pashukanis 1978.

3 Early forms of capitalism and wage labour

Lenin's polemic against the Narodniks

In this chapter, I will deal with Lenin's 1893–1900 intervention in the Russian controversy over capitalist development, which I consider to be a very fruitful contribution to Marxist theory concerning pre-industrial capitalist economic forms, and one which has not been taken into account in post-war Marxist analyses. Moreover, Lenin's analysis may be useful in exploring arguments about the genesis of capitalism, insofar as it is perceived as capitalist economic and social forms, which later Marxist theoreticians consider to be feudal or 'pre-capitalist'.

One specific point in Lenin's analyses may be used to elucidate the problems identified in contemporary Marxist approaches to the theory of capitalism and its social and economic presuppositions: the theory of formal subordination of labour to (commercial) capital as represented by the 'buyer-up', which in Lenin's view constitutes an early form of capitalist production and exploitation.

3.1 The historical context

The fierce debate that took place among Russian Marxists throughout the last two decades of the nineteenth century had to do with the social and economic *character* of the Russian social formation and the prospects for its capitalist development and/or transition to socialism. Each party that took part in the nineteenth-century Russian controversy on capitalism and capitalist development represented a different tendency of Marxist thought. As Rosa Luxemburg pointed out in 1912, in this controversy,

> for the first time, the argument centered purely in the reproduction of capital as a whole, in accumulation, […] the issue was no longer between laissez-faire and social reform, but between two varieties of socialism.
>
> (Luxemburg 1971: 274)

Russia at the end of the nineteenth century was an agrarian country, with enduring 'archaic' production forms that were extensively reproduced. According to the first official census of the empire, in 1897 (Lenin 1977,

Vol. 3: 573), the non-agrarian Russian population (inhabitants of urban areas with populations in excess of 2,000) was only 12.76% of the total population. Lenin considers this to be an underestimate, attributable to discrepancies in the methodology of the census. However, even according to his own calculations, the non-agrarian (urban and semi-urban) population of Russia did not exceed 15% of the total population in 1897 (ibid. Vol. 3: 574, 582). By way of comparison, in 1891, the non-agrarian population of the USA represented 35.3% of the total, in France 37.4% and in Germany 47.0% (Sternberg 1971: 520), whereas in 1896, it was 31% of the total population in Greece (Milios 1988: 168). Of the total working population in Russia, 74.6% were employed in the agrarian sector and only 9.8% worked in industry and manufacturing (data for 1897, Lenin 1977, Vol. 3: 513). The corresponding figures for some other countries in 1901 are as follows: 59.4% of the working population in Britain, 26.7% in France and 24.4% in the USA were employed in industry and manufacturing, and in 1907, 36.0% in Germany and 18.33% in Greece (Sternberg 1971: 425, 508, 519, 553; Milios 1988: 168–169).

More importantly, this 'agrarian' picture of the Russian economy was complicated by the presence of two types of pre-capitalist economic and social structures, or at least of their remnants. On the one hand, there were the structures inherited from feudal serfdom, and on the other those associated with the 'state-owned' communes. State intervention for the purpose of promoting capitalist social relations, especially after the political reorganization following the Crimean War of 1853–1856, which was initiated by bourgeois economic and political forces, included: protectionist measures to promote import substitution favouring domestic industrial products; the establishment of compulsory military service for all males; the creation of an independent judiciary; educational reform enabling women to attend higher educational institutions, etc. This resulted in high rates of development in the capitalist sector of the economy,[1] without precipitating the dissolution of residual pre-capitalist forms.

A programme of agrarian reform, the *Peasant Reform* of Alexander II, was initiated in 1861, abolishing serfdom and giving peasants the right to possess a land allotment on condition that they make a certain 'redemption payment' to the landlords. Pending the remittance of this 'redemption payment' (in kind, in money or even in labour), the peasant was regarded as 'temporarily bound'. Data provided by Marx indicate that on 1 January 1878, i.e. seventeen years after the reform, about 28% of the former serfs remained 'temporarily bound' (*MEW* Vol. 19, 1976: 416–417).

The agrarian population freed from serfdom in 1861 numbered 22.5 million people, out of a total agrarian population of 55 million. Discounting the 110 thousand landowners, the remaining 32 million peasants were deemed to be 'state-owned peasants', i.e. they belonged to agrarian communes (*MEW* Vol. 12: 677, *MEW* Vol. 38: 642) inhabiting a social framework that was almost entirely unrelated to feudal relations of power, but which possessed certain affinities with the Asiatic Mode of Production (see Chapter 7).

The 'Narodniks', against whom the greater part of Lenin's polemic was directed, were historically the first and most powerful current of the Russian Marxist intelligentsia until the end of the nineteenth century. One of the most distinguished representatives of the Narodniks (along with V. P. Vorontsov) was N. F. Danielson, who wrote under the pseudonym Nikolay-on or N-on (1844–1918), and who translated *Das Kapital* into Russian (the first volume was published in 1872, the second in 1885 – the same year as the German edition – and the third in 1896 – just two years after the first German edition of 1894), and corresponded with Marx and Engels up to the end of their lives.

The Narodniks considered that the reform of the 1860s, i.e. the abolition of serfdom, had in principle created the prerequisites for a 'popular', non-capitalist course of development in Russia based chiefly on the peasantry and the 'popular' agrarian sector of 'state-owned' communes. The basis for this course of development would therefore be the peasant commune, which was ardently championed by them (the Narodniks rejected all thoughts of the privatization of common lands, which would lead to the break-up of the communes). In brief, the peasant commune was the structure "in which they wanted to see the rudiments of Communism" (Lenin 1977, Vol. 1: 276).

> The Russian rural communal ownership in land, the famous *obshchina*, seemed to offer a short-cut to the blessed land of socialism, a lead direct to a higher social development of Russia, without the capitalist phase and its attendant misery as experienced in Western Europe.
>
> (Luxemburg 1971: 251)

This whole theoretical edifice was crowned by the conviction that the limitations of the domestic market (precisely because of the poverty of the popular masses in Russia, but also because of the perceived tendency of capitalism to depress the living standards of the masses) constituted a formidable impediment to, or even rendered impossible, the development of capitalism in Russia.

Initially (in the 1870s), the Narodniks were quite convinced of the impossibility of capitalism developing in Russia. Subsequently, when no one could any longer dispute the extensive reproduction of capital in certain sectors of the Russian economy, they maintained either that capitalism would not embrace 'the entirety of production in Russia' (Vorontsov), or that capitalism, to the extent that it would develop, would constitute a plague on the community (Danielson). The latter view was based on the position that capitalist development presupposes alienation of the peasantry from their means of production, the creation of a 'reserve army' of unemployed, etc., that is to say, ultimately the lowering of popular living standards and the contraction of the domestic market. There thus arises a problem of realizing capitalistically produced commodities, which is solved by the big capitalist powers creating a steep rise in the volume of exports. It was argued that this way out was not available to Russia, since it was not in a position to compete successfully with other capitalist countries on the international market. Russian capitalism, according to Danielson, could not overcome the 'problem of markets', and was therefore condemned to a low level of development, with the resulting possibility that it (capitalism) could be replaced by a communal 'popular economy'.

In the Preface to the Russian Edition of 1882 of the *Communist Manifesto*, Marx and Engels discuss the issue raised by the Narodniks: could the existing Russian commune (the obshchina) "pass directly to the higher form of communist common property"?

> But in Russia we find, face to face with the rapidly developing capitalist swindle and bourgeois landed property, just beginning to develop, more than half the land owned in common by the peasants. Now the question is: can the Russian *obshchina*, though greatly undermined, yet a form of the primeval common ownership of land, pass directly to the higher form of communist common ownership? Or on the contrary, must it first pass through the same process of dissolution as constitutes the historical evolution of the West? The only answer to that possible today is this: If the Russian Revolution becomes the signal for a proletarian revolution in the West, so that both complement each other, the present Russian common ownership of land may serve as the starting point for a communist development.
>
> (Marx and Engels 1985: 56)[2]

In the Russian development-of-capitalism controversy, participants included, apart from the 'Left social democrats' or 'orthodox Marxists' (Plekhanov, Lenin) and the Narodniks, all the currents of the Russian Left of the time, such as the Marxists of the 'new critical current' or 'legal Marxists', who were also highly critical of the Narodniks' views (for an overview of the Russian debate, see R. Luxemburg 1971: 269–326; for a detailed presentation of the dispute between Lenin and the Narodniks, see also Rosdolsky 1969 and Dutschke 1974).

In what follows, I will focus on Lenin's arguments against the Narodniks, as they can shed light on two issues closely related to the object of the present book: (i) Which social forms are to be regarded as capitalistic? (ii) What are the preconditions of capitalist development?

3.2 Capitalism prevailed as pre–capitalist exploitation forms dissolved

Lenin's theoretical intervention aimed at defending the position that Russia at the time was a *capitalist social formation*, albeit, compared with other major European capitalist powers, a less developed one. As a conclusion to his whole analysis, he writes:

> Russia is a capitalist country. […] Russia is still very backward, as compared with other capitalist countries, in her economic development.
>
> (Lenin 1977, Vol. 3: 503)

Where the one theoretical camp (the Narodniks) saw a pre-capitalist economy, a pre-capitalist state and an uncertain or weak possibility of transformation to capitalism, the other (Lenin) saw an already established capitalism.

> Capital is a certain relation between people, a relation which remains the
> same whether the categories under comparison are at a higher or a lower
> level of development.
>
> (Lenin 1977, Vol. 1: 217)

What interests us here is the way Lenin substantiates his position that Russia
was already a capitalist social formation.

Methodologically, he rejects all teleological arguments. At the beginning
of his research programme in 1894, he writes:

> No Marxist has ever argued anywhere that there 'must be' capitalism
> in Russia 'because' there was capitalism in the West, and so on [...] No
> Marxist has ever regarded Marx's theory as some universally compulsory
> philosophical scheme of history, as anything more than an explanation of
> a particular social-economic formation.
>
> (Lenin 1977, Vol. 1: 192)

On a more concrete analytical level, Lenin puts forward a twofold thesis to
support his argument that capitalism had already established itself in Russia:

a   The pre-capitalist forms of exploitation and the respective ruling classes
    had already disintegrated; self-sustaining agriculture had been substi-
    tuted by a commercialized peasant economy of increasingly divisive class
    characteristics;

> The entire mass of the agricultural population of Russia may safely
> be regarded as peasants, for the number of landlords in the sum-total
> is quite negligible. Quite a considerable section of landlords, more-
> over, are included in the category of rentiers, government officials,
> high dignitaries, etc. In the peasant mass of 97 millions, however,
> one must distinguish three main groups: the bottom group – the
> proletarian and semi-proletarian strata of the population; the middle
> group – the poor small peasant farmers; and the top group – the
> well-to-do small peasant farmers.
>
> (Lenin 1977, Vol. 3: 503)

b   The disintegration of pre-capitalist class relations of power and exploita-
    tion paved the way for capitalism to become dominant in Russia, even
    though the proportion of the total working population engaged in typ-
    ical wage labour remained relatively small. Capitalist exploitation in the
    Russian agrarian sector assumed indirect forms (see below).[3]

Commencing from the thesis that Russia was already a capitalist social formation, Lenin argues that the further evolution or development of capitalism was contingent on the class correlation of forces, on the one hand between the different fractions of the bourgeoisie,[4] and on the other between capital and labour.

Based on this argument, Lenin summarizes his arguments on the home market question as follows:

> From what has been said, it follows automatically that the problem of the home market as *a separate, self-sufficient problem* not depending on that of the degree of capitalist development does not exist at all. That is why Marx's theory does not anywhere or ever raise this problem separately. The home market appears when commodity economy appears; it is created by the development of this commodity economy, and the degree to which the social division of labour is ramified determines the level of its development.
>
> (Lenin 1977, Vol. 3: 69, emphasis added)

3.3 Production for the buyer-up as a form of capitalist manufacture

Lenin formulates his twofold argument that Russia was a capitalist social formation as follows: (i) "The basis of our economic system is commodity economy," and (ii) "the leader of which is the bourgeoisie" (Lenin 1977, Vol. 1: 250).

As a result of the reform of 1861 and the ensuing economic and social changes, the Russian economy (including its communal agricultural sector) lost its closed, self-sustaining character and was transformed into a commercialized economy. Behind the façade of commodity relations, Lenin detects capitalist domination, despite the fact that wage labour and capitalist enterprise in their full-fledged form remain a relatively limited phenomenon. He then sets out to decipher these specific forms.

Lenin's conclusion is predicated above all on finding that commodity production under certain circumstances becomes synonymous with indirect subordination of labour to capital. As the non-capitalist ruling classes disintegrate, with the feudal estates being eliminated and the state operating in the interests of capital (the Asiatic communes having lost the closed, self-sustaining characteristics that previously distinguished them), artisans and farmers are transformed into market producers and into manufacturers of commodities.

As long as the artisan or the farmer could sell his/her commodities to different merchants, he/she could retain the economic status of an independent commodity producer. However, the diversification of demand, and consequently of production, along with the need to produce not for local but for various distant markets (both tendencies created by the increasing division of labour and the increasing significance of market relations), made the producer increasingly dependent on one particular merchant, who would supply him/ her with raw materials and thus become the *buyer-up* of the producer's total output. Since the buyer-up is now the economic actor who places the product on different markets, he determines the type of product, and the quantity of products, that each artisan or farmer working for him has to produce. He places advance orders for the wares he requires, and in many cases begins to supply the direct producer with raw materials.

In this way, the buyer-up essentially *acquires control* over the production process of the individual producer, i.e. *of their means of production*. It is he who decides the extent of output and its degree of diversification as well as he who establishes the division of labour among the separate producers who are under his control, according to the productivity–profitability criteria that he sets, and changes on demand, which he then follows. The buyer-up can now lower the prices of the commodities he purchases (buys-up) from direct producers to a level that yields for the producer an income no higher than a worker's wage.

A similar analysis was put forward by I. I. Rubin in his *History of Economic Thought*, first published in 1926. Rubin argues that the putting-out– buying-up system is, historically, the first form of capitalism. He calls it a

> *cottage or domestic or decentralized system of large-scale industry*, the spread of which signified the penetration of *commercial capital into industry*, and paved the way for the complete reorganization of industry on a capitalist basis.
> (Rubin 1979: 155)

Lenin clearly comprehended and pointed out the capitalist character of an economy based on the buyer-up and the conditions that may retard the transition of this early (pre-industrial) capitalist economy to developed industrial capitalism.

> Nothing could be more absurd than the opinion that working for buyers-up is merely the result of some abuse, of some accident, *of some 'capitalization of the process of exchange' and not of production*. The contrary is true: working for a buyer-up is a special form of production, a special organization of economic relations in production. [...] In the scientific classification of forms of industry in their successive development, work for the buyers-up belongs to a considerable extent to *capitalist manufacture*, since 1) it is based on hand production and on the existence of many small establishments; 2) it introduces division of labour between these establishments and develops it also within the workshop; 3) it places the merchant at the head of production, as is always the case in manufacture, which presupposes production on an extensive scale, and the wholesale purchase of raw material and marketing of the product; 4) it reduces those who work to the status of wage-workers engaged either in a master's workshop or in their own homes [...] This form of industry, then, already

implies the deep-going rule of capitalism, being the direct predecessor of its last and highest form – large scale machine industry. *Work for the buyer-up is consequently a backward form of capitalism*, and in contemporary society this backwardness has the effect of seriously worsening the conditions of the working people, who are exploited by a host of middlemen (the sweating system), are disunited, are compelled to content themselves with the lowest wages and to work under the most insanitary conditions and for extremely long hours, and – what is most important – under conditions which render public control of production extremely difficult.

(Lenin 1977, Vol. 2: 434–435, emphasis added)

The data presented by Lenin concerning the formal subordination of handicrafts and small-scale manufacture to commercial capital are based on an analysis of the statistics then available, from which it emerges that

Merchant's and usury *capital* subordinates labour to itself in every Russian village and – without turning the producer into a wage-earner – deprives him of as much surplus-value as industrial capital takes from the working man.

(Lenin 1977, Vol. 1: 450)

Thus, in contradistinction to the position of the Narodniks, which counterposed cottage industries and small-scale manufacture (whose retention they favoured) to large-scale capitalist industry (which they held as the only existing form of capitalism), Lenin's analysis highlights the affinities between cottage industries, manufacture and large-scale industry as a development and succession of different forms of *capitalist* exploitation and dominance.

'Handicraft industry' was regarded as something economically homogeneous, something sufficient unto itself, and was 'counterposed' (sic!) to 'capitalism', which without further ado was taken to mean 'factory' industry […] The simplicity is positively touching: 'capitalism' = 'factory industry', and factory industry = what is classified under this heading in official publications. […] On the basis of this sort of 'analysis' one of the most absurd and pernicious prejudices is built up concerning the distinction between our 'handicraft' industry and our 'factory' industry, the divorcement of the latter from the former […]. It is a prejudice because no one has ever so much as attempted to examine the data, which in all branches of industry show a very close and inseparable connection between 'handicraft' industry and 'factory' industry.

(Lenin 1977, Vol. 3: 452–453)

The growth of large-scale industry accordingly takes place only as a consequence of the growth of the contradictions in and between the *different forms of capitalism* (see Lenin 1977, Vol. 3: 541–542).

3.4 Maintenance or dissolution of indirect forms of capitalist exploitation depending on class relation of forces

According to Lenin, the transition from manufacture to large-scale industrial capitalism signifies a change in the relation of forces between merchant and industrial capital. Manufacture (above all, in its primeval form of individual commercialized production by the artisan for the buyer-up) is capitalist production subordinated to merchant capital, since the latter secures capitalist centralization of the production process and its orientation towards market demand.

By contrast, large-scale industry itself embodies the typically capitalist centralization and regulation of the production process (division of labour in the factory, establishment of a hierarchy of production and mechanization, authoritarian factory discipline), and so diminishes the importance of the mediating intervention of merchant capital.

Lenin argues that this qualitative difference between the embryonic (cottage system) and the mature (large-scale industrial) forms of *capitalist production* had been analyzed by Marx himself.

> The data on Russian manufacture thus bring out in striking relief the 1aw established by the author of *Capital*, namely, that the degree of development of merchant's capital is inversely proportional to the degree of development of industrial capital. And indeed, we may characterize all the industries described [...] as follows: the fewer the big workshops in them, the more is 'buying-up' developed, and vice versa; *all that changes is the form of capital that dominates in each case* and that places the 'independent' handicraftsman in conditions which often are incomparably worse than those of the wage-worker. The fundamental error of Narodnik economics is that it ignores, or glosses over, the connection between the big and the small establishments.
>
> (Lenin 1977, Vol. 3: 440–441, emphasis added)

An analysis concerning the indirect subordination or formal subsumption of labour under merchant capital and the middleman can be found in the third volume of *Capital*, Chapter 20 (especially 452–455), and also in the first volume of *Capital*, Chapters 13 and 14 and in the *Results of the Immediate Production Process*.[5] Marx conceptualizes as "formal subsumption of labour under capital" the indirect subjection of producers to capitalist exploitation (the hybrid form of piece-wage labour, characterizing the putting-out system) and counter-poses it to the "specifically capitalist mode of production", which refers to the "real subsumption of labour under capital", or the "specifically capitalist mode of production", i.e. the full-fledged capitalist relations of production:

> The labour process becomes the instrument of the valorization process, of the process of capital's self-valorization – the process of the creation of

surplus value. The labour process is subsumed under capital (it is capital's *own* process) and the capitalist enters the process as its conductor, its director; for him it is at the same time directly a process of the exploitation of alien labour. I call this the *formal subsumption of labour under capital* […]; but at the same time it is a *particular* form alongside the developed *mode of production which is specifically capitalist*.

(Marx 1864 [§469])

As emphasized by Marx, production of both absolute surplus value, i.e. through the prolongation of the working day or the increase in the intensity of labour, and relative surplus value, i.e. through increases in labour productivity due to technological progress, represents tendencies that are permanently inherent in capitalism, having been present from the moment of the birth of capital, shaping the processes of real subordination of labour under capital (the big capitalist enterprise). Nevertheless, each tendency predominates (depending on the era) in society as a whole. The era of "formal subsumption of labour under capital" may be defined as the *era of predominance of the production of absolute surplus value*, whereas "real subsumption of labour under capital" inaugurates the era of relative surplus value:

The real subsumption of labour under capital is developed in all the forms which develop relative, as distinct from absolute, surplus value. With the real subsumption of labour under capital there takes place a complete [and a constant, continuous, and repeated] revolution in the mode of production itself, in the productivity of labour and in the relation between capitalist and worker.

(Marx 1864 [§478])

The era of capitalism of absolute surplus value will reach its end when the economic and social effects of the industrial revolution become apparent. The industrial revolution is not a 'moment' in England's or any other nation's economic history, but a transitional process (as well as a historical period) during which the real subsumption of labour under capital prevails, precisely because of the spread of industrial production into all major branches of capitalist production.

Returning to Lenin, his analysis shows that from both a social and political viewpoint, a balance of forces that allows for the retention of pre-capitalist economic remnants and political forms may, by virtue of this very fact, slow down the transition from formal to real subsumption under capital (from pre-industrial to industrial capitalism). More specifically, the existence of the Asiatic peasant commune and the limits on the free disposal of peasant labour power that are associated with that social system largely account for the tremendous power that continued to be exerted in Russia by primeval forms of capitalist exploitation and domination, as opposed to the mature forms of capitalism based on direct subordination of labour under capital.

The lack of freedom of movement, the necessity of occasionally suffering monetary loss in order to get rid of land […], the social-estate exclusiveness of the peasant community – all this artificially enlarges the sphere of application of capitalist home-work, artificially binds the peasant to these worst forms of exploitation. Obsolete institutions and an agrarian system that is thoroughly saturated with the social-estate principle thus exert a most pernicious influence in both agriculture and industry, perpetuating technically backward forms of production.

(Lenin 1977, Vol. 3: 445–446)[6]

Thus, following the line of reasoning of Lenin himself, we could assert that the transition from pre-industrial capitalist forms – characterized by formal subordination of labour to capital – to industrial capitalism, thereby consummating the real subordination of labour to capital, does not emerge from any ineluctable technological imperative or linear growth of the 'productive forces', but is a consequence of the overturning of traditional social and political relations in favour of industrial capital.

In the early stages of capitalism, the formally independent (agrarian) commodity producer and the merchant or buyer-up were the major economic agents, not only in Russia but practically in every capitalist country. The indirect subordination of labour to capital constitutes the primary form of capitalist exploitation.

As Rubin notes, commenting on this early era of capitalism:

If the spread of the domestic system was a sign of commercial capital's penetration into industry, the setting up of manufactories signified the completion of this process and the coming into being of *industrial capitalism* in the strict sense of the word. By bringing the workers together under one roof the entrepreneur rid himself of the unnecessary expense involved in distributing the materials to the individual cottage labourers and in transferring the output of some workers to others for further processing; at the same time he gained better control over the raw materials […]. On the other hand, the domestic system did relieve the entrepreneur-buyer up of all fixed-capital costs (buildings, implements of production), while it made it possible for the cottage workers to work at home and combine their activity with subsidiary occupations (agriculture, growing fruit and vegetables, etc.). *It was because of these advantages that the domestic system proved able to compete with the manufactories, all the more so since the latter held no special advantages in terms of technology.* […] Hence we very often see the *combination of the manufactory with the domestic system.*

(Rubin 1979: 156–157)

Networks of merchants, buyers-up and 'middlemen' link the farmer or artisan producer with the big merchant (and financial) enterprise through a variety of intermediary relationships involving the flows of money and commodities:

what this shows is that personal relationships and kinship links, the locality factor, linguistic affinities and, finally, ethnicity, function 'nodally' for the propagation and development of the moneyed commodity economy, that is to say for pre-industrial (merchant) capitalism. The networks of monetized communication and business dealings that end up fostering (long-distance) trade are merely an externalization of the disintegration of pre-capitalist relations of social organization and non-monetized 'natural' economies – to the advantage of the pre-industrial merchant capitalism of the first historical capitalist era.

3.5 The theoretical importance of Lenin's intervention

The strong point in Lenin's analysis, and the element that gives it its relevance as regards to the early forms of capitalism and its genesis, is that it conceives capital as a social relation of production and exploitation, and focuses on this concept. Lenin argues that a form of production relations may be considered capitalist only when labourers, freed from relations of servitude, are subordinated to the command, and subjected to the exploitation, of capitalists. This means that it is not the fact of production for a market as such that makes a form of production capitalist – it is the specific type of surplus labour extraction from the direct producer, i.e. the fact that surplus labour takes the form of surplus value, which makes exploitation capitalist. That is why it is not the traditional feudal lord exploiting the serfs and selling their product on the market that attracts Lenin's attention, but the capitalist merchant, acting as a *buyer-up*.

The buyer-up is the agent of the first, non-fully developed stage of capitalist production relations. He gains control of the direct producers' output (and in the last instance of their means of production), establishes an informal, embryonic *piece-wage relation* with them and so extracts surplus value from the labour of artisans and peasants, despite the fact that they appear to retain the status of independent commodity producers. Under certain social, economic and political circumstances, for example as a result of shifts in power relations favouring large-scale capitalist enterprises, this form of capitalist production may make the transition into the developed form of wage labour relations, the real subsumption of labour under capital.

Lenin's major methodological innovations include the simultaneous rejection of both the 'progressivist' and 'underdevelopment' prognoses, together with his analysis of the formal subordination of labour to the buyer-up, which may be seen as a critique of post-Second World War 'peripheral capitalism' – 'blocked-capitalism' approaches (Amin 1974), but also of approaches that consider capitalism as existing solely through its developed form of real subordination of labour to capital.

Lenin's approach did not aim to analyze the problem of coexistence (or 'articulation') of different modes of production, but to show under what conditions a country is to be regarded as a capitalist social formation: a social formation is not capitalist if the majority of the population is composed of wage labourers, or even labourers formally subsumed under capital, but if the dominating fraction of its ruling classes is capitalist, i.e. *if the primary form of surplus labour takes the form of surplus value.*

It is a Marxist approach that was later actualized in the work of the British historian G. E. M. de Ste. Croix:

> A class relationship, involving class *conflict*, the essence of which is exploitation, [...] (entails) *the appropriation of a surplus from the primary producer.* [...] The nature of a given mode of production is decided not according to *who does most of the work of production* but according to the specific *method of surplus appropriation*, the way in which the dominant classes extract their surplus from the producers.
>
> (Ste. Croix 1984: 101 and 107. See also de Ste. Croix 1981)

However, throughout his entire analysis, Lenin disregards the peculiarity of the agricultural economy in a *capitalist society*, i.e. the tendency towards the preservation of the viability of small- and medium-scale (commercialized) farm holdings. It is a tendency that results from the need to force down absolute rent and has a stultifying effect on any tendencies towards a concentration of holdings and domination by 'big farm capital' in the countryside, analogous to what happens in industry. This is the issue to be discussed below. I will discuss this issue in relation to Karl Kautsky's book *The Agrarian Question*, published immediately after Lenin's *The Development of Capitalism in Russia*, in the next chapter.

Notes

1 In her *Accumulation of Capital*, first published in 1913, Rosa Luxemburg wrote that in nineteenth-century Russia "the seventies and eighties represented in every respect a period of transition [...] 'Primitive accumulation' flourished splendidly, encouraged by all kinds of state subsidies, guarantees, premiums and government orders" (Luxemburg 1971: 272).

2 In his famous 1881 letter to the Russian revolutionary Vera Zasulich, Marx writes:

> I have shown in *Capital* that the transformation of feudal production into capitalist production has as a starting point the expropriation of producers, which mainly means that the expropriation of the peasants is the basis of this whole process [...] I restricted, therefore, this 'historical inevitability' to the 'countries of western Europe' [...] Surely, if capitalist production is to establish its domination in Russia, then the great majority of the peasants, that is of the Russian people, must be transformed into wage-earners and consequently expropriated, through the previous abolition of their common property. But in any way the precedent of the West will prove here absolutely nothing [...] What threatens the life of the Russian community, is neither a historical inevitability, nor a theory; it is the oppression by the side of the state and the exploitation by the intruding capitalists, who are becoming powerful with the support of this same state and to the disadvantage of the peasants.
>
> (*MEW*, Vol. 19: 396–400)

Note that Marx's argument has absolutely nothing to do with the 'PF–RP dialectic'.

3 This means that the number of wage labourers should not be considered the crucial index as to whether or not a country is capitalist.

> Marx's communist program was drawn up before 1848 [...] The smallness of the working class at that time may be judged from the fact that 27 years later, in 1875, Marx wrote that 'the majority of the toiling people in Germany consists of peasants and not of proletarians'.
>
> (Lenin 1977, Vol. 1: 319)

4 On the notion of 'class fraction' see Poulantzas 1975: 23; also Poulantzas 1973, 1980.

5 In Volume 3 of *Capital*, writes Marx:

> The transition from the feudal mode of production takes place in two different ways. The producer may become merchant and capitalist [...]. Alternatively, however, the merchant may take direct control of production himself [...]. This method [...] without revolutionising the mode of production, [....] simply worsens the conditions of the direct producers, transforms them into *mere wage-labourers and proletarians* [...] appropriating their surplus labour on the basis of the old mode of production [...]. The merchant is the *real capitalist and pockets the greater part of the surplus value*.
>
> (Marx 1991: 452–453, emphasis added)

6 For more on labour conditions in rural communities and the restriction of movement, or of private property rights, see also Lenin 1977, Vol. 2: 455, and Foreign Office, 1892, No 217: 4.

4   Capitalism and the agrarian sector

Karl Kautsky's theoretical intervention

As we saw in Chapter 3, Lenin's main thesis is that the merchant employing a certain number of household handicraftsmen or peasants through putting-out–buying-up relations is a bearer of a capitalist social relation, albeit a less-developed one compared to that of industrial capital.

What differentiates Lenin's theses on the transition from feudalism to capitalism, from those adopted in more contemporary debates (see Chapter 5), is that Lenin considers the social relations created when the merchant takes control of the craftsmen's production to be already-existing capitalist relations of production, i.e. a preliminary form of piece-wage labour, a preliminary form of surplus-value extraction. According to this view, by taking control of the craftsmen's production process, merchant capital takes control of their means of production in an informal or indirect way. Consequently, Lenin conceives industrialization as a transition from one capitalist form (the underdeveloped) to another (the developed). In contrast, most contemporary approaches conceive the initial stages of industrialization as a transition from pre-capitalism to capitalism: they conceive the merchant or buyer-up who controls handicraft production as a pre-capitalist social form facilitating the passage from pre-capitalism to capitalism. By doing so, however, they are unable to comprehend the form of surplus labour appropriated by the buyer-up, and they introduce a historical era of a supposedly non-exploitative – on the immediate economic level – 'petty mode of production'.[1]

Lenin did initially make concessions to the view, however, which is shared by most post-Second World War Marxist analyses, that with the development of capitalism in a country, and more specifically in Russia, the developed capital–wage labour relationship tended to prevail over small-scale agricultural cultivation. The conclusion that Lenin attempts to draw with the statistical data at his disposal is the following:

> The old peasantry [...] is being completely dissolved. It is ceasing to exist. It is being ousted by absolutely new types of rural inhabitants. [...] These types are the rural bourgeoisie [...] and the rural proletariat – a class of commodity producers in agriculture and a class of agricultural wage-earners.
>
> (Lenin 1977, Vol. 3: 174)

In a way, Lenin's argument reproduces Marx's conviction that the development of capitalism in the English agrarian sector was the 'classic form' of dissolution of pre-capitalist production systems[2] – but this is extremely difficult to defend. Truly, the figures quoted by Lenin himself lead to the conclusion that the growth of capitalism in Russia encouraged the division of the rural population into three separate categories of peasants. First, the rich peasants, only some of whom could be described as capitalists in the sense of the real subsumption of wage labour; these constituted approximately 28% of the rural population, and they farmed 43% of the land under cultivation. Second, the poor peasantry, a part of which was obliged to work for a wage, chiefly on a seasonal basis. The poor peasantry made up 40% of the rural population, farming 25% of the land under cultivation. And third, the middle peasantry, constituting 32% of the rural population, and farming 32% of the land under cultivation (Lenin 1977, Vol. 3: 120 ff.).

The aforementioned evidence does not justify Lenin's thesis about the division of the peasantry into a class of capitalist farmers and a class of rural wage labourers. In most capitalist countries, the development of industrial capitalism did actually oust the buyer-up and the putting-out system, but it did not lead to the formation of capitalist agriculture. Instead, an agrarian economy of small- and medium-scale (commercialized) farm holdings was formed, with large capitalist agrarian enterprises being the only exception. In some of his writings, Lenin does not attempt to deny this historical tendency:

> The distribution of allotment land among the peasant farms continues to this day to be marked by an 'equality' that is relatively very great.
>
> (Lenin 1977, Vol. 3: 628)

At the time when Lenin was writing these words, Karl Kautsky's book *Die Agrarfrage* (1899: The Agrarian Question) was published in Germany. In this book, Kautsky develops the thesis that despite the advantages in productivity of the big capitalist enterprise as compared to small- and medium-scale entrepreneurship, the agricultural economy in a capitalist society is characterized by the tendency towards the preservation of small- and medium-scale farms. The viability, in most countries, of non-capitalist commercialized holdings results from the ability of these holdings to keep prices down by forcing down absolute rent and profit, thwarting any tendencies towards the concentration of holdings and domination by 'big farm capital' in the countryside, analogous to what happens in industry.

With the publication of Kautsky's book, Lenin immediately abandoned his 'capitalist farmers vs. wage labourers' thesis and concluded alongside Kautsky, whom he cites: "As we see, the development of agriculture is quite special, quite different from the development of industrial and trading capital" (Lenin 1977, Vol. 4: 144).

Lenin celebrated Kautsky's analysis as a major breakthrough in Marxist theory, providing the following arguments:

> Kautsky's book is the most important event in present-day economic literature since the third volume of *Capital*. Until now Marxism has lacked a systematic study of capitalism in agriculture. Kautsky has filled this gap with 'The Development of Agriculture in Capitalist Society', the first part (pp. 1–300) of his voluminous (450-page) book. [...] Kautsky effectively demonstrates [...] and explains in detail how the stability of petty production in agriculture does not depend in any way on its technical rationality but on the fact that the small peasants work far harder than hired labourers and reduce their vital necessities to a level lower than that of the latter. [...] In agriculture the ousting of the small producer is hampered, primarily, by the limited size of the land area; the buying-up of small holdings to form a big holding is a very difficult matter; with intensified farming an increase in the quantity of products obtained is sometimes compatible with a reduction in the area of the land.
>
> (Lenin 1977, Vol. 4: 94, 96)

The 'agrarian question' had first been raised in the German-speaking world by Werner Sombart, in 1896, in his book *Socialism and the Social Movement in the 19th Century*.[3] Sombart had reached the conclusion that

> [...] the deductions of Marx are not applicable to agriculture without change [...] his theory of development, which rests on an assumption of [...] the proletarianising of the masses [...] does not apply to agricultural development.
>
> (Sombart 1898: 159)

According to Sombart, this very conclusion renders problematic the strategy of social democracy:

> If social democracy is to maintain its historic mission, [...] it must avoid compromise with the notoriously declining classes [...]. It will not be admissible, also, to change the programme and goal of the social movement to suit the middle-class elements that have crept in [...] because we know positively that their hand-work represents in general a low form of economy [...]. And if a man reaches the conclusion that in agrarian development, no tendency to production on a large scale exists [...] then we see before us the decisive question – Shall we now [...] change our programme and desert the communistic ideal; or shall we remain proletarian, hold fast to the communistic ideal and exclude this class from our movement?
>
> (Sombart 1898: 157–158)

Kautsky, in practice, followed the trend of thought posited by Sombart's questions. He elaborated on Marx's theory, taking into consideration, however, the empirical fact that in Germany, as in most other European capitalist countries of the time, the agrarian sector had been maintaining the character of small-scale family undertakings. Despite the commercialization of farming, there was no apparent indication of capitalist agrarian enterprises becoming dominant in the agrarian sector.

> Contrary to expectations that developments on the Continent would follow those in England they show that the small farm has not lost ground to the large since the 1850s. In fact, in terms of overall acreage, small farms seem to be growing in some areas.
>
> (Kautsky 1988: 135)

Kautsky concurs with Marx's analysis that large-scale capitalist cultivation possesses clear competitive advantages over small-scale cultivation. It has the capacity to concentrate advanced means of production, to intensify the use of machinery, to harness the benefits of workers' cooperation and thus to capitalize on a substantial and targeted division of labour. Additionally,

> the large farm is not only blessed with advantages in *production*: it also has a number of advantages in the sphere of *credit* and *commerce*.
>
> (Kautsky 1988: 104)

However, the superiority of the large farm over the small farm is not as clear-cut as in industry, as certain tendencies that are characteristic of agricultural production go against this:

> Small farms have two major weapons to set against the large. Firstly, the greater industriousness and care of their cultivators, who in contrast to wage-labourers work for themselves. And secondly, the frugality of the small independent peasant, greater even than that of the agricultural labourer.
>
> (Kautsky 1988: 110)

Marx himself had pointed out that the self-employed peasant, being satisfied with an income no higher than a worker's wage, is able to keep the price of agricultural products down, as these prices reproduce neither profit nor rent, as in the case of capitalist agriculture:

> In order for the peasant smallholder to cultivate his land or to buy land to cultivate, therefore, it is not necessary, as in the normal capitalist mode of production, for the market price of the agricultural product to rise high enough to yield him the average profit, and still less an excess over and above this average profit that is fixed in the form of rent. [...] This lower

price of corn in countries of small-scale ownership is a result of the poverty of the producers and in no way of the productivity of their labour.

(Marx 1991: 942)

The moral of the tale, which can also be extracted from other discussions of agriculture, is that the capitalist system runs counter to a rational agriculture, or that *a rational agriculture is incompatible with the capitalist system* (even if the latter promotes technical development in agriculture) and *needs either small farmers working for themselves or the control of the associated producers.*

(Marx 1991: 216, emphasis added)

The suppression of agrarian prices through the 'frugality' of the self-sustained peasant plays a positive role in the overall reproduction of a capitalist society, as it actually suppresses the price of real wages, i.e. the reproduction costs of labour power.

According to Kautsky, there are also additional reasons that favour the maintenance, and in most cases prevalence, of small-scale agriculture.

Industry is always able to multiply its means of production if conditions render it profitable. On the contrary, land of a certain level of fertility constitutes a rather fixed magnitude, despite potential improvements accruing from the use of fertilizers, etc. Accumulation of capital in industry does not presuppose the unification of enterprises. A profitable economic performance of an individual capital in the industry sector is a prerequisite for favourable access to bank loans, an increase in available money capital and large-scale investments. The same is not necessarily the case for a capitalist enterprise in the agrarian sector, as a large-scale increase in production presupposes the amassing of cultivable land. However, the centralization of capital through the unification of formerly separate individual capitals, which is a straightforward process in industry, is rather difficult to realize in the agrarian sector, as the lots to be unified must constitute an interconnected area:

Establishing a shoe factory in a particular locality does not necessitate expropriating all the local craft shoemakers. […] In contrast, where all land is private property, predominantly in the form of small-scale land-ownership, a large farm can only be established through the centralisation of a number of small property holders. The elimination of these farms is the absolute precondition for the emergence of large farms.

(Kautsky 1988: 145–146)

In addition, the historical evolution of capitalism in continental Europe did not create the necessary conditions for the full dissociation of farmers from the means of production. As Kautsky puts it:

Under such circumstances, wage-labour on the land is quite different to that in the towns. A totally propertyless wage-labourer, living in his own

> household, is a rarity. Some wage-labourers on large-scale agricultural enterprises will be members of the household as maids or manservants. Others with their own households are also usually independent farmers, on their own or rented land, devoting only part of their time to wage-labour, and the rest to working their own land.
>
> (Kautsky 1988: 161)

The fact that the agrarian household always tends to acquire its own means of production results in the large farm never being able to completely prevail in any given country.

> Even in Great Britain there were no less than 117,968 farms of less than 5 acres out of a total of 520,106 in 1895: 149,818 ranged between 5 and 20 acres, and 185,663 between 20 and 50 acres – that is, the vast majority were small farms.
>
> (Kautsky 1988: 163)

The 'agrarian question', as posited by Kautsky's theoretical intervention, challenges all the approaches that portray the genesis of capitalism as a process taking place mainly, if not exclusively, in the agrarian sector of society: in other words, as a process of transformation from feudal to capitalist relations of production *on land*.

As we have already seen in Chapter 2, Marx's own reasoning can hardly justify these approaches, which I will discuss more extensively in the next chapter. Marx clearly argues that "the formation of capital does not emerge from landed property [...] but rather from merchant's and usurer's wealth" (Marx 1993: 504–505, see Chapter 2). Kautsky's analysis on the 'agrarian question' follows Marx's trend of thought exactly:

> With the exception of a few colonies, the capitalist mode of production generally begins its development in *towns*, in *industry*, leaving agriculture largely undisturbed initially. But the development of industry in itself soon begins to affect the character of agricultural production.
>
> (Kautsky 1988: 13)

> Capitalist agriculture only began to become significant once urban capital, and hence the credit system, had become well developed.
>
> (Kautsky 1988: 88)

A final concluding remark on the articulation of small- and medium-scale agriculture in capitalism is needed before I close this chapter.

Historically, the ability of the bourgeoisie in any country to expand its power over the antagonistic (pre-capitalist) modes of production and to cause the disintegration of the latter is the most critical presumption of capitalist development (Economakis and Milios 2001). This process necessarily takes the form of *agrarian reform*, because agrarian property constitutes the basis of the pre-capitalist mode of production (Senghaas 1982). Agrarian reform is put forward by an already dominant bourgeois strategy, as capitalism prevails in the non-agrarian sectors of the economy and shapes a corresponding capitalist state apparatus. However, in most cases, as Kautsky pointed out, agrarian reform does not tend to establish capitalist relations of production in the agrarian sector of the economy; it mainly serves to develop relations of *simple commodity production* based on the land ownership of the producers.

This form of production does not constitute an economic system antagonistic to (industrial) capitalism, but on the contrary it complements the latter; it is an excellent example of an economic precondition for its accelerated development.

The subjection of simple commodity peasant production to industrial capital (the food and raw material manufacturing sector, commercial seed industry, etc.), to state economic policy (via subsidies and 'fixation' of prices of agrarian products) and to the credit system (purchase of production means through bank loans) guarantees low prices for agrarian products and a reduction, therefore, in the costs of reproduction of labour power.

Capitalist relations are 'positively articulated' with the form of simple commodity production (Milios and Economakis 2011), which enables small- and medium-scale agrarian production to be easily embedded in capitalism. The same is true for non-agrarian simple commodity production, the small-scale trade and manufacturing sectors of the economy. The magnitude of the form of simple commodity production, its preservation in various sectors of a capitalist society or, on the contrary, the rate of its dissolution depends on several factors, among which the level of profitability and the increase of labour productivity in the dominating, capitalist sector of the economy play a very important role.

Notes

1 "An interval had to elapse during which the petty mode of production, which was the legacy of feudal society, was itself partially broken up or else subordinated to capital [...]. The essence of primary accumulation is [...] the transfer of property from small owners to the ascendant bourgeoisie and the subsequent pauperization of the former" (Dobb 1975: 181, 185). Lenin has, however, shown that small-scale property can formally persist, along with the development of buying-up, with the expansion of specialized markets and of long-distance trade, and with the accumulation of wealth (surplus value) in the hands of the capitalist merchants (buyer-up).

2 According to Marx,

> The expropriation of the agricultural producer, of the peasant, from the soil, [...] in different countries, assumes different aspects, and runs through its various phases in different orders of succession, and at different periods. *In England alone*, which we take as our example, *has it the classic form.*
>
> (Marx 1887: 508, emphasis added)

3 *Sozialismus und soziale Bewegung im 19. Jahrhundert: nebst einem Anhang: Chronik der sozialen Bewegung von 1750 – 1896*, Jena: Verlag von Gustav Fischer 1896.

5   Post-Second World War Marxist approaches to the 'transition to capitalism' question

Since the Second World War, a large array of Marxist literature on the 'transition to capitalism' and the origin of capitalism has been produced. The diverse approaches reflect a variety of conceptualizations of capitalism and, in some instances, certain thoughts on its future demise. Many of these approaches constitute not only theoretical interpretations of the rise of capitalism but also specific, applied historical studies of the late medieval or early modern periods in certain countries or regions. They thus contribute diversely to our knowledge of those periods. However, I will not go into a detailed discussion of these approaches, as the aim of this book is to identify the incipient elements in capitalism, the coming "face to face and into contact [...] on the one hand, the owners of money [...] on the other hand, free labourers",[1] to use Marx's theoretical schema that I discussed in Chapter 2. Our critical presentation will therefore be necessarily eclectic, focusing mainly on certain Marxist 'traditions' that have been established on what I may refer to as the Post-Second World War Marxist theoretical scene.

As analyzed in Chapter 2 (especially Section 2.3.2), the focus of my analysis in this book is primarily on the process of *emergence* of the capital relation *in the framework of non-capitalist society*. This means that I will not be dealing with approaches that focus on transformations of labour and property relations in societies where capitalist class interests and capitalist strategies had already been consolidated or at least shaped, and where capitalist social relations and forms of exploitation have paved their way into non-capitalist sectors (or their remnants) of society. Such approaches, as, for example, those of Michael Perelman (2000)[2] or Massimo De Angelis (2007),[3] although interesting and fruitful in many aspects, do not fall within the scope of analysis of the *origins of capitalism*, which is the principal subject of this book.

With the criterion of the emergence of capital as a social relation, four Marxist theoretical traditions[4] may be identified: the 'agrarian origin of capitalism', State-Feudalism, the 'forces of production' and 'world-capitalism'. The theoretical foundations of these four traditions will be rebutted on the basis of theoretical elaboration and arguments already developed in the previous chapters.

5.1 The 'agrarian origin of capitalism' tradition

Maurice Dobb's book *Studies in the Development of Capitalism*, first published in 1946, set off an intense theoretical debate among Marxist scholars. Dobb argued that feudalism had been trapped in a fatal crisis and a process of dissolution since the fourteenth century, which was considered to be the consequence of the class struggle of serfs, who managed to strengthen their social position and to eventually free themselves from the feudal lords' seigniorage rule. However, (according to Dobb) the beginning of capitalism is to be temporally located only two centuries later, in the late sixteenth and seventeenth centuries.

Dobb's understanding of class struggle is based on a rather simplistic 'dialectic of the one contradiction': class rule transformed into something 'opposite' through accumulation of 'quantity' (i.e. resulting in the social configuration of *one* class ruling over another), which finally leads to a 'new quality' (i.e. a novel class configuration and class rule).[5]

> It is in each case a matter of quantitative growth which is at a certain stage sufficient to involve a qualitative change.
>
> (Dobb 1975: 126)

Since the principal contradiction in feudalism is between feudal lords and serfs, and it is *situated mainly on land* (in the rural areas of any social formation), the change of 'quality' from the feudal social relation to the capitalist–worker social relation also has to be situated on land. Therefore, according to Dobb, original accumulation simply means the transformation of the ownership form of *existing agrarian production assets* from the feudal to capitalist ownership form, or the creation of claims on feudal assets. The form of feudal ownership of land is hence transformed into full ownership, which is peculiar to the (emergent) capitalist ownership form. Subsequently, landowners in this new form lend their lots to producers, who gradually amass land and become capitalists, hiring wage labourers for their business.

> If any sense is to be made [...] to the notion of a primitive accumulation (in Marx's sense of the term) *prior in time* to the full flowering of capitalist production, this must be interpreted in the first place as an accumulation of capitalist *claims* of titles to existing assets which are accumulated primarily for speculative reasons; and secondly as accumulation in the hands of a class that, by virtue of its special position in society, is capable ultimately of transforming these hoarded titles to wealth into actual means of production. In other words, when one speaks of accumulation in an historical sense, one must be referring to the *ownership* of assets, and to a *transfer* of ownership, and not to the quantity of tangible instruments of production in existence.
>
> (Dobb 1975: 178)

The 'dialectic' of one-dimensional quantitative growth, which eventually leads to qualitative change, is also used as an explanatory scheme for the emergence of the capitalist relation, two centuries after the demise of serfdom. This 'transformation of quantity into quality' is expressed in

> a growth of the resources of the small man sufficient to cause him to place greater reliance on the results of hired labour than on the work of himself and his family, and in his calculations to relate the gains of his enterprise to his capital rather than to his own exertions.
>
> (Dobb 1975: 126)

> It is from the petty mode of production [...] that capitalism is born.
>
> (Dobb 2006: 59)

In contraposition to Lenin's and Kautsky's analyses that "the capitalist mode of production generally begins its development in *towns*, in *industry*, leaving agriculture largely undisturbed initially" (Kautsky 1988: 13, see Chapters 3 and 4), Dobb introduces a Marxist tradition that traces the birth of capitalism to the land. First, feudal power relations dissolve, and then, centuries later, capitalist relations are created on the land as a result of the polarization of small producers: into well-to-do peasants on the one hand, some of whom eventually become capitalists, and the decline of family cultivation on the other, out of which the class of propertyless proletarians emerge. This, according to Dobb, is the 'revolutionary path' to capitalism.

It is obvious that this approach does not even remotely acknowledge Marx's central idea of the coming "face to face and into contact" of the money-owner with the propertyless individual.

In 1950, a critique of Dobb's book by Paul Sweezy was published in *Science and Society* (Sweezy 2006), and was followed up with a reply by Dobb in the same journal (Dobb 2006). Sweezy argues that in the demise of feudalism a very decisive role was played by the development of trade and the money economy of cities, which developed as a system of "production for the market" (Sweezy 2006: 41), where "the possession of wealth soon becomes an end in itself" (ibid.: 43) as opposed to feudalism, which constituted a system of "production for use" (ibid.: 41)[6]; he concludes:

> It seems to me that Dobb has not succeeded in shaking that part of the commonly accepted theory which holds that the root cause of the decline of feudalism was the growth of trade.
>
> (Sweezy 2006: 41)

Sweezy's critique triggered the intervention of seven other Marxist scholars (Christopher Hill, Rodney Hilton, Georges Lefebvre, Kohachiro Takahashi, Giuliano Procacci, John Merrington and Eric Hobsbawm, see Hilton 2006a) who largely defended Dobb's analysis. As Sweezy – stressing the importance of trade, cities and the market – seemed to refer to a process of social change that was 'external' to the principal contradiction in the feudal system (the lord–serf relation and contradiction), he was denounced as a proponent of a 'non-Marxist' view:

> His [Sweezy's] own suggestion that feudalism had no 'prime mover' that is no internal dialectic, is in fact non-Marxist.
>
> (Hilton 2006c: 109)

The 'Dobb debate', as we may call it, practically consolidated the view introduced by Dobb himself that capitalism emerged as a 'new' *system of agrarian economy*. All Marxist analyses that stress the fact that capitalism begins in the non-agrarian economic sectors, and also that in most capitalist countries the agrarian sector tends to be dominated not by capitalist but by small- and medium-scale farming, were thrust aside. What is more, in the tradition inaugurated by Dobb's analysis, trade was considered to be a constituent element of feudalism:

> The tendency of historical enquiry since has been to situate towns within the feudal mode, arguing the compatibility of towns with feudalism in Europe, the feudal origin of towns and indeed the integral role of merchant capital within the feudal mode.
>
> (Merrington 2006: 175)

Shortly after the publication of the 'Dobb debate' in an edited collection in 1976 (see Hilton 2006a), a second debate on the 'transition to capitalism' commenced. It was labelled the 'Brenner debate' (Aston and Philpin 1985), as it was initiated following the publication of Robert Brenner's paper "Agrarian Class Structure and Economic Development in Pre-Industrial Europe" in 1976.[7]

In this paper, Brenner argues that the 'transition to capitalism' became necessary after the fatal crisis of feudalism, caused by the lords' constant striving for ever-increasing surpluses, a situation that not only put the very existence of peasants at risk, but also exhausted the reproductive capacity of society.

> Thus, the lord's surplus extraction (rent) tended to confiscate not merely the peasant's income above subsistence (and potentially even beyond) but at the same time to threaten the funds necessary to refurbish the peasant's holding and to prevent the long-term decline of its productivity. [...] This was entirely unproductive 'profit', for hardly any of it was 'ploughed back' into production; most was squandered in military expenditure and conspicuous consumption.
>
> (Brenner 1976: 48)

According to Brenner's approach, (the former feudal) lords were the instigating and leading forces in this transition. They realized the possibility of bringing the (agrarian) economy back on the development track by changing property relations and cooperating with well-to-do peasants (who were gradually becoming rural capitalists) on the basis of full ownership relations of land on the one hand, and production for market on the other. Original accumulation thus ends up being, according to Brenner, a process of 'liberation' or 'emancipation' of the peasants from the lords' coercive yoke, to the mutual benefit of both parties:

> What proved, therefore, most significant for English agricultural development was the particularly productive use of the agricultural surplus promoted by the special character of its rural class relations; in particular, the displacement of the traditionally antagonistic relationship in which landlord 'squeezing' undermined tenant initiative, by an emergent landlord-tenant symbiosis which brought mutual co-operation in investment and improvement.
>
> (Brenner 1976: 65)[8]

Two years later, in 1978, Brenner published a paper on Dobb's book in which he criticizes Dobb for erroneously portraying the landlord as a fetter to the transition to capitalism and for overemphasizing the peasants' contribution to the process as compared to the landlord's protagonistic role. According to Dobb's analysis, Brenner argues:

> there appears to be the assumption that peasant production, once freed from the controls of serfdom, will evolve more or less automatically in the direction of capitalism.
>
> (Brenner 1978: 134)

> Dobb tends to fall back toward the older conception of direct transition via the rise of the bourgeoisie, external to feudalism.
>
> (ibid.: 122)

> [...] Capitalism in early modern England [...] grew up [...] within a landlord structure – a structure which had been formed out of the fall of serfdom and the gradual undermining of peasant possession of the land.
>
> (ibid.: 138)

The whole Brenner debate, despite differences of opinion or disagreements, was firmly situated inside the 'agrarian origin of capitalism' approach. As expected, Brenner continued to support the same approach in his later works.[9]

This 'agrarian origins of capitalism' thesis, which constituted the theoretical ground of both debates already mentioned, was also predominant in a large part of post-War analyses by Marxist historians and theoreticians. A characteristic example is the work of Ellen Meiksins Wood (2002), who pushes Brenner's logic to the limit: capitalism was first born as an agrarian system in England; the rest is the result of this original genesis.

Capitalism, with all its very specific drives of accumulation and profit-maximization, was born not in the city but in the countryside.

(Wood 2002: 95)

The transformation of social property relations was firmly rooted in the countryside, and the transformation of English trade and industry was *result more than cause of England's transition to capitalism*. Merchants [...] prospered, as we have seen, in the context of European feudalism, where they profited not only from the autonomy of cities but also from the fragmentation of markets and the opportunity to conduct transactions between one market and another.

(ibid.: 129–130, emphasis added)

Both debates have been repeatedly considered and critically discussed by Marxist scholars (Holton 1985; Katz 1993; Heller 2011). However, the theoretical contributions of Kautsky and Lenin as regards the agrarian question (see Chapter 4) seem to have been set aside by the majority of contemporary Marxist writers.[10]

5.2 The 'State-Feudalism' tradition: revenge of the Narodniks?

As stated above, the proponents of the 'agrarian origin of capitalism' approach argue that a historical interim existed between the decline of feudalism and the rise of capitalism. This thesis moots the question about the character of production relations, and the class configuration between two well-defined class systems in British and European societies during this interim. Dobb alleges that the prevalent economic structure during this intermediate or transitional period was simple commodity production or petty production of a worker (or a working family), who was owner of his/her own means of production and did not employ alien salaried labour. He claims that:

the disintegration of the feudal mode of production had already reached an advanced stage before the capitalist mode of production developed, and that this disintegration did not proceed in any close association with the growth of the new mode of production within the womb of the old. The two hundred-odd years which separated Edward III and Elizabeth were certainly transitional in character. [...] one sees a mode of production which had won its independence from Feudalism: petty production of the worker-owner, artisan or peasant type.

(Dobb 1975: 20)

Brenner agrees with Dobb that a mode of 'petty production' prevailed in the place of feudal serfdom relations, which had disintegrated.[11] He only questions Dobb's view that peasant petty producers possessed the ability to create capitalism (as opposed to landlords, who actually guided the process of transition to capitalism, as he sees it):

> [...] the freeing of the petty production from the fetters of serfdom can-not directly determine a subsequent evolution to capitalism.
>
> (Brenner 1978: 136)

However, this petty production of the self-employed peasant family is by definition a non-exploitative economic form: it is impossible to define a re-lation of *direct class exploitation*, as there is no extraction of any form of surplus from one social group in favour of another. On the contrary, a rather egal-itarian society within the peasant village communities is portrayed, at least during the initial historical phase after the fall of feudal relations of exploita-tion.[12] The question thus arises as to what the class character of the social system was during this interim period.

From the fact that over the peasant communities, like all other economic actors, stood the *absolutist state*, Dobb came to the conclusion that the feudal order had continued to exist: that society continued to be feudal, in the form of *indirect* class exploitation of the peasants by the aristocracy, *through the abso-lutist state*. It is interesting how Dobb defended this thesis, while recognizing at the same time that it was not the peasant communities, but *trade*, that oc-cupied the leading role in the economy:

> The ruling class was still feudal and [...] that [absolutist, J.M.] state was still the political instrument of its rule [...]. True, since trade had come to occupy a leading place in the economy, this ruling class had itself an interest in trade [...] and took certain sections of the merchant bour-geoisie [...] into economic partnership and into political alliance with itself.
>
> (Dobb 2006: 63)

Dobb introduces a new definition of feudalism: State-Feudalism, or 'polit-ical feudalism', which abstracts from the mode of production in the strict sense, i.e. the direct exploitation and domination on the economic level (see Chapter 2, and in more detail, Chapter 7). It is not the form of sur-plus and the historically specific mode by which this surplus is extracted within the process of production that builds the foundation of a historically specific system of class exploitation *and* domination; even though these classical forms of feudalism had evaporated, the social system was suppos-edly being preserved through a state form heretofore non-existent, which emerged to save feudalism. The absolutist state is conceived by Dobb as the determining factor in the social totality and is also proclaimed as being 'feudal' in character.[13]

Brenner follows exactly the same line of thought as regards the indirect exploitation of the peasants by means of the absolutist state:

> Through the absolutist state the peasants' surplus was directly and forcefully extracted, especially by taxation, largely to the benefit of the aristocracy (Brenner 1978: 133).

However, Brenner saw in the absolutist state a modified, transitional, if not transitory, form of feudalism:

> The absolutist state was no mere guarantor of the old forms of property based on decentralized seigneurial extraction. Rather, it came to express a *transformed* version of the old system.
>
> (Brenner 1985: 289)
>
> The state which emerged during the Tudor period was, however, not absolutism.
>
> (ibid.: 298)[14]

This analysis built the basis for a certain way of interpreting expansionism and imperialism even in the era of developed capitalism in the nineteenth and twentieth centuries (see Milios and Sotiropoulos 2009: 129 ff.). Brenner's approach played an important role in this direction. As I have already mentioned, according to Brenner, a characteristic of each historical period is its own *property relations* that, once established, impose constrictive boundaries on every form of economic development. This means that property relations limit and shape the behaviour of economic actors, who are always in a position to rigorously pursue specific strategies for the reproduction of the social and economic positions they occupy. Consequently, one of the most conspicuous peculiarities in the analysis of Brenner (1982) has to do with his reappraisal of absolutism. According to this reappraisal, social property relations accompanying the period of absolutism are not yet capitalistic without being at the same time *specifically* feudal. This also determines the character of the absolutist state, which, although feudal, is caught up in the maelstrom of *geopolitical accumulation* (Brenner 1982: 36–41).

In pre-capitalist periods – consistent with Brenner's reasoning (ibid.) – for a number of reasons, there was no incentive for increasing production through the introduction of technology. As a result, the basic means at the disposal of the ruling class for improving its own material situation (apart from collecting land rent from the peasants) was through *territorial expansion*. This involved a number of prerequisites, such as, for example, expenditure on military forces and armaments, but also demanded more effective political organization of the feudal domains with a view to concentrating resources to finance military operations. Pre-capitalist social organization thus necessarily included a dynamic of territorial expansion and consolidation of states in which the dominant process is that of *geopolitical accumulation* through the conquest of new territory. This process, in essence, is accumulation through the redistribution of wealth.[15]

Several authors have drawn on the problematique of Brenner (Teschke 2003; Wood 2003; Lacher 2005; van der Pijl 2006), sharing the opinion that geopolitical competition between (absolutist) states preceded capitalism. In fact, what Brenner's followers find interesting is that via the mechanism of political accumulation, there is projection of a process for consolidating transitional states prior to the establishment of capitalism. It is a view that inevitably leads to the conclusion that

> capitalism [...] came to exist, politically, in the form of a system of territorial states – a historical legacy of the post-feudal period that continues to structure capitalism until the present day (though perhaps not beyond).
> (Lacher 2005: 34; see also Teschke and Lacher 2007)

Along the same line of thought, Brenner concludes:

> That capitalism is governed by multiple states is the result of the historical fact that it emerged against the background of a system of multiple feudal states, and, in the course of its development, transformed the component states of that system into capitalist states but failed to alter the multi-state character of the resulting international system.
> (Brenner 2006: 84)

In the opinion of these authors, absolutism did not promote a capitalist bourgeoisie; that is why the absolutist state failed to become a modern state. It was not even a precursor of, or transitional stage towards, a modern state (Teschke 2003: 189–193). Mercantilism was a strategy of rationalization of absolutist rulers who failed to promote capitalist industry. Mercantilism's social rationale was based on the persistence of non-capitalist social property relations, which necessitated the internal and external accumulation of surplus by political means, either through direct political coercion of direct producers or through politically promoted unequal exchange, that is, through political accumulation (ibid.: 210). To quote Teschke and Lacher:

> But if the countries of continental Europe, under different forms of absolutism or other non-capitalist forms of political-economic organization, were not capitalist, they nevertheless pioneered a form of state that continues to influence the organization of political space even today.
> (Teschke and Lacher 2007: 573)

The basic position of these approaches is that the geopolitical dynamic of capitalism and of imperialist competition have not entailed anything specifically capitalistic: to a significant extent, they are part of an inheritance from pre-capitalist absolutism. For a significant part of its history (until recently), capitalism has coexisted with a sort of geopolitical competition that is foreign to its specific historical character.[16]

Following this line of argumentation, Giovanni Arrighi remarked that what distinguishes capitalism from pre-capitalism can be reduced to two opposing 'modes of rule or logics of power'. In his analysis:

> Territorialist rulers identify power with the extent and populousness of their domains, and conceive of wealth/capital as a means or a by-product of the pursuit of territorial expansion. Capitalist rulers, in contrast, identify power with the extent of their command over scarce resources and consider territorial acquisitions as a means and a by-product of the accumulation of capital. Paraphrasing Marx's general formula of capitalist production (MCM'), we may render the difference between the two logics of power by the formulas TMT' and MTM', respectively. According to the first formula, abstract economic command or money (M) is a means or intermediate link in a process aimed at the acquisition of additional territories (T' minus T = +ΔT). According to the second formula, territory (T) is a means or an intermediate link in a process aimed at the acquisition of additional means of payment (M' minus M = +ΔM).
>
> (Arrighi 1996: 32–34)

I do not propose to embark on a detailed commentary of these views because it would divert me from the purpose of this book. What is worth noting here is that the tradition of State-Feudalism revives the basic idea of the Russian Narodniks, that there can be a dominant economic and social structure based on an agrarian 'petty mode of production', which is, however, rendered feudal or pre-capitalist if the absolutist state intervenes, and which can be hence considered a vehicle of rejuvenated feudal domination and exploitation.

In my view, the whole State-Feudalism problematique fails to elaborate a consistent theory of the state. It appears to oscillate theoretically between an understanding of the state as a *thing* or *instrument* in the hands of a class – which is itself a creation of this very state – and a conception of the state as an *autonomous subject*.

I have already outlined a Marxist notion of the state, according to which, unlike in the instrumentalist conception, class contradictions are not perceived as being external to the state. But, by the same token, in contrast to the conception of the state as a subject, in this view, the contradictions within the state cease to be external to class struggle.

In other words, the state, as a constituent element of the dominant class relations of power, possesses certain historically specific structural characteristics that differentiate it from state forms or forms of political domination that pertain to historically diverse systems of class power relations. The class character of the state arises, objectively, from its very structure and the thereby accruing functions.

As Nicos Poulantzas (1973: 147–184) has correctly argued in a relevant analysis, the absolutist state, although transitional, constitutes *a state with manifestly capitalist characteristics*, an institutional form already corresponding to the capitalist state power, in the historical period of formal subsumption of labour under capital:

> Capital, as an (economic) relation of property, in reality exists *before* the 'real subsumption' of the labourer under capital [...]: this is the case both for formal juridical relations of private property and for the transition state [...], the institutional form of political domination (the absolutist transition state) is a form of capitalist state [...].
>
> (Poulantzas 1973: 159)[17]

The first form of capitalist class power that emerged in the course of its historical development, capitalism of 'formal subsumption' of labour under capital, is thus linked to the emergence of the absolutist state, as a transitional form of the *bourgeois state*. It comprises the type of political power necessary to safeguard the consolidation of capitalism, subsequently stabilizing the social power of capital. But state power is imposed not only internally, within the bounds of its own territory; it is also projected outwards to safeguard the conditions for expanded reproduction of capitalist relations (of the aggregate-social capital) in the given social formation, and the resources that are required for it to become possible. What emerges, in other words, is a tendency in *every* capitalist social formation to expand beyond its boundaries:

> The transition from feudal to capitalist economy enjoyed the active promotion of *state authorities*, whose increasing centralization ran parallel with the growing strength of merchant capital [...]. To smash through the privileges of the estate holders and towns, a strong crown was essential. But the bourgeoisie also needed a powerful state to protect its international trade, to conquer colonies, and to fight for hegemony over the world market [...] Thus the age of *merchant capital* was also the age of *absolute monarchy*.
>
> (Rubin 1979: 24–25)

In this context, the absolutist state becomes the vehicle for unbridled territorial expansionism, which means colonialism by the capitalist powers. I will elaborate on this issue in Parts II and III.

5.3 The persistent 'theory of Production Forces' tradition

In Section 2.2, I critically presented the 'theory of Production Forces', or the 'Productive Forces – Relations of production dialectic', which appears sporadically in some of Marx's writings without ever actually constituting a consistent or crystallized theory. I also presented the Marxist critiques of this approach, which have shown that the 'dialectic' under question is inadequate as an explanatory scheme of historical development, particularly in regard to the question of how capital as a social relation came into existence. At this point, I do not intend to reiterate the arguments of that analysis. I only want to clarify for the reader that this mechanistic–progressivist approach has built a very strong tradition within Marxist analyses that deal with the issue of the origins of capitalism. Besides, it also proves to be fully compatible with both the 'agrarian origin of capitalism' tradition and the State-Feudalism tradition.

In both debates discussed earlier, within the context of the 'agrarian origin of capitalism' tradition, the 'theory of Production Forces' constitutes a persisting argument reinforcing ideas about class struggle, the crisis of serfdom, etc. Dobb clearly lays the groundwork for the merging of these traditions:

> The coercive relationship, consisting in the direct extraction of the surplus labour of producers by the ruling class, was conditioned *of course* by a certain level of development of the productive forces.
>
> (Dobb 2006: 58, emphasis added)

Other proponents of the same tradition use the 'development of the productive forces' thesis as a polemic,[18] or as a basis for a pastiche of different arguments, derived from diverse historical processes.[19]

However, it is Robert Brenner, once again, who radicalizes a commonly accepted thesis: according to his view, capitalism came about more or less as a result of rational choice of both lords and well-to-do peasants, when they both realized, amidst the crisis of feudalism, that a new system based not on extra-economic coercion, but on market relations, could safeguard the development of the production forces!

> In particular, reproduction by the lords through surplus extraction by means of extra-economic compulsion and by peasants through production for subsistence precluded any widespread tendencies to thorough specialization of productive units, systematic reinvestment of surpluses, or to regular technical innovation. [...] The consequence [...] was the rise of a novel social-property system, above all on the land, in which, for the first time, the organizers of production and the direct producers (sometimes the same persons) *found it* both *necessary* and *possible* to reproduce themselves through a course of economic action which was, on a system-wide scale, favourable to *the continuing development of the productive forces*.
>
> (Brenner 1985: 214, emphasis added)[20]

In all the cases discussed, the 'theory of the Productive Forces' is used as supplementary argumentation to support the main rationale of the analyses that form the 'agrarian capitalism'[21] and State-Feudalism traditions.

However, other approaches utilize it as the main explanatory line of thinking. Soviet Marxists are perhaps the most characteristic proponents of this tradition. Nevertheless, certain Western Marxists follow the same course of arguments, stressing a general Productive Forces (PF) – Relations of Production (RP) 'dialectic'. The most characteristic case is perhaps that of G. A. Cohen (1989), who claims "that history is, fundamentally, the growth of human productive power" (Cohen 1989: 3), and that:

> we must turn to the dialectic of forces and relations of production which governs class behaviour and is not explicable in terms of it, and which determines what the long-term outcome of class struggle will be.
>
> (ibid.: 14)[22]

Having thoroughly explored this approach in Chapter 2, I shall restrict myself here by reiterating my main conclusion: the 'theory of the Productive Forces' is totally inadequate as an explanatory scheme, providing heuristic theoretical inquiry into the question of the birth of capitalism.

5.4 The 'world–capitalism' tradition

During the first decades of the twentieth century, a distinct viewpoint on the *global character* of capitalism was introduced into the assemblage of Marxist theories of imperialism (by Rudolf Hilferding, Rosa Luxemburg, Nikolai Bukharin and V. I. Lenin, see Milios and Sotiropoulos 2009: 14 ff.). This viewpoint states that the capitalist mode of production, the fundamental structural relationships and class relations that characterize the capitalist system, are reproduced in their most fully developed form only at the level of the global economy and, accordingly, that the laws and the causal relationships discovered and analyzed by Marx pertain to the global economy, which consequentially takes the form of a single capitalist social structure.

After the Second World War, the notion of world-capitalism became cardinal for shaping the 'centre–periphery' Marxist stream of thought. An analysis of the global capitalist economy has been elaborated from this starting point, with Andre Gunder Frank, Samir Amin and Immanuel Wallerstein being its key exponents. According to this analysis, from the moment that the global market was created, i.e. roughly from the sixteenth century onwards, humanity as a whole (that is to say, all the areas linked to or comprising the global market) is capitalistic, polarized between the metropolis and the periphery, and pervaded by monopolistic structures. The global economy and (global) capitalism are, by this logic, synonymous terms. In Wallerstein's formulation, capitalism is:

> a mode of production in which the objective is to produce profit on the market. Capitalism has from the outset been a matter of the global economy, not of national states.
>
> (Wallerstein 1979: 63)

So it is pointless, and moot, to speak of other pre-capitalist modes of production (or of socialism), and employing as one's criterion the relation between producers and the means of production, the form of the state, etc.

At the heart of these theories is the concept of the interconnectedness of the *global system*. This interconnectedness, apart from anything else, is grounded in the structural contradiction between *centre* and *periphery*. Individual states, then, are the units par excellence of the global system, the relations between them being subject to a structural centre–periphery relationship, often utilizing the intermediate category of the *semi-periphery*. However, within this theoretical discussion on global systems, two very different sets of assumptions are encountered.

On the one hand, there are those who consider that "something distinctive occurred in (Western) Europe which was radically new somewhere in early modern times" (Wallerstein 1996: 292, see also Wallerstein 1974, 1980; Amin 1996). The modern 'world system' thus dates from around 500 years ago. Its capitalist mode of production makes it fundamentally different from 'world empires' and all previous 'world systems'.

On the other hand, there are also those who insist on speaking of a historically *unique* global system, the basic features of which have remained unchanged for at least the last 5,000 years (Frank and Gills 1996). From this point of view, there are characteristic similarities between modern world-capitalism and 'other' earlier empires, state systems or regional economies. There was no historical transition from 'something else' to capitalism because whatever happened in Europe in the sixteenth century was simply a shift within the context of a 'world system', which had already existed for several thousand years. It is argued that the essential features of the global capitalist mode of production can be extended back in time at least 5,000 years (ibid.: 11).

Within the parameters of the same schema, Frank (1969) asserted that capitalist development and underdevelopment are predicated on three fundamental antitheses: extraction/appropriation of economic surplus, polarization between metropolitan and satellite countries, and the conflict between continuity and development. Assuming that all productive processes involving the market are capitalist, Frank came out in opposition to all the theories that link the underdevelopment of the periphery to domination by, or even preservation of, expanded reproduction of certain pre-capitalist modes of production. As part of the global system, he asserted, the periphery has always been capitalistic – in the same way that the centre has always been capitalistic. The capitalism of the periphery is simply different from the capitalism of the metropolis: it is an underdeveloped capitalism. What takes place in the periphery is "the development of underdevelopment".[23] Similarly, the toiling and exploited masses belong to the (global) proletariat, but again, this proletariat differs from the proletariat of the metropolitan centres.

The global system finally takes shape, according to Frank, as an integrated colonial system whose structure may be compared to that of a solar system of planets revolving around a sun. The metropolitan centres are enriched by the satellites, but there may be other satellites revolving around a satellite, dependent on it. This is a fundamental and permanent feature of the global system.[24] One consequence of this solar-centred structure of the global system, however, is that some intermediate regions inevitably emerge between the metropolis and the periphery: the semi-peripheral states.[25]

Despite differences of opinion as regards the character of the global system between Frank, on the one hand, and Wallerstein and Amin on the other, nearly all exponents of the post-war global capitalism tradition agree that in the definition of (global) capitalism, the wage labour criterion should be relativized. As Amin puts it,

> But the proletariat at the periphery assumes different forms. It does not consist solely or even mainly of wage-earners in the large modern enterprises. It also includes the mass of the peasants who are integrated into the world trade system and who, like the urban working class, pay the price of unequal exchange. Although various types of social organization (very precapitalist in appearance) form the setting in which this mass of peasants live, they have eventually become proletarianized [...] through their integration into the world market system.
>
> (Amin 1976: 361)

What is clear up to now, and especially in the context of my elaborations in Chapters 1–3, is that it is absolutely impossible to agree with such an approach, a view that is also rather common among non-Marxist writers who deal with the issue of capitalism and its inception (as I will argue in Chapter 6). More specifically, as I have shown in Chapter 1, in accordance with Marx's analysis, 'free' labour is the *historically specific form* of *subsumption* of the direct worker under the capitalist relations of domination and exploitation.

The thesis that 'free labour' is the form of appearance of *class exploitation and domination* has been stressed by Jairus Banaji (1977, 2003), in an effort to relativize the historical specificity and significance of wage labour, as compared to that of slavery and other forms of unfree labour. The difference between these labour forms is neither ideological in character, nor does it refer to some 'essence' of 'freedom' as such. 'Free' labour reflects a different mode of social production and a *different form* of exploitation, where labour power ceases to be a production 'asset' equivalent to the means of production, and enters into the *circuit of money capital*, into a historically specific process of overall social reproduction (see also Chapter 7). As Marx puts it:

> *As a slave, the worker has exchange value*, a value; as a free wage-worker he has no value; [...] So long as the worker as such has exchange value, *industrial capital as such cannot exist*, hence nor can developed capital in general. Towards the latter, labour must exist as pure use value, which is offered as a commodity by its possessor [...]. The worker, then, finds himself only

in the relation of simple circulation, of simple exchange, and obtains only coin for his use value; subsistence; but mediated. This form of mediation is, as we saw, essential to and characteristic of the relation.

(Marx 1993: 288–289, emphasis added)

The process of 'extraction/appropriation of economic surplus' is not, as Frank and other exponents of the 'world-capitalism' tradition argue, a characteristic specific to world-capitalism, but rather a basic contradiction in every historical mode of production and in every class society. The distinguishing feature of capitalism is the production and appropriation of the surplus value of the 'free' worker by the capitalist, possessor and owner of the means of production. The exponents of the 'world-capitalism' tradition, by identifying capitalism with the extraction of any form of surplus within market relations, deploy a definition of capitalism that conceals the historically specific relationship between capital and labour.

Furthermore, the whole 'world-capitalism' problematique, in embracing a hypothesis that capitalism functions as a uniform global class structure, does not leave any room for a Marxist theory of the state; by another formulation, the role of the state is disregarded as a decisive element in capitalist class power and domination (for more, see Milios and Sotiropoulos 2009). The state is a condensation of class power of a capitalist ruling class in each and every capitalist social formation, associated, of course, with other coterminous capitalist ruling classes and, respectively, capitalist states through relations of class solidarity and simultaneously of economic, political and other ('cultural', 'ethnic', etc.) competitiveness. This is also the case for capitalist states in the so-called 'Third World', which cannot be regarded as mere appurtenances of, or accessories to, the developed capitalist states.

5.5 The birth of capitalism as an aleatory encounter: from Balibar to Deleuze-Guattari and Althusser

The first to undertake an analysis of Marx's reasoning that the birth of capitalism involved the coming "face to face and into contact" of the money-owner with the proletarian was Étienne Balibar, in the collective volume *Reading Capital* (Althusser and Balibar 1997; Althusser et al. 2015, originally published in 1965). Balibar elaborates on Marx's texts, highlighting the "relatively independent history" of "the two main elements which enter into the capitalist structure" (Balibar 1997: 280):

The formation of free labourers appears mainly in the form of transformations of agrarian structures, while the constitution of wealth is the result of merchant's capital and finance capital, whose movements take place outside those structures, 'marginally', or 'in the pores of society'.

(ibid.: 281)

This thesis begets two more important theses: (i) on the one hand, that what existed before the birth of the capital relation can be regarded as a sort of prehistory of *each of the elements*, which were eventually meant to merge, shaping the capitalist relation, but not a prehistory *of capitalism*, as this confluence was not predestined; (ii) on the other hand, that the capitalist mode of production is not the outcome of an evolution-transformation of the feudal mode of production as such, since:

> it is not the old structure which itself has transformed itself, on the contrary, it has really 'died out' as such.
>
> (ibid.: 283)

A few years after the publication of Balibar's insightful analysis, in 1972, Gilles Deleuze and Félix Guattari (1983, 1987) adopted similar arguments on the question of the origins of capitalism, coining the term 'encounter' in order to describe the coming "face to face and into contact" of the money-owner with the proletarian. In their analysis, they give special emphasis to the idea that the 'encounter' is not determined by necessity, but by historical contingency:

> The encounter might not have taken place, with the free workers and the money-capital existing 'virtually' side by side.
>
> (Deleuze and Guattari 1983: 225)

The same schema also becomes an object of intense elaboration by Louis Althusser in his later writings on the 'Materialism of the Encounter', originally published in 1993–1994.[26] One of Althusser's main theses is that

> instead of thinking contingency as a modality of necessity, or an exception to it, we must think necessity as the becoming-necessary of the encounter of contingencies.
>
> (Althusser 2006: 261)

This means that "no Cause that precedes its effects" exists (ibid.: 173). Capitalism emerged through, on the one hand, the encounter of the owner of money and the "proletarian stripped of everything but his labour power" (ibid.: 197) (two elements that pre-existed their encounter), and on the other, as a result of the historical event that enabled this encounter to take place, to 'take'. The encounter was aleatory, i.e. it was not 'predestined' to happen (it may not have taken place at all), or it was not certain that it would 'take' (it may have been but temporary and short-lived). Althusser gives special emphasis to the historical fact that the encounter did not merely take place, but, most importantly, proved to have crystallized into an enduring form, and therefore proved to be lasting:

> We can go even further, and suppose *that this encounter occurred several times in history before taking hold in the West*, but, for lack of an element or a suitable arrangement of the elements, failed to 'take'.
>
> (ibid.: 198)

I regard the notion of the 'aleatory encounter that took', shaped by Althusser, and based on the previous elaborations of Balibar and Deleuze-Guattari, most suitable for my further analysis and investigation. Nevertheless, at this point it is necessary to point out certain issues in Althusser's analysis that I consider to be ambiguous or problematic.

As a next step in his investigation into the birth of capitalism, Althusser enquired into the historical figure of the money-owner, who existed both prior to and at the moment of the encounter(s) with the proletarian. According to Marx's analysis, which I presented in Chapter 2 (an analysis reaffirmed by Balibar in *Reading Capital*, jointly written with Althusser, see above), the money-owner was the possessor of "mobile wealth piled up through usury – especially that practised against landed property – and through mercantile profits" (Marx 1993: 504). However, Althusser now strongly disputes this view:

> What holds for primitive accumulation also holds for the owner of money. Where do they come from in Marx? We cannot tell, exactly [...]. If, to define capital, one contents oneself with talking, as Marx does, about *an accumulation of money* that produces a surplus – a money profit ($M'' = M + M'$) – then it is possible to speak of money and mercantile capitalism. But these are *capitalisms without capitalists*, capitalisms *without exploitation of a labour force*, capitalisms in which exchange more or less takes the form of a levy governed not by the law of value, but by practices of pillage, either direct or indirect. Consequently, it is here that we encounter the great question of the bourgeoisie.
>
> (Althusser 2006: 200, 201)[27]

What is remarkable here is that Althusser, by writing "without exploitation of a labour force", reduces merchant profit to some 'exploitation at the expense of the trade partner(s)'. By doing so, he seems to share similar positions, as regards the irrelevance of money and trade to (the origins of) capitalism, with exponents of the Marxist traditions I discussed in the first three sections of this chapter, who fully disregard the money-owner, searching for the capitalist-in-the-making either in the well-to-do peasant or the landowner.

We touch here upon an issue that constitutes one of the most disputed chapters in Marxist literature, a subject in which Marx himself is often ambiguous. It is therefore necessary to take a closer look at the question of the merchant capital in capitalism to interrogate its productive (and exploitative) character, and to examine its alleged particularity in comparison with capital in other spheres of the economy (its alleged non-productive character). I will take up this inquiry in the next (and final) section.

5.6 The 'circulation question': Is merchant capital productive or not?

When introducing the notion of capital in Volume 1 of *Capital*, Marx stresses the unity of the 'spheres' of production and circulation. Capitalist production presupposes circulation, as the whole process is set into motion following the purchase of specific 'inputs' (means of production and labour power). The process itself is the production of commodities-for-sale, in other words, production for circulation (see also Chapter 1). In Marx's own words:

> Our friend, Moneybags, who as yet is only an embryo capitalist, must buy his commodities at their value, must sell them at their value, and yet at the end of the process must withdraw more value from circulation than he threw into it at starting. His development into a full-grown capitalist must take place, *both within the sphere of circulation and without it.*
>
> (Marx 1887: 116, emphasis added)

Marx's analysis insists that every capitalist, as an agent of the capital relation, is by definition a 'merchant' or 'trader' and at the same time a 'manager' of a labour and production process, which makes it possible for *trading* to be effective: he/she buys certain commodities (means of production and labour power) in order to sell other commodities (those accruing from a 'production process' under his/her command) at a higher price.[28] In other words, he/she strives to *buy cheap* and to *sell dear*. The use values involved in the process of capital valorization are only means for accomplishing an aim that does not depend on whether these use values are material goods or services. This point is obvious in the following rather long quotation:

> Capitalist production is not merely the production of commodities, it is essentially the production of surplus-value. [...] That labourer alone is productive, who produces surplus-value for the capitalist, and thus works for the self-expansion of capital. If we may take an example from outside the sphere of production of material objects, a schoolmaster is a productive labourer when, in addition to belabouring the heads of his scholars, he works like a horse to enrich the school proprietor. That the latter has laid out his capital in a teaching factory, instead of in a sausage factory, does not alter the relation. Hence the notion of a productive labourer implies not merely a relation between work and useful effect, [...] but also *a specific, social relation of production.*
>
> (Marx 1887: 359, emphasis added)

The above insights show us that every capitalist enterprise, regardless of the economic sector in which it is active (primary, secondary, circulation, finance), is therein equally a process of buying commodities ('creating costs'), i.e. means of production and labour power in order to sell commodities, in most cases of a different form and use value. It is a process unifying production and circulation unique to capitalist production as a whole. As Marx writes in the *Grundrisse*:

> in so far as circulation itself creates costs, itself requires surplus labour, it appears as itself included within the production process.
>
> (Marx 1993: 524)

Merchant capital "creates costs". It employs labour power and means of production to create and sell certain exchange values (commodities).[29] The fact that the same *use value* (e.g. a shipment of Coca Cola bottles) may be part of the 'inputs' of a merchant capitalist (along with the tracks that will carry it from the bottling factory to the storage facilities of a wholesale distributor, the labour power of the truck drivers and the heavers, etc.), and part of the 'outputs' of the same merchant capitalist, does not at all change the parameters of the problem. A bottle of Coca Cola is, of course, always the same use value everywhere, but it has *a different exchange value* in the facilities of the bottling company, and in the storage area of the wholesaler and even more so on the shelves of a retail merchant (as in each of the latter cases, it accumulates additional 'costs' as a result of a process "included within the production process" – Marx, ibid.).

As Marx extensively argued in Volume 2 of *Capital* (Marx 1992), the general circuit of capital is a process that comprises the confluence of three moments or individual circuit forms: the circuits of money capital, of productive capital and of commodity capital.

Certain Marxist authors argue that each single moment in the entire process epitomizes, constitutes or coheres to a particular fraction (industrial, commercial and financial) of the capitalist class.[30] However, this line of reasoning radically departs from the general spirit of Marx's analysis.

The general circuit of capital that Marx presents cannot be broken down into partial self-conscious elements. On the contrary, Marx pinpoints two important issues: on the one hand, he stresses that the valorization of capital presupposes circulation; on the other, he makes it clear that the presented circuit of 'industrial' capital resembles the circuit of social capital as a whole, and constitutes a *prototype* of the circuit of *every individual capital* regardless of the fraction or the section to which it belongs. He writes:

> Let us now consider the total movement, M–C...P...C'–M'. [...] Here capital appears as a value which goes through a sequence of connected and mutually determined transformations [...] Two of these phases belong in the circulation sphere, one to the sphere of production. [...] This total process is therefore a circuit. [...] The capital that assumes these forms in the course of its total circuit [...] is *industrial capital* – industrial here in the sense that it encompasses *every branch of production* that is pursued on a capitalist basis. [...] Money capital, commodity capital and productive capital thus *do not denote independent varieties of capital*, whose functions constitute the content of branches of business that are independent and separate from one another. They are simply particular functional forms of industrial capital, which *takes on all three forms in turn*.
>
> (Marx 1992: 132–133, emphasis added)

In this lengthy passage, one realizes that Marx defines as *'industrial' capital*, *every form of individual capital*, regardless of the sphere of production in which it is employed. He further explains that within its own circuit, each 'industrial' capital constantly passes through the successive phases of money capital, productive capital and commodity capital. In this sense, *every individual capital*, independent of its origin, employs labour power, exploits it and produces surplus value. Even if it functions in the sphere of trade services, it necessarily passes through all three stages to attain the form of money capital, commodity capital (in the form of the means of production and labour power before the production process and in the form of output after it) and productive capital (during the production process).

Marx's analysis of productive labour and the circuit of capital coexists, however, with another discourse in his mature writings, and especially in Volume 3 of *Capital*. According to this second discourse (Marx 1991: 379 ff.), two distinct divisions of non-productive capital exist, commercial capital and money-dealing capital, both of which employ wage labour but produce no surplus value, as their entire circuit remains "completely restricted to the circulation process and not interrupted by the interval of the production process" (ibid.: 381). However, it is absolutely unclear in Marx's text which "completely restricted to the circulation" and non-producing surplus-value capitalist enterprises these are, as he himself reiterates his previously formulated thesis that

> [...] the transport industry, storage and the dispersal of goods in a distributable form should be viewed as *production processes* that continue within the process of circulation.
>
> (Marx 1991: 379, emphasis added)

Beginning with the above affirmation, Marx adds that "the haulier, the railway director and the shipowner are not 'merchants'" (ibid.: 402). But, then, *who* is the merchant, given that it is impossible to conceptualize a capitalist enterprise trading goods without being involved in the "storage and dispersal" of these goods (use values), not to mention their transport.

Marx seems to have temporarily 'inherited' a rather physiocratic element from classical economists, according to which production can take place only when there is a tangible alteration in the *use value* as such. Thus, he concludes, capital and labour cannot be conceived as productive in those sectors of services, where the use value remains unaltered. However, as already discussed, in these capitalist enterprises and sectors, new value and surplus value are added to the same use value (e.g. by "storage and dispersal", not to mention transport). In this part of his work (mainly in Volume 3 of *Capital*), Marx distances himself from his own analysis that capital is "self-valorizing value" regardless of the economic sector in which it falls or the sphere of its activity, and declares that "commercial capital [...] creates neither value nor surplus-value" (Marx 1991: 392).[31]

I have already mentioned in Chapter 2 that these ambiguities in the writings of Marx do not concern solely the issue of productive and non-productive labour in capitalism. In Marx's mature writings, two theoretical discourses are presented, each of which is incompatible with the other. On the one hand, there is the theoretical system that he names 'critique of political economy' (which includes the monetary theory of value and capital); on the other, we encounter a sophisticated version of the classical (mainly Ricardian) political economy of value as 'labour expended'. In other words, Marx's writings have two souls and their accounts with classical political economy have not been decisively settled. This fact reflects the difficulty, but also the significance and the range, of Marx's theoretical revolution and is characteristic of every theoretical rupture of the kind, even in the natural sciences, and in *any* attempt to create a new theoretical discipline by critiquing an established system of thought.

It is in part due to the existence of these conceptual contradictions in Marx's writings that such diverging tendencies among Marxists have ensued. What is most important to stress, however, is the fact that many Marxists behave as if they are unaware of these contradictions in Marx, and further, that most of them present Marx's second discourse (his ambivalence towards classical labour theory and physiocracy) as the only genuine Marxist approach.

Notes

1 Marx 1887: 507.
2 Characteristically, Michael Perelman is "treating primitive accumulation as an essential theoretical concept in analyzing the ongoing process of capitalist accumulation" (Perelman 2000: 4).
3 "I argue, against traditional Marxism, that what Marx calls primitive accumulation, or, more briefly, enclosures, is a continuous feature of capitalist production" (De Angelis 2007: 14). For a similar approach, see also Bonefeld 2001.
4 Despite the fact that certain conclusions may deviate from the original theories.
5 To this simplistic one-dimensional approach, the problematique of 'overdetermination' of the principal class contradiction by a multiplicity of secondary contradictions in a social formation shall be counterposed (see Chapter 2). See also Althusser 1990: 87–128.
6 Compare the following formulation by Marx: "in the slave and serf modes of production etc., [...] use value is the chief and predominant concern, [...] the mode of production of capital, [...] is oriented directly towards exchange value, and only indirectly towards use value" (Marx 1993: 769).
7 Brenner 1976. The paper was initially presented at the annual convention of the American Historical Association in December 1974 (Brenner in Aston and Philpin 1985: 10). In the 'Brenner debate', the following scholars, besides R. Brenner, took part: R. H. Hilton, M. M. Postan and John Hatcher, Patricia Croot and David Parker, Heide Wunder, Emmanuel Le Roy Ladurie, Guy Bois, J. P. Cooper, Arnost Klima.
8 In a later book, first published in 1993 by Princeton University Press, Brenner reaffirms his main thesis as follows:

> What the transition from feudalism to capitalism on the land thus essentially amounted to was the transformation of the dominant class from one whose members depended economically, in the last analysis, on their juridical powers and their direct exercise of force over and against a peasantry that possessed its means of subsistence, into a dominant class whose members, having

ceded direct access to the means of coercion, depended economically merely on their absolute ownership of landed property and contractual relations with free, market dependent tenants.

(Brenner 2003: 650)

9   "[...] the rise of towns and the expansion of exchange cannot in themselves bring about economic development, because they cannot bring about the requisite transformation of agrarian social-property relations" (Brenner 2001: 169).

10 Interesting differentiations within the 'agrarian origin of capitalism' tradition appear in the work of Perry Anderson (1974a, 1974b). Anderson praised the Dobb debate: "The celebrated debate between Sweezy and Dobb, with contributions by Takahashi, Hilton and Hill, in *Science and Society* 1950–3, remains to this day the only systematic Marxist treatment of the central problems of the transition from feudalism to capitalism" (Anderson 1974b: 21). However, his analysis is far more complex and, in many aspects, penetrating and innovative than the majority of approaches presented here. Although Anderson does not pose the question about the coming "face to face and into contact" (Marx) of the money-owner with the proletarian, he conceptualizes the transition to capitalism not in terms of the emergence of *rural capitalism*, but as "the spread of *commodity relations in the country side* that was to define the long transition from feudalism to capitalism in the West" (Anderson 1974b: 26, emphasis added).

11 "Feudalism was dead by the 15th century, as peasant resistance and flight [...] had brought about the general collapse of the lords' rights to tallage the peasantry at will, to extract labour services, and to control peasant mobility, marriage and land transfers" (Brenner 1978: 132).

12 "English peasant communities in the thirteenth and fourteenth centuries had been capable of great resistance, even successful resistance, to attacks on their conditions by the landlords. If they allowed themselves to be evicted in the fifteenth and sixteenth centuries it was because economic and social changes had destroyed *the cohesion that had been their strength* in the past" (Hilton 1975: 173, emphasis added).

13 Perry Anderson shares the same view, following the main arguments developed in the 'Dobb debate':

Absolutism was essentially just this: *a redeployed and recharged apparatus of feudal domination*, designed to clamp the peasant masses back into their traditional social position - despite and against the gains they had won by the widespread commutation of dues. In other words, the Absolutist State was never an arbiter between the aristocracy and the bourgeoisie, still less an instrument of the nascent bourgeoisie.

(Anderson 1974b: 18)

Sweezy, in contrast, defines this interim period as a "pre-capitalist commodity-producing economy": "a social system *sui generis*, on a par with feudalism, capitalism and socialism. *There was no really dominant relation of production to put its stamp on the system as a whole*" (Sweezy 2006: 52, 51 – emphasis added).

14 The phrase 'Tudor period' refers to England between 1485 and 1603.

15 "Successful 'political accumulation' therefore required that increased military power and/or jurisdictional authority yield returns, which more than covered their increased costs, and such costs tended to grow over time. [...] The economic success of individual lords, or groups of them, did tend to depend on feudal state building, and the long-term trend, overall, does appear to have been towards greater political centralization for 'political accumulation'" (Brenner 1982: 38–39).

16 As Callinicos puts it,

Feudal relations of production therefore command a dynamic of territorial expansion and state-building. The emergence of the interstate system in late medieval and early modern Europe, therefore, was not simply a consequence of the contingent imperatives of military and political power, [...] but arose from what Brenner calls the 'rules of reproduction' specific to feudal property relations – that is, the strategies that classes of economic actors must, within a given system of property relations, pursue in order to gain access to the means of subsistence.

(Callinicos 2007: 541)

17 Poulantzas differentiates between a *dominant or hegemonic class*, which possesses class power (based on the dominant form of exploitation and the specific institutional–political form of domination) in a social formation, and a *governing class*, which is "in charge of the state apparatus" (Poulantzas 1973: 249). On the contrary, proponents of the State-Feudalism approach usually identify the dominant class with those "in charge of the state apparatus", i.e. the strata occupying the upper levels of the capitalist state bureaucracy.

18 "Sweezy does not take the break-up of a given social structure as the result of self-movement of its productive forces" (Takahashi 2006: 78).

19 "The spectacular developments in international trade, the industrialization of Flanders, Brabant, Liege, Lombardy and Tuscany, the growth of big commercial centres like Venice, Genoa, Bruges, Paris, London are chronologically secondary to the development of the forces of production in agriculture, stimulated in the process of the struggle for feudal rent" (Hilton 2006c: 116).

20 Both Dobb and Brenner portray a rather gradual, peaceful transition of the peasants from the 'mode of petty production' to capitalist relations. This contradicts Marx's view that

> capital in embryo – when, beginning to grow, it secures the right of absorbing a quantum sufficit [sufficient quantity] of surplus labour, not merely by the force of economic relations, but by the help of the State [...] It takes centuries ere the 'free' labourer, thanks to the development of capitalistic production, agrees, i.e., is compelled by social conditions, to sell the whole of his active life, his very capacity for work, for the price of the necessaries of life, his birth-right for a mess of pottage.

(Marx 1887: 181)

21 For a friendly but critical differentiation from the problematique put forward by Dobb and Brenner, see Resnick and Wolff 1979.

22 A similar argument is developed by David Laibman (2007), who writes: "In any given circumstance, the PRs [productive relations] may completely block PF [productive forces] development" (Laibman 2007: 62).

> Capitalism only comes into being when conditions for it are ripe. It plays a unique role in developing the productive forces and in the political and social maturation of the working class, but it then reveals its own immanent limits as a vehicle for human development, in the form of increasingly severe periodic instability and dislocation.

(ibid.: 94)

Chris Harman also defends this tradition:

> Changes in the forces of production encouraged changes in the relations of production. [...] Capitalism did not arise because of some unique European occurrence, but as a product of the development of the forces and relations of production on a global scale.

(Harman 2004)

23 "Economic development and underdevelopment are interrelated and the difference between them is qualitative, because they undergo structural differentiations, which are however produced by their reciprocal relation in the context of the global system" (Frank 1969: 27).

24 It is here that one finds "the continuity and the relevance of the basic structural features of economic development and underdevelopment. It is for this reason that I place primary emphasis on the continuity of the capitalist structure" (Frank 1969: 30).

25 As Wallerstein explains,

> the structural differentiations between the centre and the periphery cannot be explained adequately if we do not take it into account that there is a third structurally determined position: the position of the semi-periphery. The semi-periphery is necessary for the global economy to be able to function without friction. This semi-periphery is to some extent accorded a special economic role, which however is more necessary politically than economically [...] the absence of a semi-periphery would imply a polarized international system.
>
> (Wallerstein 1979: 50–52)

Also see Hopkins and Wallerstein (1979: 151 ff).

26 According to Althusser,

> this materialism is opposed, as a wholly different mode of thought, to the various materialisms on record, including that widely ascribed to Marx, Engels and Lenin, which, like every other materialism in the rationalist tradition, is a materialism of necessity and teleology, that is to say, a transformed, disguised form of idealism.
>
> (Althusser 2006: 167–168)

The publication of Althusser's book was the point of departure for an extensive body of Marxist literature focusing on the 'dialectics of the encounter'. See, e.g., Read 2002, Montag 2003, Morfino 2005, Fourtounis 2013.

27 Althusser's questioning of the monetary form of appearance (existence) of the capital relation leads him to the following debatable conclusion: "It was not until 1850–70 that capitalism established itself firmly in France" (Althusser 2006: 201).

28 "Since [...] the entire mass of social production – on the capitalist basis – circulates on the market as commodity capital, it is clear that both fixed and fluid elements of productive capital, and, in addition, all elements of the consumption fund, are drawn from the commodity capital; this is saying no more than that both means of production and means of consumption first appear, on the basis of capitalist production, as commodity capital, even if they are also destined later to serve as means of consumption or production" (Marx 1992: 286).

29 Marcus Rediker, in his analysis on the rise of capitalism in the Atlantic region and the role of seamen in the formation of the working class, reaches the following apt conclusion: "The wage relation, the contractual nature of seafaring, the mobility and easy change of masters, and the role of markets in defining the seaman's life all expressed and accelerated a broader movement toward capitalist relations of production" (Rediker 1989: 339).

30 The following statement by Callinicos (2010: 30) is characteristic: "Marx distinguishes between three kinds of capital – productive, commercial and money-dealing capital. [...] Commercial and money-dealing capitalists are able to secure a share of the surplus-value generated in production thanks to the economic functions they perform".

31 In his *Economic Manuscript of 1861–63*, Marx writes:

> Transporting, retailing (dividing) (measuring) and warehousing capital, which have the appearance of belonging to the circulation process, are in fact not distinguished from other productive capital […] just as agricultural, mining, manufacturing capital […] This therefore does not give rise to any new distinctions in the form of capital in general, separate from consideration of the peculiarities of its process of production which arise from the nature of the use value created by it.
>
> (Marx 2010: 41)

Contrary to this thesis, in Volume 3 of *Capital* (written in 1863–1865), he states that "[…] since the merchant, being simply an agent of circulation, produces neither value nor surplus-value […] the commercial workers whom he employs in these same functions cannot possibly create surplus-value for him directly" (Marx 1991: 406).

6 Non-Marxist approaches to the origins of capitalism

6.1 Introduction: the 'spirit of capitalism' and the riddle of monetary profit forms in pre-capitalist societies

The question of the origins of capitalism was a subject of research and controversy among the main exponents of the so-called German Historical School (Economakis and Milios 2001) for more than three decades. The period was inaugurated by the publication of Werner Sombart's *Modern Capitalism*, first published in 1902, which was critically reviewed by Gustav von Schmoller in 1903 and, one year later, denounced in a book by Jakob Strieder (1935), who rejected Sombart's main interpretation of the genesis of capitalism. In 1904, Sombart became editor of the journal *Archiv für Sozialwissenschaft und Sozialpolitik* [Archives for Social Science and Social Welfare], alongside Edgar Jaffé and Max Weber. In the first two issues of *Archiv* (November 1904 and May 1905), Max Weber published his later famous *The Protestant Ethic and the Spirit of Capitalism*, which constitutes a wholly different approach to that of Werner Sombart, despite the fact that both authors shared the opinion that the birth of modern capitalism necessitated the *pre-existence* of a certain 'spirit of capitalism' to be brought into being.

Between 1911 and 1913, Sombart published another three books in which he included certain critiques of Weber's views (Sombart 1913 [tran. Sombart 2015], 2001). In 1916, he published a revised and significantly enlarged version of *Modern Capitalism* (Sombart 1916a, 1916b). In the same year, Lujo Brentano (1916) undertook a fierce critique of both Sombart's and Weber's views on the origin of capitalism. Weber responded to his critics in the later editions of his *Protestant Ethic* (Weber 2001).

Several other economic historians of the German Historical School also took part in the debate, including Felix Rachfahl (1908), who began with a historical example of the Netherlands to develop a systematic critique of Weber's arguments, Georg von Below (1926), who criticized both Sombart and Weber, and Heinrich Sieveking (1928, 1935), who based part of his analyses on both Sombart's and Weber's elaborations. The most thorough critique of Max Weber's theoretical scheme in the non-German-speaking world was formulated by the prominent British historian Richard Henry Tawney in 1963.

Weber's book has remained a subject of debate to this day, despite the fact that most of its postulates have been repeatedly disproved, especially by historical analyses, past and recent. Weber's theoretical scheme appears to be useful for a fast-track rejection of the supposedly economistic foundation of Marxist reasoning.

The expositions of certain exponents of the so-called German Historical School, as well as the controversies among them, also seem to have bequeathed the social sciences with yet another idea that persists among certain theoreticians or schools of thought to this day: the belief that capitalism is identified with all market activities pursuing monetary earnings, and especially with large-scale trade, the historical existence of which has been traced back to antiquity. In this sense, the approach argues that (a form of) capitalism existed in Babylon, ancient Greece, Rome, etc., and its emergence is associated with the innate urges of 'human nature'. It is remarkable that John Maynard Keynes himself contributed to this tradition, as will be discussed below.

In this chapter, I will start by critically delineating the main arguments of the German Historical debate on the origins of capitalism, as it may serve to lay the groundwork for reflections on the monetary, 'entrepreneurial' and ideological–cultural (also in the sense of a specific social subjectivity) origins of capitalism, which are at times underestimated in contemporary Marxist approaches (see Chapter 5). Subsequently, I will comment on more recent non-Marxist approaches to capitalism, which, like those of the German Historical debate, superlatively underestimate the structural role of wage labour in the formation of capitalism.

Despite his fruitful distinction between a market economy and capitalism, Fernand Braudel's oeuvre gives little or no emphasis on class domination and exploitation forms, underestimates the significance of wage labour as a criterion sine qua non for the emergence of capitalism and focuses mainly on large-scale entrepreneurial activity.

6.2 Werner Sombart's *Modern Capitalism* and its critics (1902–1916)[1]

Werner Sombart was well acquainted with Marxist theory. In 1894, while being Professor at the University of Breslau, he wrote a critical review of Marx's Volume 3 of *Capital*, mainly criticizing Friedrich Engels' editorial approach.[2] Furthermore, in the foreword to his major work of the period, *Modern Capitalism* (1902), he distanced himself from his 'honoured teacher', Gustav von Schmoller, with the following words:

> What divides me from him and his followers is the construct in the arrangement of material, the radical postulate of a unified explanation of ultimate causes, the construction of all historical phenomena into a social system, in short what I call the 'specifically theoretical'. I could also say: it is Karl Marx.
> (Sombart 1902: XXIX)

Sombart views history as being a succession of various social systems, although he does not consider this succession to be determined by some genetic or general law. Historical contingency is considered crucial to the emergence of a new system in the place of an old one. He describes the different historical social systems as follows:

> Since the decline of ancient civilization, three great epochs have succeeded each other [...] agrarian culture [...] artisan organization [...]. The epoch in which we still live today follows: its innermost character is characterized by the prevalence of a commercial essence, i.e., calculative-speculative-organizational activity, which is fulfilled by the basic idea that the purpose of the economy is the earning of money. This striving has created the organization which we best call capitalistic. After the capitalist cultural epoch [...] the fourth is to follow, a socialist-cooperative epoch.
>
> (Sombart 1902: XXXI–XXXII)

According to this view, capitalism is not market-oriented activity – nor a form of entrepreneurship. Sombart clearly differentiates between the craftsman or artisan – the small and medium trader or entrepreneur – to whom he ascribes a specific pre-capitalist system ('artisan organization'), and the capitalist, who bases his activities on large-scale entrepreneurial property. In addition, from a methodological point of view, Sombart distinguishes between the capitalist *system*, the functioning and evolution of which relies on certain law-abiding regularities inherent to the system – "after it has been possible to turn the dependence on the market into a dominant system of production and distribution (the blind-acting market laws)" (ibid.: XVI) – and the *genesis* of capitalism, which he regards as an outcome of historical contingency or accidentalism.[3]

The 'accidental' event of the birth of capitalism took place, according to Sombart, when the activities of certain economic subjects possessing large amounts of money merged with the activities of other economic subjects possessing a certain *economic spirit*, which proved to be pertinent to capitalism. The owner of large sums of money (or property that could be transformed into money) belonged, according to Sombart, to a specific category of landowners, especially those who possessed real estate in cities. *The accumulation,* therefore, of such *large properties in the social system of the artisan (handicraft) economy* was a precondition to the birth of capitalism.

Through such processes, a "money plethora" took place (ibid.: 292 ff.), which, however, could not be transformed into capital because landowners did not possess any form of entrepreneurial abilities or spirit. So the birth of capitalism, according to Sombart, came through the *transfer of such large properties* (in Italy and Flanders since the thirteenth century, or even earlier) to people who by nature already possessed or could develop the suitable *calculative–speculative–organizational spirit*, or the 'spirit of capitalism'. Those were predominantly merchants, but could also be handicraftsmen, belonging to the artisan social system, who would never have become capitalists on their own, owing to their restricted economic means, if these large property *transfers* (by lending, marriage, etc.) had not taken place.

The merging of these two different social actors of the artisan era thus gave birth to capitalism. The possessor of the 'spirit of capitalism'

> could acquire property by donation, by lending, by inheritance, by marriage (a frequent case!). He could come into the possession of considerable land values or land-rents by luck or speculation – if he had bought land with his savings for agricultural use, the price of which was then increased by the expansion of the city.
>
> (ibid.: 300)

In order to explain the origins of capitalism, Sombart introduces the notion of a pre-existing 'spirit of capitalism' as an autonomous factor being the most decisive precondition for the birth of the new (capitalist) social system. This idea would later be adopted by other writers of the German Historical School. In Sombart's own words:

> The highest accumulation of money is not at all an adequate precondition even for the planning of a capitalist enterprise. What [...] has to be added to it to convert the accumulated money into capital is a specifically capitalist spirit of its owner.
>
> (ibid.: 207–208)

With this approach, Sombart rejects the interpretations of other German economic historians of the time, and most of all that of Gustav von Schmoller, who argued that capitalism had emerged out of a diversification and polarization of small producers, either into a group of prosperous entrepreneurs or into proletarians (see below). According to Sombart, the *small scale* of artisan entrepreneurship did not leave room for the accumulation of large monied properties, in other words, for the capitalist to emerge.

Besides, Sombart rejects another two conceptions that played a definitive role in the debate that followed the publication of *Modern Capitalism*: one, the idea that capitalism emerged as a consequence of, or in accordance with, 'human nature' in general; and two, that religion was the crucial factor in shaping the 'spirit of capitalism':

> References to human 'nature' and its indwelling inclinations are completely out of place. [...] I also find inadequate the explanation that the essence of modern capitalism is through its affiliation with certain religious communities. That Protestantism, especially in its varieties of Calvinism and Quakerism, has fundamentally promoted the development of capitalism is a fact too well known to be elaborated upon. But for anyone

rejecting this interpretative attempt (by making a reference to the already highly developed capitalist spirit since the Middle Ages in the Italian communes, and in the German cities of the fifteenth century): the Protestant regional systems were primarily much more an effect rather than a cause of the modern capitalist spirit, and it will not be difficult for him to show the erroneousness of [this] conception of the emergence of modern capitalism, with the exclusive help of empirical evidence accruing from concrete historical connections [...].

(Sombart 1902: 379, 380–381)[4]

It has been clear up to now that Sombart, in *Modern Capitalism*, draws certain ideas from Karl Marx's work, such as: the definition of capitalism as a social system of production based on the profit-creating activity of the capitalist enterprise (see also Sombart 1902: 195); the emergence of capitalism from a pre-existent "money-possessor" (ibid.: 207); the shaping of human behaviour (or 'nature') as an outcome or expression of the mode of functioning of a social and production system; the inherent limitless tendency of capitalist accumulation;[5] and the creation of the proletariat as "the last series of objective conditions" for the emergence of capitalism (ibid.: 217). On several other issues, however, he deviates from Marxist theoretical discourse. Of these non-Marxist views, the most important for our analysis are his theses that capitalism arose from a certain 'artisan' or 'handicraft' organization of society, and the concept of the 'spirit of capitalism', the notion that there is an ideological–cultural element that the money-owner must already possess in order for capitalism to emerge. According to Sombart, this element constitutes the most decisive precondition of capitalism: in other words, capitalism would not have appeared if this ideological–cultural element had not existed and become part of the consciousness of the money-owner. As we discussed above, for Sombart, capitalism became possible when those already possessing the 'spirit of capitalism', as a result of their social and economic roles (small- and medium-scale merchants and other entrepreneurs of the 'artisan' or 'handicraft' historical period who were unable to create large properties by their own means), came into contact or merged with the big money-owners (urban landowners or rentiers).

I will later return to this issue in order to consider another variant of the 'spirit of capitalism' approach, one developed by Max Weber, which played (and to an extent, continues to play) an important role in the non-Marxist approaches to the genesis of capitalism. At this point, I would like to focus on critical assessments of Sombart's analysis by other exponents of the German Historical School. As we will see, most critics of Sombart's *Modern Capitalism* focus on the 'money plethora' and 'landlord–merchant' fusion thesis, the idea that small- and medium-scale entrepreneurship is unable to become capitalist without the transfer of large amounts of money, originally accumulated by landlords.

The first to critically review Sombart's book was Gustav von Schmoller, Professor at the University of Berlin at the time, who contended that long-distance trade could revolutionize handicraft production and create the necessary conditions for capitalism to emerge:

> Where long-distance trade begins, the old handicraft begins to grow beyond its original character; then, the heavy struggle within the guild begins, of whether the poorer master is likely to sell his product to his rich co-master for long-distance trade. At that point the attempts, more frequently destined to fail, for cooperative far-reaching sales begin, at that point handicraft begins to transform itself into domestic industry.
>
> (von Schmoller 1903: 358, cited by Strieder 1968 [1903, 1935]: 217)

A similar critique of Sombart was posited in Jakob Strieder's book *On the Genesis of Modern Capitalism*, first published in 1903 (Strieder 1968), which investigates the formation of big bourgeoisie properties in Augsburg during the late Middle Ages. Strieder, then Doctor of History at the University of Bonn, argued that he had begun to investigate his subject by taking Sombart's hypothesis for granted, intending to apply it to the case of Augsburg. In other words, he began by implementing the 'inductive method' in order to verify the correctness of Sombart's hypothesis. Sombart's theory could not be verified, however. Through deductive reasoning, Strieder actually reached very different conclusions: big merchant or manufacture properties never had their origin in money derived from landed property or land rent. The formation of modern capitalism, with its polarization of the capitalist and the proletarian, was a long-running historical process of gradual change, which began with traditional trade and artisan activities:

> This is the beginning of a process which took place during the 15th century. In this way, heterogeneous elements came to be united in the weavers' guild. A troubled proletariat on the one hand, tormented by worries, badly nourished, born at the loom, dying at the loom, pale, grave figures, the so-called 'poor weavers'; and, on the other hand, the capitalists in this guild, men like Hans Fugger, like Hans Bimmel, like Thomas Ehem, like Jakom Hämmerlin, men with extensive commercial skills, on whom luck had smiled and who understood how to utilise it.
>
> (Strieder 1968: 218)[6]

In 1916, Lujo Brentano, Professor at the University of Munich, published a rather detailed critique of Sombart's analysis as an appendix to his own analysis of the beginnings of capitalism (Brentano 1916: 78 ff.). Brentano's critique was articulated in three main arguments:

a   The rich merchant who concentrates large amounts of money is a historical figure existing since antiquity; the assumption that the merchant was dependent on some other money-possessor in order to acquire the magnitude of property necessary for capitalist entrepreneurship is pointless.

A merchant economy is a money economy, focusing on the creation of constantly increasing monetary earnings, and is often assisted by piracy, war and (colonial) plunder. In this context, Brentano adopts a similar thesis to that of Henri Pirenne, according to which, whenever a conjoining of merchant capital with landed property took place, it kindled the investment of merchant profits in real estate, and not, as Sombart suggests, the inflow of landlord money into trade.[7]

b   A 'handicraft' historical era has never existed. What preceded capitalism was a feudal social order based on landed property and relations of personal dependence:

> Handicraft in antiquity, as in the Middle Ages and in the age of developed capitalism, was not in a dominant position, but in a subordinate position in economic life. [...] The rulers, whose will dominated economic organization, were chiefly the landlords, and alongside with them, though feeble in the beginning, the new emergent rulers, the merchants who possessed capital [...]. Capitalist domination began a struggle with feudal domination, and it is the very emergence of capitalism that led handicraft, for the first time, to be emancipated from masters both without as well as within cities.
>
> (Brentano 1916: 82–83)

c   The tendency towards unlimited monetary wealth is not the effect of a 'spirit of capitalism'. The pursuit of acquiring ever more money is a part of human nature and characterized big merchants long before the rise of capitalism. Contrary to subordinated and dependent social groups (peasants, handicraftsmen, etc.) who were accustomed to a subsistence economy, the big merchant always possessed a strong propensity for unlimited money earning:

> Long before the emergence of capitalism they were filled with a proclivity for unlimited acquisition.
>
> (Brentano 1916: 111)

We can see that the 'Sombart debate', as we may call it, introduced two positions that were later reproduced in twentieth-century Marxist debates: first, that capitalism emerged out of the gradual polarization of small-scale producers into capitalists and proletarians, and second, that trade functioned as the motivating force behind the rise of capitalism. However, it was the 'spirit of capitalism' that endured in controversies among German scholars during the first three decades of the twentieth century, and continues to be debated even to this day among social scientists all over the world. On his part, Sombart, in a way, preserves or reproduces Marx's idea that the birth of capitalism was due to an 'aleatory encounter' between a money-owner and some other economic agent. However, this other agent is not the proletariat, but the non-capitalist entrepreneur, possessor of the 'spirit of capitalism'. The neglect of wage labour is even more obvious in the works of other non-Marxist writers.

6.3 Max Weber and the 'spirit of capitalism' controversy

As we have already discussed, Werner Sombart introduced the notion of the 'spirit of capitalism' as an independent, decisive factor in the birth of the capitalist system, which, although pre-existing capitalism,[8] was *socially and economically conditioned*: it was not just certain ideas postulated by a thinker of an intellectual movement, a philosophy or a religion, that shaped the 'spirit of capitalism', but a way of life and an economic activity that necessarily tended towards the creation of the "calculative–speculative–organizational" spirit characteristic of capitalism.

In his later works of the period (Sombart 1913, 2001), Sombart broadened the idea of the 'spirit of capitalism' as he contemplated 'the spirit of the times', with a view to the wider ideological–cultural social climate during the transitional era of the late Middle Ages, noting that "the changing modes of life follow one another like waves of the sea" (Sombart 1967: 42). In this context, he traces changes in the sexual behaviour of certain social strata, which denoted the emergence of a new ethos correlated with the ideologies and practices of the 'free person', i.e. the rise of the form of subjectivity that pertains to capitalism. He writes:

> I know of no event of greater importance for the formation of medieval and modern society than the transformation of the relations between the sexes […]. A fundamentally different conception of the nature of love first becomes palpably evident in the period of the minnesinger. This would set the date in the eleventh century, which marked, in every respect, the beginning of the secularization of love.
>
> (Sombart 1967: 42, 43)

Sombart argues that the rise of this new 'spirit' regarding the attitude towards oneself and the opposite sex was strongly correlated with certain economic behaviour, and more specifically with the tendency towards luxury and consumption in aristocratic courts and the households of well-to-do merchants, manufacturers and high-ranking state officials. He concludes: "Luxury then, itself a legitimate child of illicit love […] gave birth to capitalism" (ibid.: 171).

After capitalism had been stabilized as a social system, the 'spirit of capitalism', according to Sombart, was 'naturally' propagated by the functioning of the system itself:

> The more capitalism developed the more its importance grew as a creator of the capitalist spirit […]. The system pervades the capitalist undertaking like some silent ghost; 'it' calculates, 'it' keeps the ledgers, 'it' works out prices, 'it' determines rates of wages, 'it' saves wherever possible, and so on. 'It' dominates the undertaker himself; 'it' makes demands on him; 'it' forces him to do what it requires. 'It' never rests; 'it' is always on the watch; 'it' is constantly becoming more and more perfect. 'It' lives a life of its own.
>
> (Sombart 1915: 344, 346)

In his critical review of *Modern Capitalism*, Gustav von Schmoller proposes an alternative idea, namely that capitalism was the outcome of a certain psychological attitude and certain customs and institutions, rather than of economic processes.[9] The idea of a psychological–institutional foundation of capitalism was used by Max Weber, while on sabbatical as Professor at the University of Heidelberg, to prod the notion of the 'spirit of capitalism' introduced by Sombart in a direction compatible with Nassau William Senior's theory of abstinence: that it was the ascetic spirit introduced by Calvinism after the Reformation, which functioned as the 'spirit of capitalism' and promoted the shaping of modern capitalism.

Weber reiterates Sombart's main idea that "the spirit of capitalism […] was present before the capitalistic order" (Weber 2001: 20). He further summarizes his view as follows:

> This worldly Protestant *asceticism* […] acted powerfully *against the spontaneous enjoyment of possessions*; it restricted consumption, especially of luxuries. On the other hand, it had the psychological effect of freeing the acquisition of goods from the inhibitions of traditionalistic ethics. […] The campaign against the temptations of the flesh, and the dependence on external things, was […] not a struggle against the rational acquisition, but against the irrational use of wealth […]. When the *limitation of consumption* is combined with this release of acquisitive activity, the inevitable practical result is obvious: *accumulation of capital through ascetic compulsion to save.*
> (Weber 2001: 115, 116, emphasis added)[10]

We have seen that Werner Sombart had criticized the association of the 'capitalist spirit' with the Protestant ethic even before the publication of Max Weber's book, arguing that "the Protestant regional systems were primarily much more an effect rather than a cause of the modern capitalist spirit" (Sombart 1902: 380). In his two later books, *The Jews and Modern Capitalism* and *the Quintessence of Capitalism*, he criticizes Weber on the basis of two new arguments: (i) the main ideas of Calvinism, which according to Weber, are responsible for the rise of modern capitalism, can also be traced back to Judaism; and (ii) Protestantism was born as a movement opposing already-existing capitalist relations:

> […] the dominating ideas of Puritanism which were so powerful in capitalism were more perfectly developed in Judaism, and were also of course of a much earlier date.
> (Sombart 2001: 174)[11]

> Protestantism has been all along the line a foe to capitalism, and more especially, to the capitalist economic outlook […] Puritan preachers were totally averse to all money-getting […] Puritanism hardly encouraged farsighted and adventurous enterprises; shop-keeping was the most it could achieve […] In Calvinist lands the church was distinctly hostile to capitalism […] It would be a narrow conception of the capitalist spirit thus to see its various manifestations springing from Puritanism.
> (Sombart 1915: 251–252)[12]

Other contemporary critics of Weber included Felix Rachfahl (1906, 1907, 1908, see also Mommsen and Osterhammel 1987; Bakker 2003), who argued that in seventeenth-century Holland, the rich entrepreneurs had distanced themselves from Calvinist ethics, and Lujo Brentano (1916), who formulated a detailed critique of Weber's analysis.

Brentano stressed the fact that emancipation from religious traditionalism had started in Italy long before the Reformation, and not in the Protestant or Calvinist regions.[13] He also argued that Calvinism and Puritanism were hostile towards big business and limitless money making, concluding that what Weber conceives as 'spirit of capitalism' is in reality the work ethics of the shopkeeper and petty bourgeoisie entrepreneurship:

> In my view, it presupposes a strong prejudice in order to stamp these unadventurous, absolutely petty-bourgeois prudence rules into a 'philosophy of the spirit'.
>
> (Brentano 1916: 149)[14]

Brentano's analysis inspired R. H. Tawney to write in his now famous *Religion and the Rise of Capitalism*, originally published in 1916:

> Brentano's criticisms [...] seem to me to be sound [...]. There was plenty of the 'capitalist spirit' in fifteenth-century Venice and Florence, or in south Germany and Flanders, for the simple reason that these areas were the greatest commercial and financial centers of the age, though all were, at least nominally, Catholic. [...] Of course material and psychological changes went together, and of course the second reacted on the first. But it seems a little artificial to talk as though capitalist enterprise could not appear till religious changes had produced a capitalist spirit. [...] As Brentano points out, Machiavelli was at least as powerful a solvent of traditional ethical restraints as Calvin.
>
> (Tawney 1963: 262)

More recent historical studies affirm the above-cited critics of Weber. As Luciano Pellicani (1994: 50) aptly remarks, Weber's thesis is nothing more than "a distortion of history":

> The Weber thesis is indefensible, not only for the reasons proposed by Richard Tawney, but also because nothing more antithetical to the modern capitalist spirit can be imagined than the obsessive preaching of the reformed sects about the horror of Mammon, who corrupts, degrades and prostitutes everything.
>
> (Pellicani 1994: 37)

Neither Weber nor his followers have ever persuasively responded to critics of the 'Calvinism as spirit of capitalism' thesis. However, "*The Protestant Ethic* has provoked and continues to provoke a mysterious and, at times, muddled fascination among sociologists" (Pellicani 1994: 48).[15]

In my opinion, the success of Weber's book, despite its poor documentation of historical facts and social theory, can be attributed to its being perceived as constituting an 'anti-Marxist Manifesto', through a reversal of the flow of causality and effect supposedly introduced by Marxist theory:

> Concerning the doctrine of the more naïve historical materialism, that such ideas originate as a reflection or superstructure of economic situations, [...] it will suffice for our purpose to call attention to the fact that without doubt, in the country of Benjamin Franklin's birth (Massachusetts), the spirit of capitalism [...] was present before the capitalistic order. [...] In this case the causal relation is certainly the reverse of that suggested by the materialistic standpoint.
>
> (Weber 2001: 20–21)[16]

To suppose that Massachusetts (or Philadelphia, where Franklin lived after the age of 17) in the mid-eighteenth century was not a region where the capitalist mode of production prevailed, as Weber suggests, betrays a very poor understanding of what capitalism actually is. However, it seems that for many scholars anti-Marxist prejudice has been more important than the formulation of a sound theory of capitalism and its origins.

A result of this ideological prejudice is also the fact that contemporary social science ascribes the introduction of the notion of the 'spirit of capitalism' as an indispensible precondition to the rise of capitalism to Max Weber; this notion, of course, as well as the idea that modern capitalism could not have taken hold if a certain capitalist 'spirit' had not pre-existed its emergence, was introduced by Werner Sombart in his *Modern Capitalism* (1902). It seems as though Sombart's doctrine of the 'spirit of capitalism', which we have discussed extensively in this chapter, was not 'anti-Marxist enough' to be remembered by conventional social science. And, interestingly, it was not Marxist enough to be remembered by Marxists.

6.4 'Ancient capitalism'?

As we saw in Section 6.2, Max Weber adopted and modified Werner Sombart's idea that capitalism emerged when a pre-existing 'spirit of capitalism' merged with and shaped a certain economic activity. However, Weber does not remain allegiant to this idea. He introduces an even looser concept of capitalism by differentiating between modern (or Western) capitalism and premodern (or traditional) capitalism, the latter of which allegedly existed in ancient China, India, Babylon, Greece, Rome, etc.:

> The concept spirit of capitalism is here used in this specific sense, it is the spirit of modern capitalism. For that we are here dealing only with

Western European and American capitalism is obvious from the way in which the problem was stated. Capitalism existed in China, India, Babylon, in the classic world, and in the Middle Ages. But in all these cases, as we shall see, this particular ethos was lacking.

(Weber 2001: 17)

It is remarkable that Lujo Brentano, who is a sharp critic of Weber as we have seen, who argues against Sombart's idea of a 'handicraft historical era' and who defends the thesis that capitalism was preceded by *feudalism* ("capitalist domination began to struggle with feudal domination", Brentano 1916: 83), also supports the idea of an 'ancient' capitalism. Using as a point of departure the thesis that "large-scale trade is, in its essence, capitalist" (ibid.: 190), he writes:

In the territories of the Byzantine Empire, capitalism has continued to exist, as it had developed in the land of the Phoenicians, in Greece, in Ptolemaic Egypt and after the Second Punic War in Rome. Besides, western capitalism has only been a continuation and transmission of the capitalism of the Byzantine Empire to Italy and other developed western areas.

(Brentano 1916: 7)

Brentano equated large-scale trade with capitalism, as he considered all pre-capitalist economic systems to have been based on landed property and agrarian social relations. In contrast, the merchant is the leading figure of a monetary economic form, which does not (necessarily) depend on landed property, and is constantly aiming to increase earnings. He is thus regarded as an alien, if not hostile, element to the dominant pre-capitalist social and economic relations based on landed property.

This reasoning was shared not only by adherents of the Weberian or Brentanoan approaches to economic and social evolution, but also by other currents of thought, mostly historians and economists, who equate monetary economic relations and large-scale 'entrepreneurship' with capitalism.

The following citation by the prominent historian of early Islam, Patricia Crone, is characteristic of this line of thought:

Many pre-industrial societies had a capitalist sector even though the economy at large was agrarian, but it tended to be heavily dominated by commerce rather than manufacture. [...] Such capitalism is commonly known as pre-modern. [...] More commonly the capitalist sector flourished within an agrarian economy without greatly affecting either the nature of the primacy of the latter, let alone the socio-political relations it engendered. This pattern is well attested for antiquity, the Islamic world, India, China and pre-modern Europe, and the question is how Europe came to go beyond it.

(Crone 2003: 193–194)[17]

It is clear from what has ensued in this section that within the framework of this 'ancient-capitalism' or 'premodern capitalism' approach, the question of the origins of capitalism dissipates, or is at least transformed into a matter of transition from one *form* ('premodern') of capitalism to another ('modern').

The distinction between 'modern' and 'ancient' or 'traditional' capitalism is not advocated in all cases. On the contrary, several versions of the 'ancient capitalism' view stress the uniformity of all forms of capitalism, especially when analysing the economy in Greek antiquity. Such analyses regarding the character of ancient Greek (mostly Athenian) economy and society are put forward by certain economic historians (portrayed as 'modernists'), who challenge the theorizations of Moses I. Finley, Karl Polanyi and others (the so-called 'archaists') on the archaic and 'embedded'-in-polity, pre-capitalist, character of the ancient Greek economy. Edward E. Cohen, an exponent of the 'modernist' current, writes:

> In practice maritime finance in the fourth century [BC] was extraordi-narily complex. A single ship might carry many 'traders' (emporoi), and each of these emporoi might have separate cargo securing separate loans [...]. Each of these lenders would normally require the borrower to pro-vide substantial equity subordinate to each borrowing. [...] This capital might itself be borrowed, possibly against yet other collateral.
>
> (Cohen 1992: 146)

> All these elements – the economic importance of the banks, their elusive sources of funds, the risk inherent in their activities – are consonant with the picture of Athenian banking presented consistently by Demosthenes [...]. Paley and Sandys [1896–1898] [...] observe that Phormion 'was en-abled, as a capitalist in the enjoyment of extensive credit in the commer-cial world, to advance [large] sums of money'.
>
> (Cohen 1992: 217)

Scott Meikle comments that "a powerful political agenda has lain just be-neath the surface of the dispute" (between 'archaists and modernists'), which means that in the view of neoclassical economists and conservative historians, "civilization is to be identified with the system of market economy or capi-talism" (Meikle 1992: 2, 3). This argument seems convincing, but demands further research, especially if one takes into account the views expressed by John Maynard Keynes, when he comments in "Ancient Currencies":

> Individualistic capitalism and the practices pertaining to that system were undoubtedly invented in Babylonia [...]. Perhaps the clue to the economic history of Greece from the Homeric period to the fifth cen-tury B.C. may be partly found in the gradual adaptation of the primitive economy of the tribes to the individualistic capitalism which they found in Asia Minor in a decadent and confused form but reaching back in its

origins and in the experience behind it to *a highly developed and complex system* of great antiquity. *Exactly as was the case in the Renaissance of our own era*, the discovery of traditions and fragments of ancient learning, which became the instruments of revolutionary innovations of thought in the hands of the discoverers, coincided with economic contacts strongly tending away from feudalism towards individualistic capitalism. Solon was a Renaissance character.

(Keynes 2013: 253–254, emphasis added)[18]

The merits of the various versions of the 'ancient capitalism' thesis are that they trace the existence of a high-profile economic agent in pre-capitalist societies who is external to the land-based social groups and external to the principal socio-economic relations in these societies (I will elaborate on this point in the next chapter). As we saw in Chapter 2, Marx stresses that before the emergence of capitalism, a "contrast between the power, based on the personal relations of dominion and servitude, that is conferred by landed property, and the impersonal power that is given by money" (Marx 1887: 108) already existed.

However, each and every version of this 'ancient capitalism' problematique either implicitly or explicitly fully disentangles the notion of capitalism from any connotation or hint of connection with wage labour. For example, Cohen finds that most "definitions of capitalism, and hence of 'pre-capitalism', are notoriously impressionistic", and argues in favour of a "Weberian definition" of capitalism as "an actual adaptation of economic action to a comparison of money income with money expenses" (Cohen 1992: 41).

This anachronistic approach to capitalism derives from the fact that these theories have abandoned any notion of (class) exploitation or dominance; their only focus remains on 'money creation', and so they regard the possessor of "mobile wealth piled up through usury – especially that practised against landed property – and through mercantile profits" (Marx 1993: 504, see also Chapter 2) as a historically unaltered picture of capitalism.

It goes without saying that these approaches leave no room for Marx's 'original accumulation' or 'aleatory encounter' problematique.

6.5 Fernand Braudel: market economy vs. capitalism

The French historian Fernand Braudel, the leading figure of the second generation of the 'Annales School', published an extensive oeuvre on *Material Civilization and Capitalism* (Braudel 1981, 1982, 1984), and a history of the *Mediterranean* (Braudel 1972, 1973, 2011).

In his analyses, Braudel marks a clear distinction between the *market economy* and *capitalism*, although he considers the former as constituting a precondition of the latter. He further defines capitalism as a hierarchical social and economic form with inherent monopolistic power characteristics, which is built upon pre-existing market economy forms and dominates them. In Braudel's words, "the capitalist sphere is located in the higher form" (Braudel 1979: 62).

The market itself is thus a stratified structure, at the bottom of which are self-employed or salaried simple labourers, followed by shopkeepers, small-scale manufacturers, usurers and traders, while at the top are capitalists. These capitalists are first and foremost the large (wholesale and long-distance) merchants, who are clearly distinguished from local traders or manufacturers.[19]

> The commercial or exchange world was a world of hierarchies, start-ing with the humblest jobs-porters, stevedores, peddlers, carters, and sailors – and moving up to cashiers, shopkeepers, brokers of various sorts, and moneylenders, and finally reaching the merchants.
>
> (Braudel 1979: 58–59)

However, capitalism cannot become dominant as a social system unless it dominates the state, unless "it is the state" (ibid.: 64). Through their eco-nomic and political superiority, capitalists

> grabbed up everything worth taking – land, real estate, and land rents. Who could doubt that these capitalists had monopolies at their disposal or that they simply had the power needed to eliminate competition nine times out of ten?
>
> (ibid.: 57)

As capitalism gains ground in the social and economic structure, it dissemi-nates into all economic spheres beyond large-scale trade:

> [...] the large merchant changed his activities so frequently, [...] because high profits were constantly shifting from one sector to another. Capital-ism is essentially conjunctural, that is, it flourishes according to the dic-tates of changes in the economic situation. Even today one of capitalism's greatest strengths remains its ability to adapt and to change.
>
> (ibid.: 61)

Braudel explains that he reached these findings after an intense study of em-pirical material that allowed him to evaluate different hypotheses of theoret-ical schemes and approaches.[20] As regards the emergence of capitalism, he summarizes his conclusions as follows:

> It is no accident that throughout the world a group of large merchants stands out clearly from the mass of ordinary dealers [...]. The phenom-enon can be seen by the fourteenth century in Germany, by the thir-teenth century in Paris, and by the twelfth century and probably even earlier in Italian cities. Even before the emergence in the West of the first

merchants, in the Islamic world the *tayir* was an importer-exporter who directed agents and factors from his home (here we already have business in a fixed place).

(ibid.: 56)

Although drawing from various theoretical sources and traditions, and despite his disregard for the notion of class struggle as a motivating force in history, Braudel's approach is rather friendly to Marx's analysis.[21] With respect to the genesis of capitalism, he takes a position very close to Marx's (see Chapter 2), clearly relating capitalism to wage labour. In this respect, he makes the distinction between pre-capitalist and capitalist 'enterprise':

The countryside of Western Europe was inhabited by both landlord and peasant. [...] For a capitalist system of management and economic rationalization of the land to come into being, many pre-conditions would have been necessary: the seigniorial regime would have had to be if not abolished, certainly reduced or modified [...] the system would have to be based on a wage-earning proletariat. *Unless all these conditions were fulfilled, the enterprise might be on the way to being capitalist, but it was not capitalist in the proper sense.*

(Braudel 1982: 251, emphasis added)

He then focuses on the development and territorial and global expansion of capital. In this context, he stresses the formation of domestic markets and a national economy, where he also locates England's supremacy, since the seventeenth century, over its economic rivals. The formation of a national market and national economy was thus a process that paved the way for the British Industrial Revolution to take place.

Braudel's analysis, based on the differentiation between a market and capitalist economy, is certainly fruitful, and 'corrects' the identification between monetary 'profit' forms in pre-capitalist societies and capitalism. Despite the times of superficial formulations of concepts, I regard Braudel's oeuvre as a valuable source for my analysis from this point onwards.

First, however, certain theoretical issues concerning Marx's theory of historical *modes of production* must be clarified: What was the social character of the big merchant, usurer or manufacturer in ancient Athens, Rome, Byzantium, etc.? As far as he/she also belonged to the highest level of a certain hierarchical market form, how was he/she 'entrenched' in 'ordinary', 'non-entrepreneurial' slave-owning or feudal relations? In correlation with these issues and questions, Braudel's reasoning seems to be rather deficient: by underestimating the notion of class struggle as the motive force of historical evolution, and consequently of class exploitation and domination as constituting the base of a historically specific social order, its actual significance cannot be assigned to the emergence of wage labour subsumed under capital.

Notes

1 Sombart (1902, 1916a, 1916b).
2 Sombart (1894). The publication was followed by written correspondence between Engels and Sombart. In a letter to Conrad Schmidt on 12 March 1895, Engels writes: "In Sombart's otherwise very good article on Volume 3 I also find this tendency to dilute the theory of value: he had also obviously expected a somewhat different solution?" www.marxists.org/archive/marx/works/1895/letters/95_03_12.htm.
3 "We look at the genesis of the capitalist economic subject or economic principle in terms of something accidental" (Sombart 1902: 398).
4 Sombart refers at this point to the book of Eberhard Gothein, *Wirtschaftsgeschichte des Schwarzwaldes und der angrenzenden Landschaften* [The Economic History of the Black Forest and Neighbouring Regions], where it is stated: "the Calvinist Diaspora is the nursery garden of the economy of capital" (cited in Sombart 1902: 381).
5 "The aims of the capitalist enterprise are abstract and therefore limitless" (Sombart 1902: 196).
6 A similar opinion was shared by Georg von Below, Professor of Medieval and Modern History at the University of Münster:

> I agree with Sombart that the economies of medieval merchants were not great, that their profits were not vast. But the sudden creation of huge wealth is not necessary. A grain of sand could be heaped upon a grain of sand […]. Who tells us that a capital of exorbitant amount is necessary for the founding of a capitalist enterprise? We are by no means observing that only the very rich begin industrial enterprises.
>
> (von Below 1926: 489)

7 "A new notion of wealth made its appearance: that of mercantile wealth, consisting no longer in land but in money or commodities of trade measurable in money. During the course of the eleventh century, true capitalists already existed in a number of cities […]. These city capitalists soon formed the habit of putting a part of their profits into land. The best means of consolidating their fortune and their credit was, in fact, the buying up of land. They devoted a part of their gains to the purchase of real estate, first of all in the same town where they dwelt and later in the country. But they changed themselves, especially, into money-lenders" (Pirenne 2014: 143–144).
8 "It goes without saying that in some time in the distant past, the capitalist spirit must have been in existence – in embryo, if you like – before any capitalist undertaking could become a reality" (Sombart 1915: 344).
9 "Capital plays certainly a great role in the economy as well as in the modern terms of today, but this is going to be explained only psychologically, by the men of a particular time, race, group of nations, and their spiritual powers, furthermore by the psychic results of these powers, the ideas and moral systems of the time, customs and law, institutions of the time" (von Schmoller 1903: 144 cited by Ebner 2000: 360).
10 Compare Weber's 'asceticism thesis' with Nassau Senior's 'abstinence thesis':

> To abstain from the enjoyment which is in our power, or to seek distant rather than immediate results, are among the most painful exertions of the human will […] what a *sacrifice of present enjoyment* must have been undergone by the capitalist who first opened the mine of which the carpenter's nails and hammer are the product! How much *labour directed to distant results* must have been employed by those who formed the instruments with which that mine was worked!
>
> (Senior 1951 [1836]: 60, 68)

11 This argument is, of course, fully embedded in Weber's logic (a religious group is the 'bearer' of an ethos that allows for the emergence and development of capitalism), and gives Weber the opportunity for an easy response: "The Jewish ethics, however strange that may at first sound, remained very strongly traditionalistic" (Weber 2001: 244).

12 The following excerpt from Martin Luther's writing is characteristic:

> Therefore is there, on this earth, no greater enemy of man (after the devil) than a gripe-money, and usurer, for he wants to be God over all men. [...] And since we break on the wheel, and behead highwaymen, murderers and housebreakers, how much more ought we to break on the wheel and kill [...] hunt down, curse and behead all usurers.
>
> (Martin Luther, *An die Pfarrherrn, wider den Wucher zu predigen. Vermanung* [1540], cited in Marx 1887: 428–429)

13 "Weber's theory ignores the emancipation from traditionalism in Italy which led to brilliant development of capitalism and made it the richest country in Europe in the second half of the Middle Ages" (Brentano 1916: 134). Ten years later, the same critique was repeated by Georg von Below: "Calvinism was not decisive for the development of capitalism, since the latter had been created in different places without it" (von Below 1926: 431).

14 Marx has clearly pointed out that the capitalist, in his very role, cannot abstain from a certain level of luxury:

> When a certain stage of development has been reached, a conventional degree of prodigality, which is also an exhibition of wealth, and consequently a source of credit, becomes a business necessity to the 'unfortunate' capitalist. Luxury enters into capital's expenses of representation. [...] there is at the same time developed in his breast, a Faustian conflict between the passion for accumulation, and the desire for enjoyment.
>
> (Marx 1887: 418)

15 As Fernand Braudel similarly notes in one of his later books, referring to Weber's approach: "All historians have opposed this tenuous theory, although they have not managed to be rid of it once and for all" (Braudel 1979: 66).

16 The same argument is often repeated by Weber's followers, as, for example, Heinrich Sieveking, who, when Professor at the University of Hamburg, wrote: "It is not possible, following Marx, to explain everything else starting from the production relations; on the contrary, in connection with Max Weber, the influence of the intellectual movement on the shaping of the economy must also be pursued" (Sieveking 1935: V).

17 The German archaeologist Hans Schaal wrote along similar lines:

> Capital is the pioneer of economic development. Capitalism, as it becomes clear from the early Orient, Hellenism and the Roman Empire, transformed the form of mankind [...] The diligence of the individual and the efficiency of capital are the causes which determine the extent of trade. Without them the travels of the Cretans into the Western Mediterranean, the Phoenicians into the Atlantic Ocean, the Greek and Roman merchants to nearly the north polar circle, or to the 'Middle Kingdom' [China], and its braid-bearers, would not have been possible.
>
> (Schaal 1931: 194)

18 Post-Keynesian economists Gunnar Heinsohn and Otto Steiger follow exactly this trend of thought:

> the historians, who reject Keynes's 'animal spirits' and 'hopes for profit', likewise fail in their search for an explanation of the 'individualistic capitalism' of

the ancient world, with 'money, interest, contracts, receipts and even bills of exchange' (Keynes *Collected Writings* Vol. 28: 253, 232).

(Heinsohn and Steiger 1989: 190)

19 "At an early date, from the very beginning, they went beyond 'national' boundaries and were in touch with merchants in foreign commercial centers. These men knew a thousand ways of rigging the odds in their favor: the manipulation of credit and the profitable game of good money for bad, with the 'good' silver or gold coins being used for major transactions to build up Capital and the 'bad' copper pieces being used for the lowest salaries and for daily wages, in other words, for Labor. They possessed superior knowledge, intelligence and culture. [...] Need I comment that these capitalists, both in Islam and in Christendom, were friends of the prince and helpers or exploiters of the state?" (ibid.: 57). See also Le Goff (1980).

20 "No capitalism before the Industrial Revolution, a still-young historian shouted one day: 'Capital, yes, capitalism, no!'" (Braudel 1979: 46).

21 "The 'idealist', single-factor explanation, seeing capitalism as the incarnation of a certain mentality was simply the way out adopted in desperation by Werner Sombart and Max Weber to escape the conclusions of Marx. We are in no sense obliged to follow them" (Braudel 1982: 402).

7 Modes of production and the pre-capitalist money-owner

7.1 Modes of production and social classes: basic concepts and definitions

In the previous chapter, we saw that Marx's view, according to which "the formation of capital does not emerge from landed property [...] but rather from merchant's and usurer's wealth" (Marx 1993: 504, see also Chapter 2), a thesis hardly considered by most contemporary Marxists, is in a way traceably figured in non-Marxist views. However, the majority of non-Marxist theoreticians seem not to understand capital as an exploitative class relation based on wage labour. In contrast to Marx, who comprehends these forms of wealth as "not as themselves forms of capital, but as earlier forms of wealth, as presuppositions for capital" (ibid.), non-Marxist theoreticians, from Max Weber to John Maynard Keynes and certain contemporary historians and economists, perceive large-scale merchants or usurers as capitalists. Capitalism has thus existed, according to them, since ancient times. Fernand Braudel, on his part, being much more careful in the way he uses theoretical concepts, speaks about an "enterprise [which] might be on the way to being capitalist, but it was not capitalist in the proper sense" (Braudel 1982: 251, see also Chapter 6). Does Braudel's 'anachronism' simply point to Marx's pre-capitalist money-owner?

In this chapter, I will endeavour to tackle these issues on the basis of Marxist theory of modes of production. Marx describes the mode of production as the structural interconnectedness of a certain social system of class domination and exploitation. Although focusing on the economic level of society, Marx never ignores its inherent interconnections with political, ideological and cultural forms:

> This much, however, is clear that the Middle Ages could not live on Catholicism, nor the ancient world on politics. On the contrary, it is the mode in which they gained their livelihood that explains why here politics, and there Catholicism, played the chief part.
>
> (Marx 1887: 176)

The concept of a specific (e.g. the capitalist) *pure mode of production* refers exclusively to the *core* of class relations pertaining to this specific (e.g. the capitalist) set of social relations. It entails a specific form of exploitation, that is, of appropriation by the ruling class (owners of the means of production) of the surplus product created by the 'direct labourer', and a specific form of political and ideological domination.

In line with conceptual definitions of several Marxist authors,[1] it is argued that on the economic level, the mode of production can be comprehended as the ensemble of three different relations to the means of production: *use*, *possession* and *ownership* of the means of production.

Use of the means of production is defined as the exclusive performance of actual labour, i.e. the participation of an individual or a social group in the labour process with a view to producing use values. In all modes of production, the use relation is in the hands of the 'direct labourer'.

Possession of the means of production refers to the management of the production process, namely the power to put the means of production into operation.

Ownership as an (real) *economic relationship* is the control over the means of production in the sense of having the power to dispose of the surplus obtained. In every mode of production, the ownership relation lies in the hands of the ruling class.

On the economic level, a mode of production refers to the particular combination of these three fundamental relations (Milios 2000; Economakis 2005).[2] This particular combination forms the economic structure of a mode of production and defines which of its three constituent structures (economic, juridico-political or ideological) is *predominant*.

In the capitalist mode of production, both ownership as an economic relation and possession of the means of production coexist in the hands of the ruling class. In other words, there is *homology* of ownership and possession by the capitalist, the 'carrier' of the capital relation.

By contrast, *non-homology* of ownership and possession of the means of production is characteristic of pre-capitalist modes of production. In this case, as possession of the means of production remains in the hands of direct labourers, extra-economic coercion (a relation of servitude or bond service) is rendered necessary in order for the appropriation of the surplus product by the owner of the means of production to be safeguarded. The functions of the political and ideological social levels become predominant in society. In capitalism, in contrast, homology of ownership and possession of the means of production connotes that 'free labourers' work for the benefit of the owners' class without extra-economic coercion: the economic structure becomes predominant.

According to Althusser (1976: 105 ff.) and Poulantzas (1975), social classes are formed within the modes of production as the occupants or carriers of the fundamental relations. Here, the social classes are defined as the *fundamental* social classes of a mode of production. Correspondingly, social groups that are not carriers of fundamental relations are defined as *non-fundamental* or *intermediate* social classes. The concept of relations of production involves a distributive process dividing people into classes while simultaneously constituting them as social subjects. Classes are born out of the antagonism inherent in this distributive process.

The articulation of different modes or forms of production in a social formation is always characterized by the domination of one particular mode of production. The two basic classes "of any social formation are those of the dominant mode of production in that formation" (Poulantzas 1975: 22). According to Poulantzas, the determination of social classes ("class places") must be distinguished from ideological–political "class positions", the latter of which reflect the 'stance' of a class at a specific conjuncture. A conjuncture is defined as the concrete situation of class struggle within the "unique historic individuality of a social formation" (ibid.: 14). A link between class place and class position can be achieved *provided that* 'class instinct', which corresponds to class place, is transformed into 'class consciousness' – corresponding to the interests of a class. Although class places may *potentially* indicate class positions, the opposite does not exist: *class positions cannot indicate class places*. "A social class […] may take up a class position that does not correspond to its interests" (ibid.: 15–16).

As discussed in Chapter 1, Marx defines the capitalist as the owner of the means of production who is

> able to devote the whole of the time during which he functions as a capitalist, i.e., as personified capital, to the appropriation and therefore the control of the labour of others, and to the selling of the products of this labour.
>
> (Marx 1887: 216)

With the terminology introduced in this chapter, this means that an entrepreneur must be *disentangled from the use of the means of production* in order to become a capitalist. The capitalist is directly *present* in the enterprise as the top manager who holds the possession of the means of production in the production process, personifying the enterprise as such. The same top manager shares the ownership of the means of production with the 'money capitalist', who personifies the financial form of existence of the enterprise (shareholder and bondholder, see Chapter 1).

With the emergence of capitalist enterprise, "it is not the individual worker but rather a *socially combined labour capacity* that is more and more the *real executor* of the labour process as a whole" (Marx 1864 [§481]). Within the collective worker, "an industrial army of workmen, under the command of a capitalist" is formed, which "requires, like a real army, officers (managers), and sergeants (foremen, overlookers), who, while the work is being done, command in the name of the capitalist" (Marx 1887: 232). An 'army' of a special kind of wage labourers is thus formed; whose exclusive function is the work of management–supervision (*as opposed to the performance of actual labour*).

Consequently, the wage earners belonging to this special category of wage labour do not *exclusively* perform the function of labour (use relation) but, on the contrary, also *exercise powers of capital*, that is, certain *functions* belonging to the *relation of possession* of the means of production have been conferred on them. Engineers and technicians (technologists) belong to this category, performing specific forms of management–supervision labour, which emanates from the specifically capitalist division between science and experience. Although they are productive labourers – exploited by capital – they also 'function as capital'. In other words, despite their subjection to capitalist exploitation, they are not elements of the working class (see also Poulantzas 1975, 228–229), and are consequently a part of an intermediate social class situated between the capitalist and the working class. This intermediate social class is the so-called *new petty bourgeoisie*.

Small entrepreneurs who exploit a marginal number of salaried labourers and perform similar activities as labourers in the production process are entangled in the use relation and do not therefore belong to the capitalist class. They constitute an intermediate social class (the class of the 'middle bourgeoisie', see Milios and Economakis 2011) formed in the framework of a different, non-capitalist mode of production, the 'hybrid mode of production' (ibid.), despite the fact that both capitalists and the middle bourgeoisie exploit wage labour. Intermediate classes also include all those who participate in production processes that do not entail surplus-product appropriation, like simple commodity production of the self-employed artisan, trader, peasant, scientist, etc. (who constitute the *traditional* petty-bourgeoisie class, see ibid.). According to Poulantzas (1973), such a process constitutes a *form of production*, whereas the mode of production always entails relations of exploitation.

The above remarks make it clear that in any given capitalist social formation, different modes or forms of production exist. Of course, the hybrid mode of production and simple commodity production constitute production forms non-antagonistic to the capitalist modes of production. The existence of antagonistic, pre-capitalist (e.g. feudal) modes of production in a certain social formation creates a much more complex class configuration (Milios 1999, Section VI). Political and ideological elements also play an important role in the complex class configuration characterizing a historically specific social formation.[3]

In all cases, a qualitative difference consistently exists between a dominant and non-dominant or dominated mode of production. A dominant mode of production entails a pertinent system of political and ideological dominance that restrains or even prevents the reproduction of antagonistic (to the dominant) modes of production.[4] The reproduction of non-dominant modes of production is thus in many cases confined 'in the pores of society' (see below). In nearly all modes of production, this system of political and ideological dominance takes on the form of state structure, specifically appertaining to the mode of production (ancient, Asiatic, capitalist). An exception to this was the feudal social order, which was characterized by local manorial power and the failure of monarchies ('states') to enforce royal discipline over their 'dominions'.[5]

7.2 Dominant pre-capitalist modes of production: relations of use and possession in the hands of the labouring class

A common characteristic of pre-capitalist modes of production is the non-homology of economic ownership and possession of the means of production. In other words, the ruling class does not have the possession of the means of production, which is in the hands of the ruled class, in connection with the use relation.

This is obvious in the case of feudalism: the ruling class of feudal lords had the (private) economic ownership of the land and the other means of production, that is, they appropriated the surplus labour, whereas the ruled-labouring class of serfs had not been 'freed' from the means of production, by which they produced (animals, ploughs, etc., the land itself – the serfs having been deprived of freedom of movement), but had direct possession of them, i.e. the power to put these means to work (to cultivate the land). Extra-economic coercion (surveillance by the lords' repressive apparatus, compulsory work on the lords' land, etc.) was rendered necessary for the appropriation of surplus product, which took the form of feudal rent (initially 'labour rent'; later 'rent in kind' and finally, 'money rent', see Economakis 2001).

In societies where the Asiatic mode of production was dominant,[6] the same condition of non-homology of ownership and possession existed. The Asiatic mode of production refers to the structural elements of a particular kind of pre-capitalist society, which, despite being contemporaneous with feudal societies, possessed its own peculiar characteristics, namely: (i) the absence of *private* property in the means of production, and (ii) collective organization of the subaltern (labouring) class in village communes. The land supposedly belonged to God, who had assigned it to the ruler, who personified the state. Surplus labour was appropriated by the state in the historically specific form of *tributes* paid to the state by all agrarian or urban communities.[7] The ruling class therefore attained the ownership relation collectively, organized as a state. The peasants and artisans attained possession and use of the means of production collectively as well, enjoying access to the means of production because of their belonging to a hierarchically structured (notables vs. simple peasant families) village community.

In the societies of classic Greek antiquity and the Roman Empire, where the slave mode of production prevails, things seem *at first glance* different: the master appears to own the slave in the same way that he owns a horse or any other means of production, a fact that seems to indicate that he combines both relations of ownership and possession of the means of production under his control. However, this is not the case with ancient, or 'classic', slavery, and more generally with the form of slavery that Marx describes as 'patriarchal'. In this form of ('classic') slavery, the slave-owner is *absent from the production process* and concedes the possession relation to a special category of slaves, ensuring for himself the surplus appropriation through the extra-economic coercion inherent in the master–slave relationship. Marx cites Aristotle, who writes:

> Whenever the masters are not compelled to plague themselves with supervision, the overseer assumes *this honour*, while the masters pursue public affairs or philosophy.
>
> (Aristotle, cited by Marx 1991: 509)

Marx sees further that the concession of the possession relation to a specific social group belonging to the ruled classes takes its most characteristic form in ancient societies, thus shaping the *classic* (or 'patriarchal') *slave mode of production*:

> [T]his work of supervision necessarily arises in all modes of production that are based on opposition between the worker as direct producer and the proprietor of the means of production. The greater this opposition, the greater the role that this work of supervision plays. *It reaches its high point in the slave system.*
>
> (Marx 1991: 507–508, emphasis added)

Contemporary historians have also stressed the dissociation of the slave-owning ruling class from the possession relation (the supervision and 'management' of the production process), in other words, the non-homology of ownership and possession of the means of production. The prominent Marxist historian of antiquity, G. E. M. de Ste. Croix, emphasizes the fact that "the function of slave (and freedman) overseers was essential [...] playing a very important role in the economy, perhaps far more so than has been generally realized" (de Ste. Croix 1981: 258). Perry Anderson also writes along these lines:

> Graeco-Roman Antiquity had always constituted a universe centred on cities. [...] The Graeco-Roman towns were [...], in origin and principle, urban congeries of land-owners. [...] The condition of possibility of this metropolitan grandeur in the absence of municipal industry was the existence of slave-labour in the countryside [...]; the surplus product that provided the fortunes of the possessing class could be extracted without its presence on the land. [...] The very ubiquity of slave-labour at the height of the Roman Republic and Principate had the paradoxical effect of promoting certain categories of slaves to responsible administrative or professional positions [...]. This process was [...] another index of the radical abstention of the Roman ruling class from *any* form of productive labour whatever, even of an executive type.
>
> (Anderson 1974-a: 19–20, 23, 24)

The masters (slave-owners) are absent from the production process, as in all other fundamental pre-capitalist relations of production (feudal, Asiatic). I may conclude, therefore, that in the classic slave mode of production, the possession relation is separated from the ownership relation that belongs to the ruling class of slave-owners, and remains in the hands of the labouring classes, who by definition also occupy the use relation.

This non-homology of ownership and possession on the part of the ruling class is therefore a common characteristic of all three fundamental pre-capitalist modes of production referred to. The most important element that distinguishes the classic slave mode of production from feudal and Asiatic modes of production is, above all, the fact that the ownership relation also embraces the labourer himself, who, after a certain point in time, was bought and sold exactly like any 'ordinary' means of production.

7.3 The money-begetting slave mode of production

As already mentioned, in every society (social formation), different modes and forms of production coexist under the predominance of the fundamental mode of production, which determines the character of any given society. As de Ste. Croix explains, when he defines Greek (and Roman) society as a 'slave economy':

> [T]his expression has regard, not so much to the way in which the bulk of production was done (for at most times in most areas in antiquity it was free peasants and artisans who had the largest share in production), but to the fact that the propertied classes derived their surplus above all through the exploitation of unfree labour.
>
> (de Ste. Croix 1981: 3–4)

In the ancient world, most characteristically in Athens, wage labour also existed, though to a rather limited extent, especially among the poor and in public construction plants.[8] However, this form of labour was regarded as a form of (temporary) voluntary enslavement, and was generally disdained (Kyrtatas 2002). Most historians and Marxist theoreticians seem to believe that in societies where the classic slave mode of production prevailed, other production processes were related more to non-exploitative forms of production than to divergent forms of exploitation. Characteristic again is the following formulation by de Ste. Croix:

> [A] large part of production in antiquity was always carried on, until the Later Roman Empire [...] by small free producers, mainly peasants, but also artisans and traders. In so far as *these numerous individuals neither exploited the labour of others* (outside their own families) to any appreciable extent *nor were themselves exploited* [...] they formed a kind of intermediate class, between exploiters and exploited.
>
> (ibid.: 33)[9]

However, in the societies of antiquity, as well as in other societies based on unfree labour, a self-contained exploitative mode of production based on slave labour existed, and was characterized by the concentration of both the ownership *and* the possession relation in the hands of the slave-owner. Characteristic of this mode of production is that the slave-owner is *present in the production process*, which is production for the market aiming at the appropriation of surplus in monetary form. I shall name this non-dominant pre-capitalist mode of production the *money-begetting slave mode of production*.

Let me provide a simple example: a merchant from ancient Athens (or Rome: in Rome, "members of the senatorial order themselves owed their fortunes to trade" Meikle 1995: 159) who subsumed unfree (slave) labour under his rule, bought wine from a local landlord and sold it, e.g. to the island of Milos, with the intent of acquiring monetary profit. Here we have a production process: through the combination of the means of production (e.g. vessels, carriages, the ship, etc.) and labour, the wine from the landlord's vineyard will be transformed into wine sealed in vessels or *hydrias* at the shop of local wine sellers on the island of Milos.

The money-begetting slave mode of production is thus a production process bearing monetary form. The taskmaster (money-begetting slave-owner) concentrates both ownership and possession of the means of production, and there is *homology* of ownership and possession in the hands of this particular type of slave-owner, in the same way as there is homology of ownership and possession in the hands of the capitalist. Despite this affinity in terms of homology of ownership and possession of the means of production by the taskmaster, this exploitative mode of production is by no means 'capitalism', as I will discuss below.

The production process, and its affinities with the capitalist mode of production, can be illustrated through the following scheme:

$$M \rightarrow C - [P] - C' \rightarrow M' \, [=M + \Delta M].^{10}$$

The money-begetting slave-owner (ancient merchant or manufacturer) buys with his money (M) commodities C (a ship, wine in big barrels, slaves, *hydrias*, rusks, biscuits and other food for the sailors – to a small number of whom he also pays wages). Then, he *commands* the production process: his slaves will seal the wine in *hydrias* of specific size or volume and load them onto the ship; the sailors will sail to Milos, etc. Finally, he sells the wine *hydrias* and comes up with an additional sum of money, ΔM. The same process is repeated, of course, again and again, as long as wine consumers in Milos (and other ancient cities) keep drinking Athenian wine. In the words of Aristotle, the process has:

> no limit to the end it seeks; and the end it seeks is wealth of the sort we have mentioned [...] the mere acquisition of currency [...] all who are engaged in acquisition increase their fund of money without any limit or pause.
>
> (cited by Meikle 1995: 59)

Aristotle, discussing exchange value (see Meikle 1995), described as 'spurious wealth' all forms of income accruing from a process aiming at the acquisition of a money increment of one's property (M-C-M′, see endnote 10, or M-M′: usury), as opposed to 'true wealth', which may bring on acts of barter (C-C) or simple exchange according to one's needs (C-M-C). Marx refers to Aristotle's schemes when he introduces his value-form analysis in Part I of Volume 1 of *Capital*.[11]

Furthermore, Marx clearly differentiates money-begetting slave mode of production from classic (or 'patriarchal', as he calls it) slave mode of production (of the 'absentee slave-owner', who is dissociated from the possession of the means of production): on different occasions he repeatedly stresses "the transformation of the earlier, more or less patriarchal slavery, into a *system of commercial exploitation*" (Marx 1887: 538, emphasis added). As Marx explains:

> In the ancient world, the influence of trade and the development of commercial capital always produced the result of a slave economy; or, given a different point of departure, it also meant the *transformation of a patriarchal slave system* oriented towards the production of the direct means of subsistence into one oriented towards the production of surplus-value.
>
> (Marx 1991: 449–450, emphasis added)

In the above citation, Marx uses the term 'surplus value' in a rather loose manner in order to denote the specific difference of surplus appropriation in the framework of the money-begetting slave mode of production. What is more, in order to demonstrate the difference between the money-begetting slave mode of production and other forms of pre-capitalist exploitation based on direct appropriation of surplus, he also makes use of the term 'capital', although he is referring to historic 'phases prior to the capitalist mode of production':

> In all forms where the slave economy (*not patriarchal slavery, but rather that of the later phases of the Greco-Roman era*) exists as *a means of enrichment*, and where money is thus a means for appropriating other people's labour by the purchase of slaves, land, etc., *money can be valorized as capital* and *comes to bear interest* precisely because it can be invested in this way.
>
> (Marx 1991: 728–729, emphasis added)

This passage from Volume 3 of *Capital* permits me to summarize my conclusions up to this point:

a   In the framework of the classic ('patriarchal') slave mode of production, the ruling class comprises non-working land- and slave-owners who live in cities and exercise their political power as citizens. They form the ruling class of society, concentrating the ownership of the main means of production, mainly land. The possession of these production means remains in the hands of the slave classes.

b   In contrast, within the framework of the money-begetting slave mode of production, the slave-owner, in most cases a metic, i.e. a non-citizen, concentrates both the ownership and the possession of the means of production in his hands, directing a production process that aims at creating money 'as an end in itself'. It is therefore a mode of production different from the classic ('patriarchal') slave mode of production, despite the fact that both extract their specific form of surplus from slave labour.

c   The money-begetting slave mode of production did not cease to exist with the dissolution of the classic slave mode of production and the demise of ancient societies and civilizations. On the contrary, it continued to exist throughout the entire historical era until the rise of capitalism, and to a certain extent even endures today (see the subsequent sections of this chapter for a more detailed analysis).

The money-begetting slave-owner is therefore a pre-capitalist *money-owner* who, theoretically speaking, could play the role of the one pole of the 'encounter' (see Chapter 5) out of which the capitalist mode of production is born. The above-cited passage from Marx's *Capital* continues as follows:

> Two of the forms in which usurer's *capital* exists *in phases prior to the capitalist mode of production* are particularly characteristic. [...] These two forms are, *firstly*, usury by lending money to extravagant magnates, essentially to landed proprietors; *secondly*, usury by lending money to small producers who possess their own conditions of labour, including artisans, but particularly and especially peasants [...]. Both of these things, the ruining of rich landed proprietors by usury and the impoverishment of the small producers, lead to the *formation and concentration of large money capitals*.
>
> (Marx 1991: 729, emphasis added)

d   However, capitalism cannot emerge unless the second pole, the proletariat, emerges, and the encounter between the two poles takes hold:

> But the extent to which this process abolishes the old mode of production, as was the *case in modern Europe*, and whether it establishes the capitalist mode of production in its place, depends entirely on the historical level of development and the conditions that this provides.
>
> (ibid.)

7.4 A dominated non-capitalist mode of production persisting through time

To avoid any misinterpretation, it is necessary at this point to stress once more that the money-begetting slave mode of production never became the dominant system in antiquity or in any other form of pre-capitalist society, but consistently remained embedded in fundamental (pre-capitalist) social relations that prevailed in each era. In other words, it was always subordinated to the dominant mode of production.

In ancient Greece and Rome, the non-monetary character of the dominant classic slave mode of production had, as a consequence, as de Ste. Croix explains, that "money income cannot be directly equated with income in kind from land for assessment purposes" (de Ste. Croix 2004: 41).[12]

The dominant slave mode of production (and later feudal or Asiatic modes of production) assigned the money-begetting slave mode of production to the 'intermundia' of society, that is, interstitially, in spaces between the basic social structures:

> The trading peoples of old existed like the gods of Epicurus in the *intermundia*, or like the Jews in the pores of Polish society.
>
> (Marx 1991: 447)[13]

Despite its non-central role in ancient societies, the money-begetting slave mode of production fuelled, at certain historical conjunctures, events of some significance. One of various examples from ancient Greek literature refers to the role of Cephalus II of Syracuse and his son Lysias, a famous logographer.

Cephalus II, a non-citizen (metic) in Pericles' Athens in the second half of the fifth century BC, was a rich trader and shield manufacturer (Nails 2002). Plato's *Republic* begins with Socrates visiting Cephalus at his house in Pireaus and starting a conversation with him about justice. However, Socrates very soon and rather unexpectedly abandons Cephalus as his interlocutor, an evolution that raises the question of the meaning of Cephalus' very brief appearance in the *Republic* for the development of Plato's argument. According to Kaveh Rafie:

> Plato bans people like Cephalus from being involved in the active political life of a just city. This, however, does not mean that Plato regards Cephalus as unjust or ethically perverted. He has qualms about the wealth of these people that may corrupt a city when they come to power; [...] Thus Cephalus belongs to the class of people who should be ruled by a prudent ruler, namely, a philosopher-ruler.
>
> (Rafie 2013: 1)[14]

Subsequent political events in Athens give the Cephalus family the opportunity to play a very important role in the city. After the Peloponnesian War, the oligarchic regime of the Thirty Tyrants was imposed in Athens (404–403 BC). The new regime decided to confiscate the property of certain metics who had opposed their rule. From Cephalus' family's factory, run by Lysias and his two brothers,

[t]he Thirty had confiscated seven hundred shields and 120 slaves; from the brothers' houses, they had taken copper, jewelry, furniture, and women's clothing [...]. In spite of losing the armory and the income derived from it [...], after fleeing Athens, Lysias was able to give substantial material assistance – three hundred mercenaries, currency in excess of two *talents*, et al. [...] – to the exiled democrats who were seeking to topple the Thirty, an indication that he had access to assets elsewhere.

(Nails 2002: 92)

After the overthrow of the Thirty Tyrants in 403 BC, an Athenian citizen proposed to the city that citizenship should be granted to Lysias for his definitive contribution to the restoration of democracy. The proposition was opposed, however, and never introduced to the city assembly (*ecclesia*). Citizenship remained a privilege of Athenian landowners.

What is more important, though, is that this money-begetting slave mode of production continued to exist, as already mentioned, after the classic slave mode of production had dissolved. I will deal with this issue in the next chapters. At this point, we should mention that the Crusades were not only a story of religious war but also of enslavement and slave trade.[15] During the Middle Ages, the trade of Christian slaves among Christians flourished in Italian cities and colonies. In the Venetian colony of Crete,

in the first half of the fourteenth century, the majority of slaves were Christian Greeks captured in Asia Minor, mainland Greece or the Aegean islands. The end of the century witnessed the replacement of Greek slaves by more and more people from the Black Sea region: Tatars, Circassians, Bulgars, Turks, Russians and others.

(McKee 2004: 40)[16]

Karl Marx argues that "the *continuity of the relation* between slave and slave holder is preserved by the direct compulsion exerted upon the slave" (Marx 1864 [§476]), whereas Friedrich Engels, who very often supports the progressivist problematique of ascending succession of modes of production, nevertheless also emphasizes the historic persistence of slavery.[17] In any case, it was the social figure not of the classic, but of the money-begetting, slave-owner, active as merchant, manufacturer, or usurer, who persisted or recurred in pre-capitalist societies that followed the dissolution of Greco-Roman antiquity. Marx portrays the money-begetting pre-capitalist merchant as 'trapping' the wealth not only of the classic slave-owner, but also of the feudal lord and the Asiatic state:

[I]n those earlier modes of production the principal proprietors of the surplus product whom the *merchant* trades with, *i.e. the slaveowner*, the *feudal lord* and the *state* (e.g. the oriental despot), represent the consumption wealth which the merchant sets out to trap, as Adam Smith correctly perceived [...] with regard to the feudal period.

(Marx 1991: 448, emphasis added)

7.5 The money-begetting slave mode of production and the capitalist mode of production

In Chapter 6, we saw a number of historians, social scientists and economists, most notably Max Weber and John Maynard Keynes, describe certain ancient societies as capitalist (Babylon, ancient Athens, the Roman Empire, etc.) solely because they possessed a discernible 'entrepreneurial' economic sector. It is obvious from what has been developed in the present chapter that this thesis constitutes an obvious mistake: the confusion of the money-begetting slave mode of production with the capitalist mode of production. A corollary of this mistake is the false impression that this supposed capitalist mode of production had become dominant in ancient societies.

I have already explained that the money-begetting slave mode of production is different from the capitalist one, as in the former, the labourer is still bound to the taskmaster by a relation of direct personal dependence, and his individual consumption does not depend directly on monetary market relations. As a consequence, exchange value and money cannot become universal, that is, it cannot become the motivating force in the economy, the capital relation cannot take shape. Pre-capitalist societies "follow a different economic logic", as Ernest Mandel aptly stresses.[18]

I would like to elaborate a bit further on the difference between the two modes of production, since the 'ancient capitalism' thesis remains powerful among certain parts of academia.

Scott Meikle reviewed a vast array of literature on the ancient Greek economy and concluded that the low development of *productive* credit in the ancient world constrained the role of money to a medium of circulation and a treasure to be hoarded (Meikle 1995: 147–179). The absence of inclusive capital and labour markets ruled out the possibility of exchange value becoming the regulating principle of the economy.

> There were no credit instruments of any kind, and each individual transaction was settled almost always by physical transfers in person, either by the principal himself or by an accredited agent. [...] There was no double-entry bookkeeping; notions of debit and credit were unknown; there was no accounting of debits and credits through strings of transactions to be settled at the end of a period, and there were no settlement days, quarterly or otherwise.
>
> (Meikle 1995: 160)

Alain Bresson questions approaches claiming that in antiquity productive credit was insignificant, and argues that in ancient Athens people borrowed money "to acquire land, to improve their farms or their equipment, or to buy slaves" (Bresson 2016: 280). Taking such loan transactions for granted, the picture of a *non-capitalist* economy still does not change. As Paul Millett's detailed analysis has shown, loans in ancient Athens were twofold in character: on the one hand, there were those between relatives or friends who were part of a broader reciprocal relationship; and on the other, there were credit agreements between two non-affiliated persons (who in most cases were non-citizens) who were charged interest payment.

> The two systems were complementary and where they interlocked, as in the law courts, it was the ideology of reciprocity that generally prevailed. In a Western, capitalist economy, that would be unthinkable.
>
> (Millett 1991: 220)

It must be stressed at this point that even the second category of loans, which carried an interest payment obligation, in cases where it had the character of 'productive credit', never lost its (inter)personal character in Greco-Roman antiquity. By contrast, credit under the prevalence of the capitalist mode of production is characterized by the 'reification' of the given economic relationship into a tradable 'thing', i.e. a security, bill of exchange, mortgage deed, etc., that functions as a 'sui-generis commodity' (see Sotiropoulos, Milios, Lapatsioras 2013: 134–179).[19]

The subordination of monetary relations to pre-capitalist structures, and the prevalent position of politics maintained in ancient societies, resulted in economic relations and processes being perceived as issues of politics or ethics. As Dimitris Kyrtatas aptly stresses:

> The idea of exploitation as a general economic category in human relations was absent in ancient Greek thought. What Aristotle and other authors stressed was domination. [...] [T]opics that we would examine as aspects of the economy, the Greeks examined as aspects of politics and ethics. And instead of seeking profit-maximization, the Greeks were mostly after honour-maximization.
>
> (Kyrtatas 2002: 153–154)[20]

Karl Polanyi has highlighted the issue of the 'invisibility' of the economy as depicted by ancient Greek writers in order to emphasize the difference and incompatibility between ancient Greek society (where the economic sphere was "embedded" or bound in the overall social structure) and modern capitalist societies (where the economy is regarded to have been extracted and to stand 'above' the political or cultural social structures). In his own words, the incongruity between ancient and modern economies can be epitomized in "the distinction between the embedded and the disembedded condition of the economy in relation to society" (Polanyi 1971: 69). However, rather unexpectedly, Polanyi, referring to Aristotle, argues in the same text that the ancient Greek economy was the "embryo" of the capitalist economy, which was to emerge "twenty centuries later":

> The economy, when it first attracted the conscious awareness of the philosopher in the shape of commercial trading and price differentials, was already *destined* to run its variegated course *toward its fulfilment some twenty centuries later*. Aristotle divined the full-fledged specimen from the embryo.
>
> (Polanyi 1971: 67–68, emphasis added)

It is clear from what has been developed in Chapters 2 and 5 that I reject any viewpoint that capitalism was 'destined' to prevail or that the 'fulfilment' of the money-begetting mode of production is in fact capitalism: the 'encounter' of the money-owner with the proletarian was not a 'necessity', but a historical contingency.

However, in the statement cited above, Polanyi also traces the affinity (or 'similarity') of the money-begetting slave mode of production with the capitalist mode of production – the concentration of both ownership and possession of the means of production in the hands of the taskmaster, i.e. the 'entrepreneurial' character of both production processes: market-oriented activities aiming at a monetary revenue as an end in itself, "without any limit or pause" (Aristotle).

This affinity allowed for the coexistence, and to a certain extent coalescence, of the money-begetting slave mode of production and the capitalist mode of production. After the latter had been established and had gained momentum in certain geographical regions of Europe, the former very often functioned as its support and a presupposition for its further expansion, especially where the wage relationship had not been established as an acceptable or reasonable form of labour among the poor.

Commenting on the economic order created by transatlantic colonialism, Fernand Braudel notes:

> With the exception of Canada and the young English colonies in America, the entire New World was a world based upon slavery.
>
> (Braudel 1979: 91–92)

When the Spanish and Portuguese colonized South America, European settlers in those territories of the New World were not willing to become workers, at least not in the numbers needed for the formation of a fast-growing internal capitalist market and capitalist economy. The indigenous populations, having lived in a pre-capitalist social framework, which was absolutely extraneous to wage labour until the colonial invasion, were now drafted into forced labour (and Christianization) under slave conditions, mostly in silver and gold mines and on huge plantations. The dramatic demographic decline of these indigenous populations due to the harshness of their new living conditions and the illnesses imported from Europe was compensated for by slave trade, with the massive importation of African slaves to the Spanish and Portuguese colonies. Similar conditions of slave labour were established in other European colonies, for example in the Dutch colony in Java (see Marx 1887: 534).

But it was not only in the colonies where the money-begetting slave mode of production functioned as a buttress for capitalism. In England as well, slave relations supported the stabilization of capitalism and disciplined the poor into new labour relations:

> Edward VI.: A statute of the first year of his reign, 1547, ordains that if anyone refuses to work, he shall be condemned as a slave to the person who has denounced him as an idler. The master shall feed his slave on bread and water, weak broth and such refuse meat as he thinks fit. He has the right to force him to do any work, no matter how disgusting, with whip and chains. If the slave is absent a fortnight, he is condemned to slavery for life and is to be branded on forehead or back with the letter S; if he runs away thrice, he is to be executed as a felon. The master can sell him, bequeath him, let him out on hire as a slave, just as any other personal chattel or cattle. If the slaves attempt anything against the masters, they are also to be executed.
>
> (Marx 1887: 522)

Three centuries later, the Industrial Revolution generalized wage labour in Britain, but at the same time gave a boost to the money-begetting slave mode of production in the South of the United States:

> The rise of industrial capitalism thus rested on the maintenance of slavery in another part of the world, even though that slavery was no longer dependent on the continuation of the slave trade.
>
> (Wolf, 1982: 316, cited in Brass 2011: 146)[21]

In order to promote capitalism, capitalist states also had to promote the money-begetting slave mode of production, which functioned as capitalism's social buttress. This fact was reflected in the thought of classical economists, many of whom elaborated on the commensurable character of money-begetting slavery and capitalism:

> E.g., when Steuart says: 'Here, in slavery, was a forcible method of making mankind diligent' (for the nonworkers).
>
> (Marx 1887: 496)

It is characteristic that Adam Smith and classical economists of the nineteenth century compare the money-begetting and capitalist modes of production as comparable systems of production on the basis of productivity and effectiveness criteria (for a detailed presentation, see Brass 2011). Adam Smith claims:

It appears, accordingly, from the experience of all ages and nations, I believe, that the work done by freemen comes cheaper in the end than that performed by slaves. It is found to do so even at Boston, New York, and Philadelphia, where the wages of common labour are so very high.

(Smith 2007: 67)[22]

On the basis of such arguments, if one were to choose to follow Werner Sombart's or Max Weber's idea that a 'spirit of capitalism' must have existed beforehand in order for capitalism to be able to emerge, then one is obliged to accept that the pre-existing 'spirit of capitalism' is the *'soul' of slavery*, that is, the 'soul' of the money-begetting slave mode of production. Adam Smith is, in his manner, crystal clear on this issue when he compares the economic situation of a British worker and an African-American slave:

The blacks, indeed, who make the greater part of the inhabitants both of the southern colonies upon the continent and of the West India islands, as they are in a state of slavery, are, no doubt, in a worse condition than the poorest people either in Scotland or Ireland. We must not, however, upon that account, imagine that they are worse fed, or that their consumption of articles which might be subjected to moderate duties is less than that even of the lower ranks of people in England. In order that they may work well, it is the interest of their master that they should be fed well and kept in good heart in the same manner as it is his interest that his working cattle should be so.

(Smith 2007: 733–734)

Capitalism is not the realm of 'freedom'. It is a social system in which *direct coercion guaranteeing economic exploitation* of the ruled by the rulers *has been incorporated into the economic relation itself.* 'Freedom' is then nothing but the *form of appearance* of a historically specific (the capitalist!) system *of class domination and exploitation.*

Karl Marx had no doubts about this. That is why he conceptualized the dissemination of the proletarian condition among the poor in terms of processes of coercion and expropriation (the violent expropriation of peasants from land possession, the bloody legislation against the expropriated peasants, the suppression of wages, etc. – see Chapter 2), and not as a process of liberation, as some post-Second World War historians seem to think (see Chapter 5). The proletarian condition appears (and 'functions') as 'freedom' only *after* the capital relation has been established and extra-economic coercion has been incorporated and concealed in the economic relation per se.[23] Marx explains:

It is not enough that the conditions of labour are concentrated in a mass, in the shape of capital, at the one pole of society, while at the other are grouped masses of men, who have nothing to sell but their labour-power.

Neither is it enough that they are compelled to sell it voluntarily. The advance of capitalist production develops a working class, which by education, tradition, habit, looks upon the conditions of that mode of production as self-evident laws of Nature. The organisation of the capitalist process of production, once fully developed, breaks down all resistance. [...] It is otherwise during the historic genesis of capitalist production. *The bourgeoisie, at its rise, wants and uses the power of the state* to "regulate" wages, [...] to lengthen the working day and *to keep the labourer himself in the normal degree of dependence.* This is an essential element of the so-called primitive accumulation.

(Marx 1887: 523, emphasis added)

7.6 Economic partnerships as forms of pre-capitalist money-begetting activities

7.6.1 Pre-capitalist coinage and finance

As already stated, money in the form of coinage or precious metals was common, and in many aspects important, in pre-capitalist societies such as ancient Greece, Rome and the Byzantine Empire. It was also accompanied by interest-bearing loans, 'banking' and other forms of finance.

Those same financial forms have been much discussed and disputed among historians, economists and other social scientists as to if they actually indicate early manifestations of capitalist forms, or were at least economic forms transitioning towards capitalism. Notably, as early as 1928, Joseph A. Schumpeter articulated the concept that credit constitutes the *differentia specifica* that distinguishes capitalism from other social systems based on private property and market-oriented production. By capitalism, he writes:

[w]e mean an economic system characterised by private property (private initiative), by production for a market and by the phenomenon of credit, this phenomenon being the *differentia specifica* distinguishing the "capitalist" system from other species, historical or possible, of the larger genus defined by the first two characteristics.

(Schumpeter 1928: 362)

In my previous analysis, I argued that in pre-capitalist societies, money and finance forms remained embedded in political, ideological and social structures pertaining to the prevailing relations of class exploitation and domination, which were non-monetary in their inner structure (the coercive relation of master and slave, of lord and serf, or of peasant and city community and the state). The money-begetting slave mode of production, the only pre-capitalist exploitation relation of the antiquity that aimed at maximizing monetary earnings, never became dominant in ancient Greece or Rome. The only case where pre-capitalist money-begetting became dominant was during the High Middle Ages in the northern Italian city states of Amalfi, Venice, Genoa, etc., where it eventually transformed itself into other social forms not based on slave labour, as we will see below.

In this section, I will focus on the character of pre-capitalist financial schemes, which developed from the period of the Roman Empire up through the High Middle Ages, and I will examine the extent to which their historical evolution and transformation shaped them into adaptable bearers of capitalist relations of production and exploitation.

After the dissolution of the Western Roman Empire, and up to the early thirteenth century, coinage reached its most highly developed form in the Byzantine Empire:

> The Byzantine monetary system had two main features. It was first and foremost a multidenominational system. Its structure was far more sophisticated than those of contemporary western coinages, which only featured the silver denarius and its half fraction, the obol, at least until the commercial revolution in the thirteenth century and the ensuing monetary evolution. It also demonstrated a great capacity for adapting, since every major monetary crisis was followed by a stabilization process that lasted for longer or shorter periods, but always for at least a century.
>
> (Morrisson 2002: 920)

The Byzantine state monitored and administered its mints centrally for more than a thousand years (imperial coinage) and never made concessions of minting rights to local political or religious authorities, as was the case in the Western European territories. The hegemonic role of Byzantine coinage up until the end of the twelfth century was reflected in the fact that even after the Arab conquest of large parts of the Empire, the fifth Umayyad caliph, Abd al-Malik ibn Marwan, minted "a bilingual Arab-Byzantine coinage ca. 680 or later" (Morrisson 2002: 913). According to Angeliki E. Laiou, in the twelfth century, prior to the conquest of Constantinople by the Crusaders in 1204, a relatively high, for the (medieval) period, degree of monetization of the Byzantine economy existed, which first and foremost reflected the dominant role of the state in the Byzantine economy, as in all societies where the Asiatic mode played an important role.[24]

In any case, with the massive introduction of coinage in pre-capitalist societies (see also Howgego 1995), different forms of credit contracts were formed. Among the first credit schemes mentioned in literature are those based on an 'association' or partnership between an owner of mobile wealth (coinage, precious metals, commodities or any of these – to which we will refer hereafter as 'money'), and an owner of 'labour', a taskmaster commanding a number of sailors and/or other labourers. In antiquity, as well as in the early phases of the Middle Ages, this taskmaster coincided with the money-begetting slave-owner; in later times, he could be a merchant or a 'commission agent' who also commanded over other forms of dependent labour.

The rationale behind these forms of 'association' was that one party contributes the money (or a part of it) necessary for a particular commercial voyage, while the other contributes the labour needed for the fulfilment of the venture (and the rest of the money needed). Upon completion of the voyage, both parties divide the proceeds according to their overall contribution (in money and labour) as interpreted by certain rules or according to their prior agreement.

The most well-known variants of such 'associations' or contracts were the Babylonian *tappūtim*, the Athenian *heteroploun*, the Roman *societas* and *fenus nauticum*, the Byzantine *chreokoinonia*, the Jewish '*isqa*, the Arab *qirād*, and the *commenda*, or *collegantia*, or *colleganza* of the northern Italian communes (Lane 1966, 1973; Abulafia 1977; Pryor 1977). In what follows, I will begin my exposition of these pre-capitalist 'financial' schemes with the *societas*, as it alone survived the dissolution of the Roman Empire and most probably influenced the formation of later schemes.

The Roman *societas* of money and labour was a consensual agreement contracted for the duration of a voyage between a party 'investing' money, and another 'investing' labour – and possibly money as well, in a commercial expedition (voyage); it had been widespread throughout the Mediterranean region since the era of the Roman Empire. In the contract, commensurability was recognized between the mobile property (money) and labour invested in a commercial expedition, and thereafter the distribution of gain or loss was defined according to the assessed magnitude of 'investment' provided by each party. The 'labour investor' was not liable for any loss of money on condition that his labour had been assessed equal to the amount of money put up by the 'money investor'. In such a case, the latter acquired up to half of the gains. The whole commercial enterprise was planned and directed jointly by the 'money investor' and the 'labour investor'. *Societas* contracts were often agreements between partners or relatives, not only as forms of credit but also as instruments for hedging risk, as two or more taskmasters would invest money in one another's voyages instead of keeping all their 'assets' in one – their own – expedition. *Societas* contracts survived the fall of the Western Roman Empire, and even the increasing perils of sea trade that followed the multiple invasions and wars from the fifth century AD onwards.[25]

In contrast, the *fenus nauticum* was not a partnership agreement of invested labour and money and the sharing of proceeds, but a sea loan bearing interest to be paid upon completion of the voyage, independent of the magnitude of profits reaped. In this case, the management of the expedition was not shared, but remained in the hands of the debtor (taskmaster); however, the money lender was liable for all losses incurred at sea, an arrangement that proved unfavourable to the creditor when sea trade became perilous.

The Byzantine *chreokoinonia*, which was also used as a loan and investment form in maritime commerce,[26] bore a lot of similarities to the Roman *societas*: the one partner contributed money and the other labour (and possibly money as well), and each one acquired gains or bore losses "in proportion to the shares according to the agreements" (Pryor 1977: 24). Its main innovation in contrast to the *societas* is that it allowed practically any division of proceeds among the partners, according to their prior agreement.

> Either in writing or not in writing, a partnership is constituted between two, or even more, whenever each of them contributes his own, either equal or lesser, share; or when some contribute capital and others their own labour. [They ought] to divide the profit accruing to them according to the agreements reached between them with subtraction of the initial capital funds (κεφαλαίων), clearly. And if such a partnership should sustain a loss to the *capital*, each partner ought to meet it according to his own proper share of the gain.
>
> > (*Ecloga*, a compilation of laws formulated during the reign of Leo III, 717–741, cited in Pryor 1977: 25)

The Jewish *'isqa* is referred to as "a semi loan and semi trust" (*Babylonian Talmud*, cited by Pryor 1977: 26). The invested money comprised two equal parts: (i) an interest-free *'loan'*, which the taskmaster ('labour investor') was obliged to return in full regardless of the outcome of the voyage, and (ii) a 'trust' that was to be returned to the 'money investor' with the profit accruing from it. In case of loss, the 'labour investor' was not liable for this 'trust'. This arrangement meant that if the economic outcome of the venture was lucrative, proceeds were divided in half. However, in case of loss, the 'money investor' bore two-thirds of it. Alternatively, he could agree to receive only one-third of the yield so as to be liable for half of the loss. Nevertheless, with changing economic relations in the Mediterranean, the *'isqa* became more flexible beginning in the late twelfth century and "almost any division of profit and loss was permissible provided that the labor-investor's share of profit remained greater than his share of loss" (Pryor 1977: 27).

In contrast to the above forms of association, two other forms of contracts emerged in the Mediterranean that possessed their own peculiarities beyond those commonly shared with the *societas* or the *chreokoinonia*: the Arab *qirād* (in existence since the eighth century) and the Italian *commenda* (since the tenth century). The *qirād*, which predated the *commenda*, was common not only in maritime but also in land commerce, whereas *commendae* for land trade rarely appeared. Religious restrictions and Muslim law rendered it necessary that the *qirād* be defined as a partnership and hire of labour, and not as a loan.[27]

The similarities between these two types of contracts, and the way they differed *from other associations* between 'investors' of money and 'investors' of labour, are the following:

a   The taskmaster of the commercial journey acquires full control of all money invested; he becomes the sole 'manager' of the venture. As 'manager', he is bound to certain pre-agreed upon obligations and objectives.

b   Although the taskmaster alone 'manages' the commercial voyages and obtains full possession of the money invested, the ownership of the money remains in the hands of its investor. This means that labour provided by the taskmaster ceases to be conceived of as an 'investment' commensurate with money. However, the taskmaster can also invest money in the *commenda* or the *qirād*. In this case, the contract is described as *bilateral*, and is distinguished from the *unilateral qirād* or *commenda*, where the 'money investor(s)' do(es) not participate directly in the commercial expedition as such.

The taskmaster is granted the authority to make the best use of the money invested in the venture in order to achieve the objectives set by the 'investor'. However, the mandate to the taskmaster is not always unlimited:

> When the labor-investor was not given such an unlimited mandate, his freedom of action was somewhat restricted, especially with respect to third parties [...] [he] was not permitted to combine *commenda* capital with other property in his possession and was not permitted to invest it in a *commenda* with a third party.
>
> (Pryor 1977: 34)

c   Upon completion of the commercial voyage, the taskmaster is obliged to return all money to the investor. Then both partners divide the earnings or losses according to their previous agreement.

> Generally, and in the archetypal case, in a unilateral *commenda* the *commendator* ('money investor', J.M.) received ¾ of any profit and bore all liability for loss while the *tractator* (taskmaster, J.M.) received ¼ of any profit and bore no liability for loss of capital. [...] In a bilateral *commenda* any profit was usually divided ½-½ while the *commendator* bore 2/3 of any loss.
>
> (Pryor 1977: 7)

Despite their major similarities, certain differences between the *commenda* and the *qirād* did exist, which concerned both the liability of the 'money investor' in special cases of money loss, and the rules of profit sharing between 'money investor' and taskmaster, which, in the case of the *qirād*, did not obey standardized conventional codes as in the case of the *commenda* (Pryor 1977: 30–32).[28] However, most writers dealing with forms of 'entrepreneurial' partnership and trade in the Mediterranean stick to the similarities and identify the *commenda* with the *qirād*, sometimes ascribing to them capitalist content. Jairus Banaji, following Abraham Udovitch, writes:

> Islamic commercial law and business practice knew both *commenda* agreements [*muḍāraba*, *qirād*] and investment partnerships [*mufāwaḍa*], and, as Udovitch says, "virtually *all* the features of partnership and *commenda* law are already found fully developed in the earliest Hanafite legal

compendium, Shaybānī's *Kitāb al-Aṣl*, composed toward the end of the 8th century". Thus, the major institutions of long-distance trade were firmly in place, certainly well before the end of the eighth century. But even more interesting, is the implication that the capitalism of the Mediterranean was preceded by (and could build on) an earlier *tradition of capitalist activity* which has so far received considerably less attention.

(Banaji 2010: 262, emphasis added)

7.6.2 Transitional money-begetting production forms

Both the *qirād* and *commenda* contracts are indications of the beginning of a process of separation between mobile wealth (money or 'capital', which is concentrated exclusively in the hands of 'resident investors') and labour. Labour is no longer conceived as 'investment' commensurable with, or even equivalent to, 'money investment'. On the contrary, money is advanced to hire labour that will set the commercial venture into motion.[29] From the point of view of the resident (non-travelling) investor or "static partner" (Abulafia 1977: 14), the earnings of trade appear as yield from the money he has advanced.

This process of separation between 'money investment' and 'labour investment' is more apparent in the unilateral *commenda*, in which all money was advanced by static merchants or other money-owners not taking part in the commercial voyage, as opposed to the bilateral *commenda*, in which the travelling partner or even members of the crew participated as 'money investor(s)' as well.

The unilateral *commenda* had been rapidly displacing the bilateral one in the northern Italian cities since the end of the twelfth century. In Genoa, "the ratio of unilateral to bilateral *commendae* climbed from 0.38:1 in the period 1156–1164 to 5.54:1 in 1200" (Pryor 1977: 13). In Venice, the bilateral *commenda* was banned in 1242, in the statutes published by vice doge Raniero Dandolo (ibid.: 10), in an effort by state authorities to check foreigners who attempted to exploit Venetian maritime trade, among other reasons.[30] The unilateral *commenda* became popular not only among merchants but, more generally, among prosperous people "men and women of widely diverse occupations and conditions" (Lane 1966: 61). In a way, as there were no limits to the number of people who could jointly finance a unilateral *commenda*, it also functioned as a joint stock fund giving participants the opportunity of raising income, especially after retirement.

However, even the unilateral *commenda* continued to bear features of partnership or association between one or more money-investing static partner(s) and an active partner (the travelling taskmaster). This was even more pronounced when the taskmaster ceased to utilize unfree labour (as a money-begetting slave-owner), when sailors began to be recruited from among free men: the 'association' then expanded into a relationship between the taskmaster (travelling partner) and the members of the crew, who were also remunerated as 'partners' ('profit sailing'), being paid a percentage of the final yield of the venture that exceeded the level of any salary paid by the taskmaster or the money-owner. Besides, sailors were also *partners as traders*, carrying their own merchandise on each commercial voyage, and even if they received a wage, they had not yet been transformed into proletarians, as they owned part of the commercial 'capital invested' in the venture.

As Frederic C. Lane writes, referring to pre-fourteenth-century Venice, "[t]he daily wage was only a part of what a seaman expected to gain from a voyage" (Lane 1973: 168).

> At sea, they were traders as well as sailors or oarsmen, so that it must have been difficult in the twelfth and even in the thirteenth century to draw the line between travelling merchant and merchant-seaman. [...] A gap between seamen and merchants opened when travelling merchants were transformed into resident merchants.
>
> (Lane 1973: 168)

After slave labour lost out to free labour, it was not capitalism but a new pre-capitalist money-begetting mode of production that emerged in relation to the *commenda* and other more or less similar financial schemes based on partnerships or associations.

I name this new pre-capitalist mode of production the *contractual money-begetting mode of production*, to denote the 'contract' between the money-owner and the labourer, which allowed the latter to have access to 'capital' and 'profit'.

The money-owner met a labourer who was free from all forms of personal servitude or bondage, but who was not 'free' from the means of production. In other words, he was not a proletarian, even if part of his income came from wage payment. The contractual money-begetting mode of production entailed a relation of economic exploitation of the labourer by the money-owner, who appropriated the labourer's surplus labour. The money-owner and the taskmaster concentrated both the ownership and the possession (the management) of the means of production. However, the labourer also had (limited) access to the ownership of the means of production (of 'capital') through both 'profit sharing' and the right to trade merchandise.

Access to the ownership of 'capital' by the labourers was an expression of their ability to resist the increase in exploitation by a money-begetting oligarchy, within a state expressing the class interests of this very oligarchy.

I will further elaborate on this issue in Part II, while also referring to the buying-up–putting-out system (see Chapter 3) that developed in parallel with the contractual money-begetting mode of production. Furthermore, I will present the historical contingencies that finally led to the transformation of the labourer into a proletarian. More specifically, in Chapters 9 and 10, I will discuss the characteristics of the contractual money-begetting mode of production and its withering away, as capitalist social relations gained ground.

At this point, I will only reiterate that I disagree with any attempt to interpret the *commenda*, the *qirād* or any form of finance based on a money–labour partnership as forms of capitalist finance.[31] I will agree, however, that trade as well as financial schemes like the *commenda* or the *qirād* belonged to an array of decisive factors, which paved the way for the emergence of capitalism.[32]

The *commenda* was not capitalist finance, although it facilitated and supported its formation. The same is true for the other forms of 'association' or credit discussed in this chapter. Capitalism is, above all, a historically specific relation between the owner of the means of production and the direct labourer. Although pre-capitalist finance preceded the formation of the capitalist relation (in direct contrast to Schumpeter's affirmation to the contrary), *capitalist* finance is a facet of this relation.

7.7 Concluding remarks

Having completed my theoretical inquiry into the question of the origins of capitalism, I can formulate my first conclusions as follows:

1   Historically, pre-capitalist money-begetting modes of production existed long before the emergence of the free (from means of production and relations of personal coercion) proletarian and, therefore, of capitalism. Money-owners commanding economic processes that aimed at a money revenue as an end in itself were not capitalists, but pre-capitalist taskmasters or lenders, in most cases living 'at the pores' of societies. The money-begetting slave mode of production is the oldest and most enduring pre-capitalist monetary production form. The contractual money-begetting mode of production appeared many centuries later and, as we will discuss in Part II, was sustained by means of a state power consolidating the money-owners' interests.

2   Given their entrepreneurial character, the money-begetting modes of production themselves can be transformed into the capitalist mode of production when the slave or the 'partner' is converted into a wage earner whose encounter with the money-owner takes hold.[33] This encounter, aleatory in essence, that is, historically contingent, gave birth to the capital relation and thereupon to capitalism as a social system.

3   The money-begetting modes of production may coexist with the capitalist mode of production and pave the way for it in all societies and historical conjunctures where wage labour has not yet been established as a normal social condition.

4   The condition of freedom and equality in capitalism is the form of operation of class domination and exploitation, resulting from the 'inclusion' of direct coercion into the economic relation as such. It is a condition that makes class rule (exploitation and domination) invisible.[34]

In the next chapters, I will focus my analysis on the historical contingencies that made possible the prevalence of the aleatory encounter of the money-owner with the proletarian – in other words, the birth of capitalism. It goes without saying that the city states on the Italian peninsula and their broader spheres of influence in the Mediterranean will constitute the epicentre of my analysis, as it is known that

> in Italy, where capitalistic production developed earliest, the dissolution of serfdom also took place earlier than elsewhere. The serf was emancipated in that country before he had acquired any prescriptive right to the soil. His emancipation at once transformed him into a free proletarian, who, moreover, found his master ready waiting for him in the towns.
>
> (Marx 1887: 508–509)

Notes

1 See mainly Althusser (1976, 1984-a, 1984-b), Althusser & Balibar 1997, Balibar (1983, 1986), Bettelheim (1968, 1974, 1975), Harnecker (2000), Poulantzas (1973, 1975, 1976), Rey (1973), Carchedi (1977), Godelier (1978).

2 These relations must not be considered as invariable regarding concrete content (and functions), from one mode of production to the other (see Poulantzas 1976: 78, Gerstein 1989: 123, 125).

3 As a result, social "classes are defined principally (but not exclusively) by their place in the relations of production" (Jessop 1985, 165); i.e. "a complete definition of classes must be worked out in terms of economic, political and the ideological [factors]" (Carchedi 1977: 43), with the precondition that *any class definition in contrast to the structural definition on the economic level cannot exist.*

4 In this context, I remind the reader of the principal element defining a certain (dominant) mode of production:

> The nature of a given mode of production is decided not according to *who does most of the work of production* but according to the specific *method of surplus appropriation*, the way in which the dominant classes extract their surplus from the producers.
>
> (de Ste. Croix 1984: 107, see also Chapter 3)

5 "The entrenchment of local counts and landowners in the provinces, through the nascent fief system, and the consolidation of their manorial estates and lordships over the peasantry, proved to be the bedrock of the feudalism that slowly solidified across Europe in the next two centuries" (Anderson 1974-a: 142).

6 On the Marxist notion of the Asiatic mode of production, see Mandel (1971: 116–139), Brook (1989), Milios (1989, 1997, 1999).

7 Marx distinguishes "Asiatic landforms" from all other precapitalist production forms:

> Amidst oriental despotism and the propertylessness which seems legally to exist there, this clan or communal property exists in fact as the foundation, created mostly by a combination of manufactures and agriculture within the small commune […]. A part of their surplus labour belongs to the higher community, which exists ultimately as a person, and this surplus labour takes the form of tribute etc., as well as of common labour for the exaltation of the unity.
>
> (Marx 1993: 473)

Marx argued that the tribute is a historically specific form of surplus, which shall be distinguished from rent, i.e. it shall not be "erroneously include[d] in this economic category" (Marx 1887: 519). The notion of the Asiatic mode of production is obviously not compatible with the evolutionist four-stage scheme of dogmatic Marxism (see Chapter 2). Besides, as Ernest Mandel (1971: 118) notes, the notion of the Asiatic mode of production was denounced by Soviet leaders as early as 1931 for reasons that had to do with the so-called "anti-feudal tasks" of Communist parties in less developed countries, and especially in China.

8 "By the end of the fifth century, as we know from the Erechtheum accounts, wage rates of one drachma per day were common. The daily pay of sailors in the fleet was also between one drachma per day [...] and half a drachma [...] and the daily pay of dicasts was half a drachma from 425 onwards" (de Ste. Croix 2004: 43). "The poorer women of Athens and, presumably, of other cities also worked for wages" (Kyrtatas 2011: 105).

9 A similar approach is put forward by Perry Anderson: "Free peasants, dependent tenants, and urban artisans always coexisted with slaves [...] in the different city-states of Greece. [...] Small-holders never disappeared generally or completely in the Italy [...] of ascendant landowners" (Anderson 1974-a: 21–22).

10 The same scheme can be formulated in a clipped form as: M-C-M′, as opposed to C-M-C, which refers to simple exchange (selling a commodity in order to obtain another one).

11 "The two [...] peculiarities of the equivalent form will become more intelligible if we go back to the great thinker who was the first to analyse so many forms, whether of thought, society, or Nature, and amongst them also the form of value. I mean Aristotle" (Marx 1887: 40).

12 "A manufacturer or trader, even when the use of money became general, would simply not know what his 'income' or his 'profits' expressed in terms of drachmae were. This is one of the basic facts about the economy of the Greek world (and the Roman world) that many modern historians have entirely overlooked, because they persist, quite unconsciously, in conceiving the ancient economic systems in terms taken over directly from the modern or the medieval world. No characteristic of the economy of modern or even medieval Europe can safely be assumed to have been present in that of ancient Greece until actual evidence of its existence there has been found" (de Ste. Croix 2004: 42–43).

13 In the antiquity,

> no single statesman is known to have been a practising merchant, and no merchant is known to have played a prominent part in politics, even at Athens. The merchants were not all [...] both non-citizens and men of little or no property; but [...] their influence on politics, as merchants, was certainly infinitesimal.
>
> (de Ste. Croix 2004: 356)

14 The distrust of money in mainstream ancient Greek thinking is delineated in the following excerpt from a well-known tragedy:

> Nothing so evil as money ever grew to be current among men. This destroys cities, this drives men from their homes, this trains and warps honest minds to set themselves to works of shame, this teaches people to practice villainies, and to know every act of unholiness.
>
> Sophocles, *Antigone* [441 BC], Sir Richard Jebb, Ed., Perseus Digital Library, www.perseus.tufts.edu/hopper/verses 295–300

15 "In the 1220s Prussians overran Culm, the one Prussian province Conrad [Poland's most powerful duke] had been able to conquer, and attacked Polish

villages and abbeys, seizing people to be sold as slaves or put to work on the warriors' farms" (Madden 2004: 128).

16 Adam Smith describes the persistence of slavery in Western Europe as follows:

> so early as the twelfth century, Alexander III published a bull for the general emancipation of slaves. It seems, however, to have been rather a pious exhortation than a law to which exact obedience was required from the faithful. Slavery continued to take place almost universally for several centuries afterwards.
>
> (Smith 2007: 304)

Regarding the Byzantine Empire, Michael Kaplan writes:

> The slaves employed in the workshops were of varying condition. Some were placed by their masters at the head of the workshop; as such, they had wage-earners or other slaves under their command. [...] On the other hand, amongst the bankers or money-changers, slaves were not permitted to become the head of an enterprise. In contrast, other slaves were workers placed on the same level as wage-earners or apprentices and charged with unskilled tasks. That said, even at the head of a workshop, the slave did [not] have any of his own property, could not accumulate profit, and could not build up any savings.
>
> (Kaplan in Haldon 2009: 161–162)

Sally McKee writes about fifteenth-century Venice:

> Despite the high cost of slaves, all levels of society participated in slave owning. Nobles, priests, notaries, master craftsmen, spice merchants, sailors, and textile workers are the principal vendors while just as wide a variety of people bought slaves. In Venice, patricians, not surprisingly, constituted the largest group of sellers and buyers, since as a group they were more likely to have the capital necessary to buy slaves.
>
> (McKee 2008: 319)

17 "Slavery is the first form of exploitation, the form peculiar to the ancient world; it is succeeded by serfdom in the Middle Ages and wage labour in the more recent period. These are the three great forms of servitude characteristic of the three great epochs of civilization; open, and in recent times disguised, slavery always accompanies them" (Engels 2010: 427).

18 "It is true that the capitalist mode of production is the only social organization of the economy which implies *generalized* commodity production. It would thus be completely mistaken to consider for example Hellenistic slave society or the classical Islamic Empire – two forms of society with strongly developed petty commodity production, money economy and international trade – as being *ruled* by the 'law of value'. Commodity production in these pre-capitalist modes of production is intertwined with, and in the last analysis subordinated to, organizations of production (in the first place agricultural production) of a clearly non-capitalist nature, which follow a different economic logic from that which governs exchanges between commodities or the accumulation of capital" (Mandel 1991: 14–15).

19 "[In] capitalism, credit became standardized. That is to say, that whereas before indebtedness arose as the result of an agreement between two people who knew each other, it was now rearranged on a systematic basis [...]. The new relationship is expressed by negotiable instruments, whether as a bill of exchange or security or banknote or mortgage deed" (Sombart 2001: 46). For more on this issue, see also Wray 1993, Semenova and Wray 2015.

20 Karl Marx has also stressed this view:

> Do we never find in antiquity an inquiry into which form of landed prop-
> erty etc. is the most productive, creates the greatest wealth? Wealth does not
> appear as the aim of production, although Cato may well investigate which
> manner of cultivating a field brings the greatest rewards, and Brutus may even
> lend out his money at the best rates of interest. The question is always which
> mode of property creates the best citizens.
>
> (Marx 1993: 487)

The focus of ancient Greek societies on political and moral issues and objectives,
rather than on economic ones, created a certain ambiguity as regards the meaning of words that later acquired an economic connotation. As Wolfgang Müller
observes:

> Even the word *chrémata*, often translated as money, is manifold; its origin
> points to the usefulness in use, to the need; it can then be the mass of useful
> objects, the property, the possession, the means; in a certain sense then also
> the money, the money-sum, even the debt or the commodities.
>
> (Müller 1975: 17)

21 Marx stresses on several occasions the complementarity of slavery (the money-
begetting slave mode of production) to capitalism:

> [A]s soon as people, whose production still moves within the lower forms of
> slave-labour, corvée-labour, &c., are drawn into the whirlpool of an interna-
> tional market dominated by the capitalistic mode of production, the sale of
> their products for export becoming their principal interest, the civilised hor-
> rors of overwork are grafted on the barbaric horrors of slavery, serfdom, &c.
> Hence the negro labour in the Southern States of the American Union pre-
> served something of a patriarchal character, so long as production was chiefly
> directed to immediate local consumption. But in proportion, as the export of
> cotton became of vital interest to these states, the over-working of the negro
> [...] became a factor in a calculated and calculating system.
>
> (Marx 1887: 164)

"When, in 1790, the first census of slaves was taken in the United States, their
number was 697,000; in 1861, it had nearly reached four millions" (Marx 1887:
296).

22 As Tom Brass writes,

> like most other economists, Malthus, Mill and Bright recognized that the
> presence of slaves in the labour market undercut the demand for workers who
> were free. Unfree labour was regarded by them as unproductive and ineffi-
> cient, and – like Adam Smith – more costly than its free equivalent.
>
> (Brass 2011: 18)

Max Weber does not trace the superiority of wage labour over slavery in the
higher productivity of labour, but on the fact that the slave relationship limits the
power of the entrepreneur over the labour force he utilizes:

> According to Weberian sociological theory, however, the most important
> obstacle posed by the presence of unfreedom to the process of economic ra-
> tionalization on which capitalist development depends was the consequent
> inability of employers to recruit/dismiss workers in keeping with business
> requirements. For this and the above reasons, Weber maintained that it was
> possible to employ unfree labour only when the following three conditions

were met: where slaves could be maintained cheaply, where a large and continuous supply of such workers was assured, and in large-scale agricultural
enterprises (e.g., plantations) or technologically underdeveloped (= 'simple')
industrial labour processes.

(Brass 2011: 23)

23 Anderson, for example, seems not to understand the fact that slavery (or 'voluntary enslavement': hired labour for a wage) was the only possible form of *dependent labour* in antiquity, and so claims that "loss of liberty" undermined the morale
of the labourer and curtailed the productivity of "manual labour". He writes:

Once manual labour became deeply associated with *loss of liberty*, there was no
free social rationale for invention. The stifling effects of slavery on technique
were not a simple function of the low average productivity of slave-labour
itself, or even of the volume of its use: they subtly affected all forms of labour.

(Anderson 1974-a: 26–27, emphasis added)

However, when the classic slave mode of production dominates, social rationality
regards slavery as just, and no dependent labour can be 'free', in contemporary terms:

The content is just so long as it corresponds to the mode of production and is
adequate to it. It is unjust as soon as it contradicts it. Slavery, on the basis of
the capitalist mode of production, is unjust.

(Marx 1991: 461)

As Kyrtatas aptly argues, "a farmer could farm his land with the aid of either a
slave, or a hired man from the neighbourhood, or the assistance of a neighbour,
or alone, with [...] the help of family members" (Kyrtatas 2011: 98). The use of
slave labour was an outcome of the core structure of ancient societies, i.e. the
domination of the classic slave mode of production and the dissociation of the
master from the possession of the means of production:

Possessing slaves made leisured lives possible and secured the position of
slave-owners in the social structure. In this sense, by securing the dominance
of the dominant classes, slavery can be seen as the principal if not exclusive
mode of production in the classical Greek world.

(Kyrtatas 2011: 110)

24 "The state structured the command economy, whereby a very considerable
part of the surplus (in proportions that varied with time) was appropriated
by the state and redistributed in the form of salaries, a system that facilitated
monetization in the countryside. In what is perhaps the first sign of impending
recovery, the state ordered the payment of taxes in cash, already in 769" (Laiou
2002-b: 1146).

25 "A contract of 27 September 1186, arguably one of the most significant of all the
Genoese contracts for business in Sicily, ties together many strands. [...] Now, in
this instance the original contract of *societas* may still exist" (Abulafia 1977: 274).

26 "Special mention should be made of the financing of maritime trade via the
formation of partnerships whose sole purpose was entrepreneurial activity at sea.
The beginnings of the maritime partnership are regarded as being the profit-
sharing system (*kerdokoinonia*) referred to in the index to the *Rhodian Sea Law* or
the system of debt-sharing (*chreokoinonia*) defined in the relevant provision of the
same collection" (Maridaki-Karatza 2002: 1117).

27 Similar religious restrictions applied to loans in the Christian world:

The early commercial documents show the use at Venice on the one hand of
the kind of ordinary loans on security which the church fathers censored as

usurious and on the other hand of real partnerships, a form of contract that was never condemned.

(Lane 1966: 67)

28 Schemes similar to the *commendae* were also introduced in the Byzantine Empire during the eleventh and twelfth centuries:

In the late Byzantine period, commerce as an occupation began to attract more and more people of 'noble' descent, perhaps because the loss of many of the imperial territories had brought to an end the prosperity of landowners. On the other hand, the increased influence of Venetian and Genoese merchants on the economic life of Constantinople had led to the creation of Byzantine replicas of the forms of partnership that trade took in the West. Among such partnerships were the *societates* (*syntrophiai*) that operated on land and the unilateral and bilateral *commenda* active in maritime trade; aristocrats were commonly involved in many of these partnerships, being fully aware, as members of a society in decline, of the power that money could bestow.

(Papagianni 2002: 1093)

29 "The *qirād* became hire of labor if the labor-investor was given a fixed return in place of a share of the profit" (Pryor 1977: 32).

30 Surviving historical data do not provide a clear picture of the extent of *commenda* contracts as compared with voyages financed solely by travelling partners:

The contracts are, of course, partnership contracts, involving two or more individuals. There is no way of knowing what proportion of trade in Genoa and Venice was financed by partnerships, and what proportion was financed by individual merchants who travelled overseas free of obligation to a second party.

(Abulafia 1977: 13)

31 Such an attempt is undertaken by Gene Heck, who argues that capitalism has Arab roots and that Islamic credit partnerships were capitalistic:

Accordingly, if the ultimate goal of commercial capitalism is, indeed, 'capital augmentation', then the motivations that underlay the medieval Islamic credit partnerships can, almost by definition, retrospectively be described as 'capitalistic'.

(Heck 2006: 103)

Patricia Crone comments on the emergence of a so-called Muslim bourgeoisie as follows:

[...] the Marwanid period [683–743, J.M.] saw the formation of the so-called Muslim bourgeoisie. The ex-tribesmen became shopkeepers, craftsmen and merchants, and the *Sharia* which they wrote is accordingly marked by a high regard for mercantile activities which landed nobilities usually despise.

(Crone 2003: 51)

The ruling landed nobilities and political elites considered commerce to be "the lowest activity" (ibid.: 239).

32 As Jairus Banaji correctly stresses,

Islam made a *powerful contribution to the growth of capitalism in the Mediterranean*, in part because it preserved and expanded the monetary economy of late antiquity and innovated business techniques that became the staple of Mediterranean commerce (in particular, partnerships and *commenda* agreements), and also because the seaports of the Muslim world became a rich source of the plundered money-capital which largely financed the growth of maritime capitalism in Europe.

(Banaji 2010: 267–268)

I would add that the contribution of Byzantine trade and financial traditions were equally powerful! Besides, the conquest and division of the Byzantine Empire following the Fourth Crusade enabled the plundering and usurpation by the Venetians and Genoese of economic resources, which were at least equally important as those taken from the 'Muslim world'!

33 Referring to the slave, Marx writes:

> when the man who was previously a slaveholder employs his former slaves as wage labourers, etc., production processes with a different social determination are thereby converted into the production process of capital. [...] The slave ceases to be an instrument of production belonging to the owner of that instrument. [...] Before the production process they all confront each other as owners of commodities, having only a *monetary relation* in common.
>
> (Marx 1864 [§470])

34 "In slave labour, even that part of the working day in which the slave is only replacing the value of his own means of existence, in which, therefore, in fact, he works for himself alone, appears as labour for his master. [...] In wage-labour, on the contrary, even surplus labour, or unpaid labour, appears as paid. There the property-relation conceals the labour of the slave for himself; here the money-relation conceals the unrequited labour of the wage labourer" (Marx 1887: 381).

Part II

Venice and the Mediterranean

A discourse on the birth of capitalism

8 From a Byzantine exarchate to a major colonial power in the Mediterranean

A historical sketch of the rise of Venice up to 1204

8.1 The emergence of the Italian maritime republics: an overview

After the collapse of the Western Roman Empire in the wake of the invasion of the Goths and the Huns in the fifth century AD, the Byzantine forces of the Eastern Roman Empire recaptured most of the Italian peninsula in the sixth century. However, later in the sixth century and in the first decades of the seventh, a large part of the Italian peninsula was subjected to Lombard rule. The Byzantines still kept areas of Northern and Southern Italy, with Ravenna being their main stronghold in the North, governed by an imperial deputy with the title of 'Exarch'.

A Byzantine exarchate was a province that kept looser connections with the rest of the empire as compared with ordinary imperial provinces in the sense that, among other concerns, it would defend itself primarily by its own means, without relying upon the imperial army or navy. Ravenna eventually fell under Lombard rule in 751, and shortly thereafter the Pope abandoned Byzantium to ally himself with the King of the Franks, Pippin III (Pepin the Short). By the end of the eighth century, Pippin's son and heir to the Frankish throne, Charlemagne, had conquered the Lombard kingdom, absorbing into his suzerainty most of the territories of the former Byzantine exarchate of Ravenna. On Christmas day 800, Pope Leo III crowned him 'Holy Roman Emperor'.

The Holy Roman Empire comprised several kingdoms, among which was the Kingdom of Italy. Kings, acting as overlords, granted fiefs to local lords, who in turn functioned as their vassals and owed fealty to them. At this new historical conjuncture, a number of Italian cities still under Byzantine suzerainty gradually developed their own forms of self-government, in a process that finally led to their evolution into independent city *states*. Some, like Amalfi, Ancona, Gaete, Genoa, Noli, Pisa, Ragusa and Venice, emerged as maritime republics, as they were shaped in accordance with the social interests of a ruling class of nobles focused almost exclusively on money-begetting maritime activities such as trade, slave trade, rapine and piracy, creating corresponding institutional and government forms (Abulafia 2012).

A variety of contingent historical occurrences such as the Arab conquest of the Southern Mediterranean; social and economic change in Byzantium; the initial alliances of the emerging Italian maritime republics with Byzantium in order to draw benefits from the more highly developed Byzantine economy; the social tensions in Byzantium, which, at a crucial moment, found expression in iconoclasm; the Norman invasion of southern Italy; the Crusades; the Schism between the Western and Eastern Christian Churches; the conflict between the Holy Roman Emperors and the Popes; the disintegration and conquest of Byzantine territories since the eleventh and twelfth centuries; the rivalries and wars between the emerging independent Italian cities and other factors *all* contributed to the city states' becoming independent, and to their later miraculous economic development.

Fernand Braudel portrays the emergence of the Italian city states as follows:

> [...] in the eighth and ninth centuries, trading revived: shipping was once more seen in the Mediterranean, and all coastal dwellers benefited, rich and poor alike. Along the coasts of Italy, small seaports began to thrive – not only Venice which was still insignificant at this time, but ten or twenty little Venices. Prominent among them was Amalfi [...]. The rise of Amalfi, though not easily comprehensible at first sight, is explained by the port's early privileged contacts with Islam, as well as by the very poverty of its infertile hinterland, which drove the little town to commit itself single-mindedly to maritime ventures.
>
> (Braudel 1984: 106)

After the decline of Amalfi in the early twelfth century, due in part to its having been sacked and conquered first by the Normans, and shortly thereafter by the Pisans, three other Italian city states played a decisive role in the Mediterranean: Pisa, Genoa and Venice.

In Chapter 7, I presented facets of Mediterranean maritime ventures during the Middle Ages, focusing on their monetary and financial features. We saw that up until the twelfth century, nearly all economic (merchants) and political (states) actors in the region (the Byzantine Empire; the Islamic and Italian states; Christian, Jewish and Muslim traders; etc.) had developed similar economic practices and financial tools. These practices and tools boosted the 'monetization' of economic structures, and in this sense created an economic environment that might have facilitated the emergence of capitalism in the event that the encounter of the money-owner and the propertyless proletarian had taken place. However, they should not be regarded as capitalist by any means; they were economic forms subsumed under the predominant – in each historical period or social formation – pre-capitalist mode of production, which had been inherited from the money-begetting slave mode of production.

In this chapter, I will focus on the first phase of the history of Venice, up to 1204, outlining the main historical events that allowed her to be transformed from a former Byzantine province into an independent social formation and, despite being a 'late bloomer', to "reign supreme" (Braudel 1984: 119) as a political, economic and colonial power.

This historical sketch of Venice's economic and political rise will allow me, in Chapter 9, to analyze the historically unique class relations of power in the Venetian social formation, which functioned as prerequisites to her success. Then, in Chapter 10, the historical contingencies and social transformations that led to the prevalence of the capitalist mode of production in the Venetian social formation will be discussed.

Of course, Venice was not alone. As already mentioned, analogous historical development had been taking place in other city states on the Italian peninsula, Genoa being the most characteristic example. However, in order to give my analysis the character of a 'concrete analysis of the concrete situation',[1] and to avoid 'average reasoning' generalizations, I have decided to focus on Venice, which, besides, was the only Italian city state to remain independent for nearly a thousand years, until 1797.

8.2 Building a merchant tradition on salt, slaves and timber

After Constantinople became the 'New Rome', that is, the new capital of the Roman Empire, the province of *Venetia* on the Adriatic Sea consisted of three major cities: Padua, Aquileia and Oderzo. When the Goths invaded the region in 403 AD, destroying Aquileia, many *Veneti*, among whom were several of Roman nobility, took refuge on the offshore islands of the muddy lagoons where Venice would eventually be built. A new influx of immigrants reached the islands of the lagoons after the invasion of the Huns in Venetia in 452. Less than a century later, the province became Roman (Byzantine) again, following the victorious wars of the Emperor Justinian against the Vandals and the Goths. However, when at the turn of the sixth and seventh centuries the Lombards conquered Aquileia, Padua and Oderzo, the offshore islands of the lagoons, among which Torcello was the most prosperous, and the city of Venice, which had been built around a trading post at the harbour of the lagoons by Paduan authorities as early as the fifth century, became once more ports of entry for many refugees. During the same period, the Arab conquest of parts of the Byzantine Empire began. By the mid-seventh century, Syria, Palestine and Egypt had come under Arab rule. Venice remained part of the Byzantine Empire, belonging to the province of Ravenna.[2]

In the late seventh century, the province of Ravenna became an exarchate of the Byzantine Empire, a move that gave its governor (the exarch) the authority and responsibility to concentrate both civil and military administrations in his hands, minimizing the need for supervision and guidance from the central Byzantine imperial administration.

While Byzantium was losing territories to the Lombards in the West and to the Arabs in the East and South, religious turmoil and civil war were spreading throughout the empire. In 730, the Emperor Leo III introduced iconoclasm, and the Byzantine territories on the Italian peninsula joined a rebellion against central imperial authorities to support the Pope, who rallied against iconoclasm.

> But the Emperor Leo tactfully conceded a measure of local autonomy to what he described as 'the province of Venetia conserved by God'. He recognised Orso as the first native governor or *dux* of Venice and granted him the Byzantine title of *hypatos* or consul. This was a first step towards the emancipation of Venice from the exarchate of Ravenna.
>
> (Nicol 1988: 10–11)

After Ravenna fell under Lombard rule in 751, "the province of Venice stood alone under the management of its own *dux*" (Nicol 1988: 11). Despite having gained such political autonomy, the *dux* (doge) of Venice remained loyal to the Byzantine Empire, especially after 787, when iconoclasm was defeated and declared a heresy.

The Venetian allegiance to Byzantium, especially following the rapid rise of the Holy Roman Empire in the early ninth century, was thought not to be a matter of religious, but rather of political and economic affairs and interests. Venice's ruling patrician class comprised at the time mainly feudal landlord families, many of whom were refugees from Italian regions under 'barbaric' rule claiming noble Roman ancestry.[3] However, a fast-growing fraction of merchants was rapidly developing among Venice's ruling aristocracy of nobles, whose interests could be safeguarded best through adherence to the more highly developed maritime trade – that of Byzantium, along with the protection offered by the Byzantine emperor. Others combined landowning with 'investment' in trade, through schemes like the *societas* and the *commenda* (see Chapter 7).

Venetian merchants had initially been bargemen on the Po and other rivers in the region, as well as caravan transit traders travelling to and from mainland Italy and northern European territories via the Alps. Later, in the ninth and tenth centuries, they started trading in the Adriatic, carrying merchandise to and from the Istrian coasts. Their main trade was salt, Slavic slaves[4] and later, timber.

In the ninth century, these merchants became middlemen between 'the West' and the Byzantine Empire:

> They quickly adapted to the larger role of middlemen between east and west. Byzantine merchants would bring luxury goods from the east to the market at Torcello and Venetian traders would then distribute them in the west, in Italy, France and Germany. The means of exchange was barter. The Byzantines would take payment in the form of timber for shipbuilding, of slaves, of metal, or of salt and fish, which were the two staple products of Venetian waters.
>
> (Nicol 1988: 21)

So, despite an internal split in the ruling Venetian nobility evolving into two factions, one favouring the Holy Roman Emperor, who promised Venetian landowners the concession of fiefs on the Italian mainland, and the other favouring Byzantium,[5] the hegemonic interests of Venice's money-begetting oligarchy increasingly bound her to an alliance with Byzantium. Byzantium could guarantee Venice's high degree of independence and its access to 'world trade',[6] whereas the Holy Roman Empire was a rather loose political entity based on changing and unstable power relations between local feudal lords.

A treaty between Byzantium and the Holy Roman Empire in 812 constituted a further step in Venetian autonomy: on the one hand, it recognized Byzantine suzerainty over Venice; on the other, it obliged Venice to pay a tribute to the Holy Roman Emperor, who thus resigned from any further demands on the city.[7] A period of peace began for Venice, during which the new city of Venice was built in Rialto.

When Venetian trade started expanding on the River Po and in the Adriatic, it confronted a significant rival that threatened its hegemonic role in the region: the city of Comacchio, situated "nearer Ravenna than Venice and equally near the shifting mouths of the Po" (Lane 1973: 5–6); and, having the support of local vassals of the Holy Roman Empire, it challenged Venetian commercial supremacy. Venice sacked and subjugated Comacchio twice, in 854 (Chisholm 1911: 749) and in 886 (Lane 1973: 6).

Frederic C. Lane, commenting on the historically contingent character of Venice's political and economic rise, reaches the following apt conclusion:

> Had Comacchio defeated the Venetians and established its control over the mouths of the Adige and the Po, it instead of Venice might have become the Queen of the Adriatic, and Venice might now be an inconspicuous village in a stagnant lagoon, as dead as the lagoon of Comacchio, famous only for its eels.
>
> (ibid.: 6)

The destruction of Comacchio was a clear step towards Venetian political independence and, of course, her maritime economic supremacy in the Adriatic Sea. The Venetians undertook a second similar initiative in 871, when their military fleet joined Christian forces under Frankish leadership to reconquer Bari from the Arabs. By the end of the ninth century, Byzantine suzerainty over Venice was growing feeble. Venice was becoming more of an ally to, and less a province or protectorate of, Byzantium. Donald M. Nicol assesses this historical shift:

> The Venetians had not rebelled. Nor had they come out with a formal declaration of independence. [...] The Emperor Basil I [...] would have preferred his relationship with Venice to be more closely defined as that between master and servant. [...] With the creation of the theme of Dalmatia and the collapse of his plan for co-operation with the Franks,

Basil needed the friendship of Venice. In 879 he [...] conferred upon the Doge the imperial title of *protospatharios*. The enhanced status of the dignity did not pass unnoticed. [...] Orso had been promoted in the ranks of the Byzantine family. He returned the compliment by sending twelve bells to Constantinople.

(Nicol 1988: 33)

In 828, two merchants had supposedly brought the relics of St Mark, or Mark the Evangelist, to Venice from Alexandria. By worshipping these 'holy relics', the city inaugurated its own unique identity in the Christian world. According to legend, an angel prophesized to St Mark himself that the Venetian lagoons would be the final resting place of his body. The winged lion of St Mark would eventually become the state emblem of the Republic of Venice in the twelfth century.

By the end of the tenth century, Venetian warships had dominated the Dalmatian coasts of the upper and middle Adriatic, had sacked Comacchio for a third time, and Venetian merchants had gained the upper hand in the slave trade of the region, the latter in cooperation with the Slavic pirates at the mouth of the Narenta River.

Export of slaves from the interior was then at its peak, and the Narentants were slave traders as well as pirates. The Venetians were their best customers, when not themselves collecting slave in warlike raids.

(Lane 1973: 26)

The Venetian ruling patricians nevertheless continued to be divided between a faction seeking mainly territorial possessions and feudal rents, and another directed mainly towards maritime trade and other profits from the sea. This division overlapped and to an extent reflected the split between a pro-Western faction and a pro-Byzantine one within the aristocracy. The conflict reached its peak in 976, when a mass revolt overthrew doge Pietro IV Candiano, son-in-law of the German Emperor Otto I, whose "interests, [...] friends and [...] property lay in Italy and the west" (Nicol 1988: 37). The crowd besieged the doge's palace, setting fire to it and killing the doge and his infant son.[8] The conflicts among rivalling Venetian noble factions continued until 991, when the thirty-year-old Pietro II Orseolo was elected as Venice's doge. The new doge, "was rightly convinced that trade was the life blood of Venice" and that "[t]he most lucrative markets were in the east" (Nicol 1988: 39). Nevertheless, he tried to maintain balanced relations with both the Byzantine and Holy Roman Empires.

8.3 Gaining power through alliance with Byzantium

By the end of the tenth century, Venice had gained political autonomy as an independent city state and her naval power had significantly increased. She was acting as an ally of Byzantium in the Adriatic and beyond, and her merchants had expanded their business all over the Mediterranean, benefitting from the alliance with the empire and the naval strength of their own city.

In 992, the year after Pietro II Orseolo's election as Venice's doge, the Byzantine emperor issued a chrysobull, an imperial act bearing the golden imperial bull, granting commercial privileges to Venice in Constantinople and throughout 'Romania' (i.e. the Byzantine Empire). It is worth mentioning that this was the first such imperial chrysobull issued in favour of a trade partner, and more specifically in favour of an Italian city state, as "Pisa received its first Byzantine privilege act in 1111 and Genoa only in 1169" (Penna 2012: 12). By 1204, ten chrysobulls had been issued in favour of Venice, five in favour of Genoa and three in favour of Pisa.

The main benefit provided by the chrysobull of 992 for Venetian merchants was a reduction of the custom duty they had been paying in the ports of Constantinople (import–export tariffs) by nearly half, from thirty to seventeen *solidi*. Moreover, the chrysobull offered Venetians additional legal protection, as it determined that not ordinary judges but only the *Logothetes tou Dromou*, the higher Byzantine officers who administered foreign affairs, could serve as judges in all civil and criminal cases that involved Venetian subjects, even if the legal cases were mixed ones, implicating both Venetian and Byzantine (or other) subjects. In return, the Venetians agreed to provide military assistance to the empire in southern Italy.

Although this first chrysobull resembled more a decree of imperial benefits, it also constituted a prototype of official recognition of Venice's independence from the Byzantine emperor. As regards its economic consequences, it gave Venice significant advantages in Constantinople, which at the time was the centre of maritime trade, over her main economic rivals, especially Pisa and Genoa.

The tension between the Italian maritime states intensified over the decades and centuries to come. Notably, importantly, the eleventh century constituted a turning point in European history, as many historians have pointed out: during this historical period, a shift of power from East to West began taking root. The military power and the political cohesiveness of Byzantine territories gradually declined, due in part to military setbacks, and in part to a 'feudal tendency' gradually developing within society, which eroded its political and economic cohesiveness, based until then on state centralism and Asiatic social relations of class exploitation and domination (see Chapter 7). This process had begun in the tenth century, as internal social polarization gradually developed within the Asiatic agrarian community (*chorion* = village community paying various forms of tributes to higher state administrative units). Apart from stratification within village communities and the emergence of a stratum of wealthy peasants employing slave and wage labour, large estates outside communal land started being concentrated in the hands of 'quasi-feudal' landlords (*chorooikodespotai*).[9] I use the terms 'feudal tendency' and 'quasi-feudal' landlords because, prior to 1204, Byzantine landlords did not possess the juridical and economic power and relative autonomy that characterized feudal social relations, as they were still incorporated into the Asiatic system of centralized state authority and tribute payment.

Donald M. Nicol portrays the historical shift that took place during the eleventh century as follows:

> In the wider context of European history the eleventh century was the age in which the balance of power began to shift decisively from east to west. [...] The decline of Byzantium after the death of Basil II was partly due to the radical changes in the social and economic structure of the empire brought about by its own prosperity. The rich had become richer through the years of conquest and expansion. [...] The neat division of the provinces into military, economic and administrative units known as themes broke down, as did the centralisation of all authority in the person and the office of the emperor in Constantinople. [...] Constantinople was still by far the richest and most agreeable Christian city in the world.
>
> (Nicol 1988: 50–51)

From the beginning of the eleventh century, Venice offered military support and served as an ally of Byzantium, policing the seas against both piracy in the Adriatic, and Muslim and Norman invaders. In 1004, the Venetians pushed the Arabs out of Bari. Throughout the next decade, they fought Slavic and Saracen piracy in the Adriatic and the Mediterranean Seas. At the beginning of the 1080s, they fought victorious naval battles against the Normans, who had been invading Byzantine territories on several fronts, as at the harbour of Dyrrachion (Durazzo) on the eastern coastline of the Adriatic, off Corfu, and elsewhere, significantly delaying the Norman military advance before eventually being bitterly defeated by them.

By taking such actions, the Venetians were protecting their own economic and military interests: the city state's ruling class was by that time already oriented towards profits from long-distance maritime trade and other forms of maritime profits in the Mediterranean, with Constantinople being the most significant commercial hub of the Christian world.

> The Venetians sought sea power, not territorial possessions from which to draw tribute. Their wars were fought to effect political arrangements which would be disadvantageous to rival sea powers, which would make Venice's established trades more secure in Levantine waters, and which would gain them trading privileges permitting commercial expansion into new seas.
>
> (Lane 1973: 27)

To reward the Venetians for their assistance, Emperor Alexios I Komnenos issued a new chrysobull in 1082 granting them commercial and other privileges: Venetian merchants were excluded from any payment of taxes to the Byzantine Empire;[10] Venice was granted three piers in the port of

Constantinople for loading and unloading merchandise; the Venetian district in Constantinople was expanded, and certain buildings in the capital and in the city of Dyrrachion were reserved for Venetian use; every doge of Venice was thereafter to bear the title of '*protosebastos*', a most distinguished title connected with an annual salary; the Patriarch of Venice was decorated as '*hypertimos*', a most distinguished ecclesiastical title; an annual payment was granted to the church of St Mark and to other Venetian churches (Penna 2012: 26–34). In 1108, a Venetian fleet joined the Byzantine forces off the eastern Adriatic coast and finally beat the Normans, re-establishing Byzantine rule in Dyrrachion.

8.4 The new geopolitical landscape after the First Crusade: phases of alliance and conflict up to the final clash of arms

As is clear from what has preceded, Venice, in becoming a 'maritime republic', became a 'naval power' as well, in a state of perpetual preparedness for military action that would result in paving the way for her interests at sea, including the protection of merchant trade routes. I will elaborate on this point in the next chapter. At this point, I would like to again stress that the engagement of Venice's naval power on behalf of Byzantium up to the end of the eleventh century was a strategy aimed at safeguarding her own trade and interests in the eastern Mediterranean,[11] whence an extensive array of merchandise came to Western Europe, as did merchandise from the Black Sea area, which had become the new centre of slave trade.

The Venetian strategy became rather ambiguous, however, in the aftermath of the First Crusade (1096–1099), which had led to the creation of the Latin Kingdom of Jerusalem. The active involvement of Pisan and Genoese warships in the crusade, which gave merchants and looters from both cities an advantageous position in the ports of the new Christian kingdom, threatened the trade supremacy of Venice in the Levant and created second thoughts for Venetian patricians as regards their allegiance to the Byzantine Empire. Finally, in 1110, Venice sent a fleet to Palestine to support the King of Jerusalem, despite mounting tensions between Byzantium and the lords of the crusader territories.

In the coming year, 1111, the Byzantine Emperor Alexios I issued a chrysobull granting trade privileges to Pisa. Although the privileges granted were less important than those already conceded to Venice, the Pisan authorities took an oath that the Pisan population as a whole would be loyal to the Byzantine emperor, supporting his plans to regain control over Antioch and other territories of the crusader states.[12] Pisa exchanged access to Byzantine markets with 'vassalage' to the Byzantine emperor.

The Byzantine attack on Antioch had been planned for 1113, but an invasion of the Seljuk Turks in the eastern territories of the empire cancelled those plans (Lilie 1994: 87–94). The new Byzantine emperor, John II Komnenos, who came to the throne in 1118, refused to ratify the chrysobull of 1082, which had granted special privileges to Venice. Beginning in 1122, Venetian war ships, taking part in a crusade fleet whose mission was to protect Antioch from Muslim threats, attacked and plundered Byzantine islands in the Aegean and Ionian Seas and port cities on the mainland shores repeatedly for at least four consecutive years. Venice's policy had changed from policing the seas to profiting from piracy. However, her main objective was to negotiate peace in the seas with Byzantium in order to regain her past preferential trade benefits in the empire. At that time, the rivalry between Pisa and Venice was escalating, as economic competition between the two city states in the Levant was taking on a religious and political form, with Venice supporting the Pope (the so-called Guelph camp) and Pisa allying herself with the German emperor (the so-called Ghibelline camp) in his confrontation with the Pope.

The Byzantine emperor eventually yielded to Venetian pressure, and in 1126 ratified the 1082 chrysobull of his predecessor. By his decree of the year 1126,

> the emperor also allowed the Venetians to trade freely in Crete and in Cyprus. As a result, the Venetians gained better access to the markets of Syria and Palestine.
>
> (Penna 2012: 35)

A new period of alliance between Byzantium and Venice now started, which would last for more than forty years, despite frequent tensions between Byzantine and Venetian subjects. During 1148–1149, Venice's war fleet assisted Byzantine forces in reconquering Corfu from the Normans, who had sacked and occupied the island in 1147 during the Second Crusade. With two new chrysobulls in the years 1147 and 1148, the Byzantine emperor confirmed the previous trade privileges of Venice in the empire and further expanded the Venetian district in Constantinople. However, when in 1167, Byzantine forces conquered Croatia and Dalmatia from the Kingdom of Hungary, tensions arose between Byzantium and Venice, as the Italian maritime republic coveted those same territories. In the next years, piratic attacks by Venetian ships against Byzantine territories became commonplace.

During 1169–1170, the Byzantine Emperor Manuel I Komnenos issued three chrysobulls granting trade and tax privileges, as well as areas in Constantinople (which included piers for the loading and unloading of merchandise), to the Genoese (Penna 2012: 133–156). As compensation, the Genoese swore an oath of loyalty and allegiance to Byzantium.[13]

In the next year, 1171, after the Venetians living in Constantinople had attacked and heavily damaged the Genoese district of the city, the Byzantine emperor ordered the arrest of all Venetians living in the empire and the confiscation of their property, according to a previously well-organized plan.[14] War broke out between Byzantium and Venice. A Venetian fleet, led by the doge himself, had some initial success in attacking Byzantine towns on the Dalmatian coast and in the Aegean Sea, but was eventually compelled to retreat back to Venice. As the cost of both war and exclusion from Byzantine markets, especially those of Constantinople, was enormous for the Venetians, the new doge chose to follow a diplomatic path: in 1775, he signed a peace treaty with the Normans, which in essence served as a catalyst for a rapprochement between Venice and Byzantium. Negotiations between the two powers started in the second half of the 1170s, and in 1179 a peace agreement was reached, which provided the release of all Venetians imprisoned in the Byzantine Empire, the re-establishment of all the pre-1171 benefits of Venice in Byzantium and financial (monetary) compensation for damages suffered since 1171. In 1184, the Byzantine Emperor Andronikos agreed to pay Venice 1,500 pounds of gold as compensation for the losses incurred in 1171.

In 1187, the new Byzantine Emperor Isaac II Angelos issued three chrysobulls granting privileges to Venice, and in 1189 another two, practically restoring Venice's preferred status in the empire. The latter two re-affirmed the monetary compensation for the losses incurred during the 1171 events agreed upon by Andronikos in 1184, while also further granting Venetians access to the French and German quarters in Constantinople. It was a period when Byzantium was in dire need of an alliance with Venice: following the death of Emperor Manuel I Komnenos in 1180, the alliance of the empire with Pisa and Genoa had been shaken when a mob massacred the Pisans and Genoese in Constantinople as a result of growing anti-Latin sentiment among the Byzantine populace, periodically inflated by Latin piratic raids against Byzantine ships and coastal settlements.[15] Besides, the 'feudal tendency' that had been developing throughout the empire since the early eleventh century was now creating conspicuously debilitating effects, and despite some military victories of the Byzantine army in the Balkans, the threats from the west were once again noticeable:

> In 1184 the island of Cyprus was seized by Isaac Komnenos, a nephew of the late Manuel, who adopted the imperial title; and in Asia Minor a number of cities, such as Philadelphia, proclaimed their independence under their own local archons. The emperor's problems were compounded by the announcement of a new crusade from the west.
>
> (Nicol 1988: 114–115)

According to Daphne Penna (2012: 12, 47 ff.), these chrysobulls (and especially the second of the year 1187) bear less a character of an imperial decree of privileges and more that of a treaty between two states, as a detailed description of each party's obligation to the other is incorporated in them.[16]

Throughout the twelfth century, conflict between Venice and Pisa over maritime routes in the Mediterranean and trading privileges in the Byzantine Empire escalated; the first naval battle between fleets of the two city states is recorded to have been in 1099, in the waters off Rhodes (Lane 1973: 32). Genoa was to become Venice's main commercial rival and naval enemy by the middle of the thirteenth century.

As we have already seen, the Byzantine emperors, although generally guaranteeing a preferential position to Venice (as it aided in the promotion of their own strategic interests), at times tried to exploit the rivalries between the Italian maritime republics, either due to the peculiarities of a certain conjuncture or as a form of the 'divide and conquer' policy. At the end of the twelfth century, the attempt of two successive Byzantine emperors to exploit once more these rivalries between the Italian city states proved disastrous for the empire.

Emperor Isaac II Angelos issued two chrysobulls in 1192, one offering privileges to Pisa and the other to Genoa. In the next year, 1193, he issued another chrysobull in favour of Genoa. All three chrysobulls restored the privileges previously granted to both city states, further expanding their respective districts in Constantinople, and bestowing on them a sum of money on condition that the Italian city states check and (make an effort to) contain piracy by their subjects in the Byzantine territories. However, in 1195, Isaac II Angelos was overthrown, blinded and imprisoned by his brother Alexios III Angelos. The new emperor appeared to be rather reluctant to serve the debt payments of Byzantium to Venice agreed upon by the Emperors Andronikos in 1184 and Isaac II Angelos between 1187 and 1189.[17] In 1198, he issued three new chrysobulls, thus ratifying the previous trading privileges assigned to each of the three Italian city states, Venice, Pisa and Genoa, and dealing with a number of related legal issues. By this initiative, the emperor seemed to establish and maintain a position of equidistance from the three maritime rivals. In the chrysobull granted to Venice, "the provisions [...] concerning the debts between Venetians and Byzantines mentioned in the act of Isaac II Angelos are not included" (Penna 2012: 63), whereas the Byzantine authorities were "taxing Venetians in spite of the treaty" (Lane 1973: 38).

It was during this period that the internal situation in Byzantium deteriorated: a faction of the Byzantine elites regarded the new emperor as an illegal usurper of power.[18] When after the unsuccessful end of the Third Crusade in 1199 Pope Innocent III called for a new crusade, Alexios III Angelos endorsed his initiative in an effort to stabilize his rule by means of new alliances. However, a number of historical occurrences forced the Fourth Crusade to deviate from its original objective, ostensibly 'the liberation of the holy land of Jerusalem from the infidels', to the conquest of Constantinople in 1204 by the crusaders, under the command of Venice's aged doge Enrico Dandolo.

Considering the outcome of the Fourth Crusade, Donald M. Nicol stresses the historical contingencies (including the sudden death of Theobald III Count of Champagne, who had been accepted by all participating parties as leader of the crusade). He writes:

> In assessing what went wrong and why the crusade went to Constantinople and not to its proper destination, the modern historian [...] may [...] be driven to conclude that the event of 1204 came about simply by a concatenation of circumstances, a series of mishaps and human errors whose predestined conclusion neither the pope nor any other power could prevent.
> (Nicol 1988: 125)

A concatenation of historical coincidences or a merging and melding together of historical contradictions could not, however, lead to any such concrete military and political outcomes if an abiding concrete strategy of the Venetians had not already been in place to economically dominate in the realm of the Byzantine Empire and the broader Mediterranean region. Such a strategy had been pursued for centuries by implementing all means available: through trade, preferential treaties, piracy and war.

The Venetians were initially reluctant to support the Fourth Crusade. They only agreed to provide ships to carry the crusaders to Egypt after their envoy, Geoffrey of Villehardouin, promised them 85,000 silver marks for transportation and food for the 33,500 crusaders who were supposed to have gathered in Venice by 1202 (Brentano 1916: 65 ff.; Lane 1973: 36 ff.; Nicol 1988: 125 ff.). However, by 1202 in fact fewer than 10,000 crusaders had assembled in Venice and the money amassed was less than 51,000 silver marks. The doge thereupon proposed that the crusader fleet make a detour to the Dalmatian coast to restore Venetian rule in the city of Zara, which at the time was under the suzerainty of the King of Hungary. Venice would take part in the expedition with fifty galleys, and the rest of the money owed to her by the crusaders would be provided by the booty earned in the conquest of Zara. Despite the Pope's reservations about the prospect of a crusade attacking Christian territory, Zara was conquered in November 1202. A year before, the Byzantine Prince Alexios Angelos, son of the overthrown, blinded and jailed Emperor Isaac II Angelos, had escaped from Constantinople on a Pisan ship. When the Pope refused to support him in repossessing his father's throne, Alexios Angelos exploited his kinship with his brother-in-law Philip of Swabia to negotiate with the crusaders who were still docked at Zara:

> If the crusaders would go by way of Constantinople and restore Alexios and his father Isaac to their inheritance they would be generously rewarded. Alexios would pay them 200,000 marks, supply provisions for their onward journey to Egypt, send an army of 10,000 Byzantine troops with them, and maintain a permanent force of 500 men in the Holy Land. In addition, he promised that his whole empire would recognise the supremacy of the See of Rome, from which it had long been separated.
>
> (Nicol 1988: 133)

The doge seized the opportunity and convinced the crusaders' leaders to undertake the operation. Prince Alexios soon joined the crusaders. When their fleet reached the Byzantine city of Dyrrachion, the local population hailed Alexios as their legitimate emperor. In contrast, when they entered the Golden Horn of Constantinople, they were met by only hostile crowds on the walls of the city. Being terrified at the sight of such a large fleet, the Byzantine emperor secretly abandoned the city. The blind Isaac II Angelos took back the emperor's throne. On 1 August 1203, Prince Alexios was crowned as his co-emperor.

The crusader fleet would not leave Constantinople's waters until the promises given by Alexios Angelos, now a co-emperor of Byzantium, were fulfilled. Anti-Latin sentiment and unrest in Constantinople were nevertheless constantly on the rise. Angry crowds had begun attacking the Venetian and other Latin districts in the city, and finally, in January 1204, a Byzantine nobleman, Alexios Mourtzouflos, overthrew Alexios Angelos and his father and became the new emperor of Byzantium under the name Alexios V Doukas.

When it became clear that the new emperor was not willing to meet the promises given to the crusaders by Alexios Angelos, who in the meantime had been strangled in jail, the crusaders' attack against Constantinople began. The city was captured and sacked[19] in April 1204 and the empire was divided among its new rulers. In May 1204, Baldwin, Count of Flanders and Hainaut, was crowned emperor of the 'Latin Empire of Constantinople'. Three-eighths of Constantinople came under Venetian rule, including the city's Arsenal and piers, and three-eighths of the empire's territories, including the island of Crete, Negroponte (Euboea) and Corfu, and the southern Peloponnesian stronghold towns of Modon and Coron.

The success of Venice was unprecedented. Within two centuries, she had transformed herself from a provincial commercial town in the Adriatic into a major colonial power across the Mediterranean; she had gone from seeking the protection and alliance of Byzantium to safeguard her integrity and existence, to being a major commercial centre in Europe (see Chapter 9). Having been a city of roughly 100,000 inhabitants, in 1204 Venice brought 'the three-eighths' of an imperial capital under her rule, the world's richest and largest Christian city, a population four or five times larger than her own.

An explanation for this miraculous ascent shall be partly sought in the social character, or the internal structure and cohesiveness, of Venetian society and the thereof derived strength of the Venetian state.

Notes

1 "*For Marxists the concrete analysis of the concrete situation* is not the opposite of 'pure' theory; on the contrary, it is *the culmination of all genuine theory*, its consummation [...]" (Lukács 2009: 41–42).

2 "Venetia in its new form remained a province of the Byzantine Empire. It was governed by a *magister militum*, or military official, answerable to the Prefect of Ravenna who, for the time being, upheld what was left of Roman authority in this far-flung outpost" (Nicol 1988: 5).

3 "[...] the few deeds, wills, and other documents that survive from before A.D. 1000 show that within the lagoons there were rich landlords with dependent tenants owing payments in kind such as eggs and chickens. Some property owners had sizeable herds of cattle, horses or pigs, as well as vineyards, gardens and orchards. Salt pans and choice fishing spots were in private hands" (Lane 1973: 4).

4 "Men could do without gold but not without salt" (Nicol 1988: 21). "In the sixth century, pagan Angles and Saxons had reached the Italian slave market [...] in the ninth century slaves ranked almost with salt and fish as the mainstay of Venetian commerce" (Lane 1973: 7).

5 "When John, the Patriarch of Grado, proclaimed his allegiance to Charlemagne, the Doge Maurizio had him hunted down and murdered as a traitor. The feuds between the ruling families and the islands of Venice were now more than ever fought under the banners of the Frankish and the Byzantine factions" (Nicol 1988: 15).

6 "Byzantium's trade routes linked three continents in a network of caravan tracks, rivers, seaways and Roman-style paved roads. The empire controlled only a part of these routes, yet Byzantine merchants imported products from as far away as Iceland, Ethiopia, northern Russia, Ceylon and China. Even in times of peace, goods passed through many hands along the way. [...] The center of almost all commerce was Constantinople, which prospered by receiving, refining and re-exporting the goods that passed through its markets. Eventually, however, Moslem invasions disrupted many of Byzantium's lifelines" (Sherrard 1966: 32).

Trade was embedded in the dominant Asiatic mode of production (see Chapter 7) in the Byzantine social formation. The state-organized ruling class considered trade as one of its sources of tribute and tax collection. See also below.

7 "The treaty of 812 guaranteed their protection against enemies from the mainland, fixed their boundaries with the Kingdom of Italy, and above all recognised the rights of their merchant ships to sail freely about their business. These privileges had been achieved not through the efforts of the Venetians themselves but through Byzantine diplomacy; [...] Their submission to Byzantium assured their immunity from harm in Italy" (Nicol 1988: 19).

8 The fire that burnt the doge's Palace also destroyed the Basilica of St Mark, where the holy relics of Venice's protector were kept. The relics vanished in the fire, but they miraculously re-appeared in 1094, during the consecration of the new basilica.

9 "A variety of forms of agricultural exploitation is revealed in the Fiscal Treatise, a tenth-century document which outlines the basic workings of the land-tax. [...] [The] concentrated settlement and complicated tenurial pattern was probably an irritant to a wealthier peasant who owned slaves and large numbers of cattle, but if sufficient land was available he could move elsewhere in the fiscal unit [...]. The Fiscal Treatise also defines the *proasteion* (estate), which differed significantly from other lands in the fiscal unit. Its owner was not a resident of the territory, and the estate was cultivated by slaves, wage labourers or (although the treatise does not say so specifically) by tenant farmers. The range in social status was great: slaves, wage labourers, independent peasant farmers and large landowners. [...] The Fiscal Treatise also discusses another category of peasant cultivators, the *chorooikodespotai* [...]. They were farmers in the *ktesis*, a separate fiscal unit identical to the *chorion* for all practical purposes of tax-collecting. The [...]*ktesis* consisted of scattered settlements instead of a nucleated village, indicating a larger area of land in the ownership of the *chorooikodespotes* and possibly a greater concentration on pastoral farming" (Harvey 1989: 34–37).

10 "The trade in Romania employed the larger number of ships and merchants. Privileges which the Venetians had gained by aiding the Byzantine emperors against the Normans gave them preferential treatment; [...] The native Greeks themselves paid 10 percent, whereas the Venetians paid nothing" (Lane 1973: 68).

11 "The third and still existing church of St Mark was begun by the Doge Domenico Contarini and continued and completed by his successors, Domenico Silvio (1070–1084) and Vitale Falier (1084–1096). [...] The motive was civic pride. The new building was a public demonstration of the new wealth and strength of Venice. [...] The church was modelled on that of the Holy Apostles in Constantinople [...] and there can be no doubt that the master architect of the eleventh-century St Mark's was a Greek from Constantinople. *Nothing could more obviously proclaim to all the Christian world the special relationship between Venice and Byzantium*" (Nicol 1988: 51–52, emphasis added).

12 "[...] the Pisans were to take the side of the Emperor in any war between Byzantium and the crusader states. The end effect was thus an alliance with the purpose of overthrowing the Frankish states" (Lilie 1994: 90).

13 Amico, the Genoese envoy,

> promises, on behalf of Genoa, that this city will not help any nation that is an enemy of the Byzantines. Moreover, the Genoese living within the empire will help defend the Byzantines if attacks are mounted against the empire. [...] For their loyalty, the Genoese receive immovable property in Constantinople, as well as money. Provisions regarding the tax of kommerkion are also included.
>
> (Penna 2012: 134)

A similar chrysobull was issued in 1170 granting privileges to Pisa (Penna 2012: 115 ff.).

14 "On the appointed day, 12 March 1171, the plan was put into action in every corner of the empire. All Venetians were arrested at precisely the same moment in Constantinople and elsewhere. The prisons could not hold them all. There were more than 10,000 in the capital alone. Some had to be confined in monasteries. But the overcrowding was so acute that some had to be set free on parole after a few days" (Nicol 1988: 97).

15 "The periodic street fights in Constantinople reflected the situation at sea. By the end of the twelfth century, piracy had become general. [...] Unlike downright pirates, they limited to a certain extent their looting according to their political hates and loyalties [...] none of the governments took any severe action against pirates who were their own subjects" (Lane 1973: 35).

16 "It is provided that in case Romania is attacked by a fleet consisting of 40 ships or more, Venice must provide 40 ships or more (up to 100) to Romania within six months; these ships will be constructed in Venice at the expenses of Romania. [...] Oath provisions are also included here both for the Venetians who undertake the construction of ships and for the captains who sail them. It is mentioned that the emperor reserves the right to use three quarters of the number of Venetians living within Romania for the fleet, paying them the corresponding salary; [...] It is also stated that the crews have to be loyal to the emperor and should fight the enemies, Christians or not, for the glory of Romania" (Penna 2012: 47–48). According to Donald M. Nicol, however,

> the carefully worded clauses and conditions of Isaac's four agreements with Venice are mainly of academic interest, for they were never implemented. No Venetian fleet of between forty and 100 ships was ever called upon to defend Byzantine interests. Venetian residents in the empire were never conscripted into service.
>
> (Nicol 1988: 117)

17 "On the larger issue of the compensation for damages which the Emperor Andronikos had promised, Isaac agreed that 1400 pounds of gold remained outstanding. Andronikos had paid 100 pounds on account. Isaac [...] undertook to settle the bill for the entire sum of 1500 pounds and made over to the Doge's ambassadors a first instalment of 250 pounds. The remaining 1250 pounds would be paid in annual instalments over a period of six years until the debt was fully honoured. [...] Venetian documents tell of the receipt of the first 250 pounds and of further payments from the imperial treasury in 1191 and 1193. These were distributed *pro rata* to the merchants who had submitted claims for compensation. But the six years were up in 1195 when Isaac lost his throne and the debt was still far from being cleared" (Nicol 1988: 116–117).

18 "The decentralisation and separatism which had already undermined the structure of the empire became uncontrollable" (Nicol 1988: 117).

19 After the fall of Constantinople,

> there followed three days of murder, rapine, rape, and sacrilege. Churches and
> houses were thoroughly plundered. When Boniface of Montferrat ordered all
> the booty collected for division, it was valued (apart from what may have been
> secretly held back) at 400,000 marks and 10,000 suits of armor. There was no
> trouble then in paying the overdue debt to the Venetians, besides giving them
> their half of the booty.
>
> (Lane 1973: 41–42)

9 The Venetian social formation until the end of the thirteenth century

An unconsummated process of original accumulation

9.1 The rule of a state-organized money-begetting oligarchy

9.1.1 The myth of 'private initiative'

In his presentation of the history of Venice, Frederic C. Lane refers to the myths that have accompanied (or which supposedly interpret) Venice's spectacular rise: her alleged independence since her very foundation (ignoring the fact that from her inception she was just a mere Byzantine territory), and the supposed lack of factions and internal divides, etc. (Lane 1973: 87–91). I dealt with these issues in Chapter 8, where I recounted Venice's historical evolution prior to the Fourth Crusade.

I will now turn to yet another myth, one more enduring than any other, and applicable not only to Venice, but also to every other city state or European region that emerged as an early centre of trade and manufacture and was thereafter to become an epicentre of capitalist development: the myth of 'private initiative' and of the 'individual entrepreneur' as bearer of a specific type of economic and social 'rationality', which flourishes in an environment of 'freedom', and consequently becomes the 'rational drive' of an entire society. Luciano Pellicani, although well acquainted with Marx's work and the Marxist literature on controversies surrounding the 'transition from feudalism to capitalism', is a characteristic proponent of this approach. He writes:

> The idea of investing capital to augment wealth […] was strange to the dominant class. It was not, however, strange to the newcomer, the *Mercator*. This typical self-made man […] engendered and spread the entrepreneurial spirit. His chief motive, and in a sense his only motive, was to enrich himself.
>
> (Pellicani 1994: 150)

A miracle had happened. In some places in Europe, the merchant and manufacturing cities, the method of performing the daily multiplication of loaves and fish had been perfected. It was *a peaceful method, in sharp contrast with traditional warlike ones* of piracy and looting.

(ibid.: 152, emphasis added)

However, Venice, just as Pisa and Genoa, did not climb to the top of economic and political power in Europe by way of peaceful methods. On the contrary, even during her first ascending steps on the ladder of economic pre-eminence in the Adriatic, Venice relied on the trading of slaves, with all the "traditional warlike methods" on which this special trade is established. Her success was also founded on plunder, as, for example, on the repeated destruction and sacking of Comacchio (see Chapter 8).[1]

Besides, and of equal importance, the economic upswing of Venice never had as its 'prime mover' the 'private initiative' of certain ingenious 'mercators' or any other 'self-made' and 'risk-taking' individuals. The 'instigator' of Venice's economic rise was the collectivity of a patrician class, having organized itself from the onset of the eleventh century as a militarized naval state that functioned as both coordinator and main undertaker of a multiplicity of money-begetting 'ventures': trade, piracy,[2] plunder, slave trade, war, etc.

The structure of the Venetian state was modelled on a centralized state prototype, which the local nobility had inherited from the Byzantine exarchate to which they had initially belonged.[3] Also relevant was the Venetian legal framework, which reflected the prevalence of Roman law, another inherited element from the city state's Byzantine past.[4]

The Venetian aristocracy functioned both privately and (mostly) collectively as members of a class of money-owners; at the same time, they functioned collectively as *the* state. In this section, I will elaborate on both facets of class power in the Venetian social formation, beginning with an exposition of the main features of the Venetian state power structure.

9.1.2 State apparatuses as 'committees' manned by members of the ruling class

Up until the mid-thirteenth century, the Venetian state had been administered by a group of about 500 men, all from approximately a hundred noble families. A good number belonged to the 'old nobility' of landowners, and the rest were 'newcomers', mostly rich merchants. Twenty to fifty of these families were the most prominent as regards their immovable property and movable (monetary) wealth, upon which they justified and maintained their 'noble' status; some also claimed ancestry from Roman tribunes. It was a rather narrowly manned central state for a population of nearly 100,000 inhabitants. There were also a number of quite prominent local authorities who supported this central state apparatus.

At the top of the Venetian state stood the *doge*. Until the beginning of the eleventh century, all executive, juridical and military authority was concentrated in the hands of the doge, essentially in the tradition of a Byzantine exarch, whose rule the Venetians had imitated. The exarchs, having been granted increased political, military and ecclesiastical autonomy and authority by the Byzantine emperor, and aspiring to better defend their remote territories from foreign invaders, had developed a monarchical form of government.[5] In 1032, the authority of the doge was to a certain extent restricted through the presence of a group of councillors and judges around him. From the mid-twelfth century onwards, these councillors and judges acquired well-defined jurisdictions that gave them actual authority, in fact allowing them to share power with the doge. Venice adopted the name *Commune Veneciarum* in 1143.

In theory, the doge was elected by the 'General Assembly' of the Venetian people. In practice, after the death of a doge, the ruling families would take the decision of who his successor would be, and a few of them would cry out his name before a crowd assembled in the church of St Mark. The crowd, the 'General Assembly' only in name, would greet the new doge with applause.[6]

Things changed rapidly after 1172, however, when the Venetian navy returned home after an unsuccessful war against Byzantium (see Chapter 8), a war the doge had waged despite the adverse opinion of his councillors. The doge thus faced an angry crowd, tried to flee to a monastery and was assassinated. With the election of the new doge, the decision was taken that no doge in the future could take any initiative without the consent of his councillors. Besides, the election of a doge was thereafter based on the decision of an official nominating committee, the members of which were elected among the Venetian nobles by a rather complicated process, which combined voting with casting lots.

Venice's new institutional framework comprised: (i) the *Great Council* of several hundred members (mostly 'nobles') out of which other, diversified councils emerged; (ii) the *Council of Forty* and the *Senate*, two committees possessing increased powers in matters of commerce, navigation, war fleets, international affairs, etc.; (iii) six *Ducal Councillors*; and, of course, (iv) the doge.

Ten men, that is, the doge with his councillors and three 'heads' of the Council of Forty and the Senate, comprised the *Signoria*, the highest executive institution of the state. Besides being simply the head of the *Signoria*, and not a despot, the doge's authority was also limited by an oath, the adherence to which was audited by a special committee.

With the exception of the doge, who was elected for life, the members of all other state institutions and committees were elected for a limited time period, from several months to up to three years, from among the male members of the roughly one hundred noble families.[7] "The doge could not remove or directly punish the members of these administrative committees" (Lane 1973: 98); those responsible for prosecuting officials and committee members for abuse were the State Attorneys, bringing cases to trial by the Forty (ibid. 100).

The members of the different committees were generally elected by lot, the holding of an office being obligatory[8] and always remunerated by a salary paid by the Commune. The committee responsible for policing the city, the 'Lords of the Night-watch', had the authority to hire more than a hundred other officers with no association with the aristocracy. Other committees were responsible for managing state finances, inspecting ships and entire fleets, policing markets, commanding merchant ship convoys or Venice's war fleet, etc.

> The management of the Arsenal, of the mint, of the grain warehouse, the collection of taxes, and the inspection of ships [...] were one after another assigned to elected committees of from three to six nobles who held office for only a few years at most and were not eligible to succeed themselves.
>
> (Lane 1973: 98)

On a local level, Venice was divided into sixty to seventy districts (parishes), and a special officer ('*capo*') was appointed as the head of each district. Each *capo*, who in most cases belonged to one of the ruling families, was assigned the responsibility of assessing the property of inhabitants in the event that a forced loan was demanded of property owners by the Commune, of registering all adult males for military conscription and naval service and of safeguarding order in the district by policing taverns and foreigners, etc.

Higher office holders, as members of the ruling class of Venice's merchants, ship-owners, *commenda* traders, usurers, real estate proprietors, etc., very often held office for only a very limited time period, subsequently returning to their money-begetting activities. The more elderly among them, who had assigned these activities to younger members of their family, often chose to rotate from one state committee to another, given the limited time of service allowed for each position. By being active in the state apparatuses, Venetian noblemen and their families ensured certain advantages and earnings for their private affairs as well.

9.2 The economic functions of the Venetian state

Maritime trade, Venice's main economic endeavour, was closely connected with, as I have already written, military operations, whether for protecting Byzantine territories, or for supplementing commercial profits with profits from piracy and the sacking of coastal towns, or for protecting sea routes and Venetian merchant ships, or, finally, for pillaging Byzantium. Maritime trade therefore presupposed the development of a commensurate naval force and state policies conducive to supporting merchant and war fleets and to safeguarding maritime supremacy.

However, the state did not restrict itself to the role of guardian and organizer of the money-begetting activities of the Venetian nobility, but directly undertook significant economic activities itself, acting as a 'collective entrepreneur'.

In 1104, the Arsenal was built as a state-owned shipyard and manufactory of arms, alongside already-existing private shipyards. The state occasionally took control of all shipbuilding activities in the city by conscripting labourers from privately owned shipyards.[9] Next to the Arsenal, another state-owned enterprise for the production of rope and storage of hemp was built, the Tana. Other state-owned enterprises and state institutions that produced revenues for the Commune were the mint, the Zecca, where Venetian coins were produced, and the Salt Office, which controlled all private salt production and the regulation of its prices and the quantities of exports, as well as all duties and tariffs associated with the import and export of salt. Also worth mentioning is the Grain Office, which monitored wheat stores, assuring adequate reserves for the city through the regulation of prices and a steady inflow of imports, at times even by organizing naval operations in the Adriatic in order to 'persuade' ships carrying wheat to other destinations to detour their cargo to Venice. It also had control over the city's bakers, distributing wheat to them and fixing their prices. In times of shortage, the Office offered high prices to foreign merchants so as to facilitate the import of wheat from all over the Mediterranean and the Italian mainland, and "Venetians were both urged and ordered to do so" (Lane 1973: 59). The Office also kept stocks of wheat, by which it could increase supply in order to check inflated prices (if need be).

To the extent that Venetian sea power was growing, ships, the main means of production in the Venetian social formation, were built and licenced to navigate as long as they complied with strict regulations.[10] Merchant journeys were also subject to thorough state regulation.

> Frequently the doge and his council ordered that no ships leave port until they received further orders. [...] Sometimes all big ships were ordered to join a military expedition such as the crusade of Enrico Dandolo. [...] [S]pecified ports may be banned for specified periods. [...] And as often as not, the ships going on the most heavily travelled routes were ordered to sail in convoy, under an admiral appointed by the doge. [...] [F]or centuries oversea voyages were treated as community enterprises subject to government approval.
>
> (Lane 1973: 49)

The Venetian merchant fleet was partly under state ownership, and some of the state-owned ships were auctioned off to individual merchants for private enterprising, while the rest remained state-operated. As I will discuss in the next chapter, state ownership of merchant ships was actually standardized in the late thirteenth and fourteenth centuries. Until the end of the twelfth century, even the majority of privately owned ships, especially those active on major sea routes in the Mediterranean (sailing to and from Constantinople or other destinations in the Levant, the Black Sea, the Arab and crusader states), travelled as part of either *regulated*, or *licenced*, voyages.

On a regulated voyage, the government not only specified the schedule of the voyage, but also often determined the freight rates for it. Being licensed, ships travelled as a fleet under the command of an admiral and other state officials, and financially were subject to the guidelines of a unified business plan.

State control over merchant ships satisfied two strategic objectives of the Venetian ruling class: on the one hand, it boosted state and class cohesiveness, as it aimed at increasing state revenues and cutting back on antagonisms within the aristocracy;[11] on the other, it directly bolstered ruling class interests, as it provided protection to Venetian commerce and therefore greater comparative advantage, aside from tax exemption in the Byzantine ports, vis-à-vis Venice's trade competitors.

The trade balance between Western Europe and Byzantium recorded huge surpluses in the latter so there was a constant inflow of 'money' (coinage and precious metals) into the Byzantine Empire.[12] The Byzantines imported metals, timber, slaves and foodstuffs, and exported expensive luxury items such as spices, dyes, sugar, silks, pearls and precious stones, as well as potash, wheat, furs, skins, pitch, etc. (Day 2002: 808). Venetian and other Latin intermediaries and transporters of merchandise to and from the Byzantine Empire and other destinations in the Levant constantly profited from East–West trade, regardless of Western trade deficits and the outflow of precious metals. This does not mean they were without competitors, however.

Michael F. Hendy argues that from the second half of the eleventh century, there "gradually developed a conscious political division in the dominant class" of Byzantium, "with the military/regional administration on the one hand, and with the civil magnates/Constantinopolitan bureaucracy on the other" (Hendy 1985: 570). The latter favoured Byzantine merchants and supported commercial treaties between the empire and the northern Italian city states. A "metropolitan mercantile class and artisanate" (ibid.: 590) thus emerged in Constantinople, which "began to break out of the constraints hitherto imposed upon them by the prevailing ideology of the dominant class and by the mechanisms of the state", and which "was not depressed or killed off by the Latin competition" (ibid.).

Venetian merchants were therefore facing growing competition not only with Pisan and Genoese traders, but also with Orthodox Christian and Jewish merchants of the Byzantine Empire. The protection provided to them by state regulations and interventionism, licenced commercial fleets and by state ownership of part of Venice's merchant fleet, however, created yet another lever for augmenting profits for the Venetian ruling class and her state revenues,[13] not to mention the benefits accruing from tax exemption granted to Venice by Byzantine imperial chrysobulls.

It seems that Venetian trade fleets were very often in a position to negotiate cargo at higher freight rates than their Byzantine or Latin competitors simply because of the higher protection they could guarantee their ships. These benefits of protection were shared by both merchants and the Venetian state, as revenues for the Commune surpassed the expenses involved in creating protection. Frederic C. Lane stresses the role of state-organized protection for Venice's economic rise up until the thirteenth century:

> Any effort to explain why Venice was more prosperous than its rivals, or more prosperous at some times than at others, must consider how far the

Venetians were more secure, at less cost, from disruption by violence in their purchases of wares in one place, their shipments, and their sales in good markets.

(Lane 1979: 58)

The state budget was financed by a consumption tax (on salt, wine, oil, meat, etc.) of about 1% on every wholesale transaction, yielding very high revenues for the state, given "the flow of goods through Venice" (Lane 1973: 150), and by fines and penalties imposed on all those who violated the maritime codes and other state regulations of shipping, trade, guilds, etc. As no income tax or other direct taxes were levied, the tax burden fell mainly on the lower classes, whose income simply covered their consumption needs.

9.3 Complex forms of class exploitation and domination in a commercialized pre-capitalist society

9.3.1 The Venetian economy: a brief overview of production relations

The Venetian economy and society were dominated, from the eleventh century or even earlier, by an ensemble of money-begetting relations of production and exploitation, without, however, having been transformed into a capitalist economy and society.

On the surface, Venice was chiefly a maritime economy and society, as maritime trade and navigation, along with shipbuilding, were the main economic activities of her ruling class,[14] and a large part of her society's workforce was engaged in these economic sectors. Nevertheless, under the façade of 'maritime economy', several patterns of exploitation and modes and forms of production were reproducing themselves. In anticipation of what I will be presenting in the subsequent sections of this chapter, I will hereby sum up the following forms of production and exploitation.

The form of petty commodity production and a primordial pattern of the hybrid mode of production of small-scale entrepreneurship (see Chapter 7) covered the larger part of economic activity. The money-begetting slave mode of production (see ibid.) was of course present, but played an inferior role. Feudal relations still existed, as wealthy landowners possessed large estates on the mainland that exploited serf labour, but they were definitely of marginal significance compared with non-agrarian, maritime and artisan-manufacturing activities. Besides, landowners, being part of the Venetian ruling class, were generally also active in sea trade, as well as in the collective administration of the state and its entrepreneurial activities. A feudal tendency within Venice, emanating from its colonial system, was reinvigorated in the wake of the Fourth Crusade, as I intend to discuss in Chapter 10.

Most importantly, along with a concentration of individual and communal wealth, contractually organized wage labour and the putting-out system were constantly gaining ground in the economic relations between money-owners and the state on the one hand, and sailors, master craftsmen and unskilled labourers on the other. However, until the fourteenth century, these wage forms were intermingled with elements of 'association' and 'participation' of the wage earners in the 'capital invested' to set into motion the money-begetting activities under discussion (e.g. 'profit sailing', see Chapter 7). In other words, wage earners maintained certain 'institutionalized' expectations that they would acquire a share of the proceeds of a commercial, piratic or war expedition. And, perhaps most importantly, they themselves participated in the commercial voyages as 'traders', carrying and selling their own merchandise.

The basis of these 'institutionalized' expectations was the fact that wage earners (exactly as labourers subjected to the putting-out–buying-up system) *had not (yet) been fully separated from the ownership of the means of production*. The condition of being a wage earner in and of itself also entailed a claim on the proceeds of the economic activity in question, via enduring pre-capitalist 'partnership' connections between the money-owner and the labourer and via ownership of a portion of merchant capital. In addition, wage relations sometimes cloaked other forms of pre-capitalist relations, as in cases where a wage-remunerated seaman could take part in an economic venture along with his slaves.

I discussed the mingling of these facets of 'association' relations with money-begetting activities in Chapter 7, where I proposed the term *contractual money-begetting mode of production* to denote that these economic forms, although exploitative (as the shipowner or taskmaster of the commercial expedition appropriated the surplus product of the labourers), were not (yet) capitalist, as the labourers were not (yet) proletarians. At this point, I shall stress that to the extent that these forms of production and employment not only boosted the monetization of the economy but, additionally, created the preconditions for the detachment of labourers from the means of production (the creation of the *propertyless proletarian*), can be regarded as an unconsummated and *unsettled process of original accumulation*.

In this sense, both contractually organized labour and the putting-out system of the twelfth and thirteenth centuries constituted *potentially* transitional forms towards capitalist social relations, despite the fact that their very existence did not indicate the prevalence of capitalism, or even necessarily a more or less predestined capitalist future, that is, an evolution towards capitalism. Their evolution towards a capitalist or pre-capitalist direction was contingent upon a variety of factors, both internal and external to Venetian society.

9.3.2 Venice's social strata: the spurious bourgeoisie, the guilds, the middle classes, the labourers and the slaves

Venice had been amongst Europe's largest cities since the tenth century;[15] the population included those living in the lagoon area under Venetian control.

The money-begetting character of the city's chief activities functioned as a magnet drawing populations into Venice from other parts of the Italian peninsula, Western Europe and the Mediterranean. As Fernand Braudel stresses:

> Venice's activities all fell into the sectors which economists would nowadays describe as secondary and tertiary: industry, commerce, services – sectors where labour was more profitably employed than in rural activities.
>
> (Braudel 1984: 108)

If one excludes the aristocracy, at the maximum a couple of thousand, the city's population of 80,000–100,000 inhabitants (including those living in the lagoon area) at the beginning of the thirteenth century comprised five main categories of people: (i) the new rich, or 'fat people', that is, merchants, manufacturers and/or landowners having levels of wealth comparable to those of noble status, but not belonging to them, despite some limited integration of 'fat' families into Venetian 'nobility'; (ii) the 'little people', that is, the upper middle class who did not perform 'manual work' (and who in the fourteenth century were granted the legal right to 'citizenship' – see Chapter 10), as, for example, less important international traders, well-off shopkeepers, lawyers, civil servants below the highest hierarchy – notaries, clerks, members of the Ducal Chancery, etc.; (iii) the lower middle class of guild masters performing 'manual work', that is, artisans and craftsmen; (iv) the labourers, unskilled or of different skill levels, who constituted the large majority of the population, and also comprised the main workforce on Venice's merchant ships; (v) the servants and slaves, including debt slaves (see below).

According to existing historical evidence, "the artisans, shopkeepers, and workers", that is, categories (iii), (iv) and (v), "accounted for the [...] 90 percent of the city's inhabitants" (Martin and Romano: 16). Before endeavouring to theoretically analyze these social categories on the basis of more well-defined class criteria, I will take a look at the role of guilds in the Venetian economy and society, an issue that can shed light on the prevailing class relations of exploitation and domination in the city state.

Guilds in medieval cities were of three kinds: *religious* guilds, or *brotherhoods*, "for the purpose of worship and prayer" (Brentano 1969: lxvi), which developed into associations of mutual assistance;[16] *craft guilds*, which set regulations and production rules for the protection of artisan goods, uniting master craftsmen of a specific occupation (each of whom worked with a number of apprentices);[17] *merchant guilds*, which aimed at "protecting property, liberty, and trade, against the violence of neighbouring nobles, the arbitrary aggressions of the bishops or the burgrave, or the bold onsets of robbers" (Brentano 1969: xciii).

What should be stressed regarding guilds in Venice is, first of all, the absence of any merchants' guilds. Venice was not just 'another medieval city', whose merchants fought for 'freedom' against local feudal lords or royal suzerains. Venice was a city *state*, under the social and political rule of a class of patrician money-owners and merchants.

> Venetian merchants engaged in international trade felt no need of any special organizations, such as guilds, to look after their commercial interests, for their Communal government made that its chief concern. No rival in that field was needed or would have been tolerated.
>
> (Lane 1973: 104)

The absence of guilds did not concern only the ruling class of patrician merchants; in the entire shipping sector, "Venice's biggest industry" (Lane 1973: 166), there existed not even one guild organization.[18] The relations between 'investors', taskmasters, officers and ordinary seamen were regulated on a different basis, on which I will elaborate below.

Finally, the craft guilds, which in most other medieval social formations managed "to regulate production and to take whatever measures were necessary to eliminate competition" (Rubin 1989: 20), were at least by the mid-thirteenth century put under the supervision and control of the Venetian Justices, the authority established in the mid-twelfth century in order to police markets.[19]

Of equal importance was the fact that many of Venice's craft guilds, which in other European regions or cities maintained their power or even supremacy in urban manufacturing activities until the sixteenth, and even seventeenth, centuries, precluding the development of the putting-out economic scheme,[20] had been, since the late twelfth century, subordinated under a putting-out–buying-up system advanced by wealthy merchants.

> Moreover, the political subordination of the guilds was matched by an economic subordination of many guildsmen to merchants who drew their main profits from foreign trade. [...] In short, the suppliers of capital were in control of many branches of industry, and the chief suppliers of capital were in the governing merchant aristocracy.
>
> (Lane 1973: 107)

To clarify this point, I shall elaborate on the structure of Venice's manufacturing sector. The Venetian economy was, in the twelfth and thirteenth centuries, governed by small-scale enterprise: a guild master or a specialized craftsman hired workers or apprentices and organized the production process; he maintained the ownership and possession relations over the means of production, being directly involved in the production process as such, or, in other words, being entangled as well in the use relation (see Chapter 7). This production form, which prevailed in Venice's manufacture along with the *simple commodity production* of single household units, may be comprehended as a *primordial*[21] *hybrid mode of production* (consistent with the concepts introduced in Chapter 7).

However, these small production units corresponding to the primordial hybrid mode of production were in many sectors and cases subsumed under well-off money-owners, mostly merchants and ship-owners, who functioned as putter-out–buyer-up.[22] In other words, the ownership of the means of production partly passed into the hands of these money-owners, who supplied masters with raw materials and other means of production and bought up their whole output, thus appropriating the larger part of the surplus created by direct labour.

> The shipwrights, for example, were employed my merchant owners who supplied the capital for the construction and outfitting of ships. Cordage makers were largely dependent on merchant employers who imported the hemp.
>
> (ibid.)

However, until the late thirteenth century, this subordination of craft guilds and craftsmen to the putting-out–buying-up system had not created an authentic cottage system, or, in other words, the direct producers had not been transformed into a form of piece-wage labourers (see Chapters 3 and 7). On the one hand, the putting-out–buying-up system did not destroy, but absorbed existing guilds and small enterprises, which means that production continued to be organized (as regards the possession relation) by masters or specialized craftsmen who themselves hired a small number of workers or apprentices;[23] on the other hand, direct producers (guilds, small enterprises or independent household producers) also maintained access to the local market parallel to the putting-out–buying-up relation. This means that they partially maintained the ownership relation over the means of production as well, which they only temporarily ceded to or shared with the buyer-up. This was the case with carpenters and caulkers, who were hired by merchants in the framework of putting-out–buying-up contracts for the production or repair of a ship or boat, but were also able to keep a retail store for selling on the local market furniture that they had produced.

The tendency of the putting-out–buying-up system to acquire both ownership and possession of the means of production and to convert the direct producer into a piece-wage earner (see Chapters 3 and 7) was thus hampered.

This means that the money-owners who functioned as buyer-ups had not yet been transformed into capitalists. We may call them *spurious bourgeoisie* in the sense that by advancing money and means of production, they temporarily acquired from (or shared with) the master the ownership of the means of production. Even though these putter-out sometimes participated in the possession relation as well (the management of the production process), they mostly capitulated the latter to small-scale taskmasters (guild masters or specialized craftsmen), who themselves directly hired and commanded wage labour, and so also appropriated a part of the surplus product.

It is noteworthy that even at a later date, large-scale production was organized on the basis of the primordial hybrid mode of production, subjected to the putting-out–buying-up relation:

> In 1304, for example, a contract to supply the Commune with 20,000 steel bolts for crossbows was awarded to three men who then subcontracted the manufacture to master ironsmiths employing six to seven workers each.
>
> (Lane 1973: 161)

The only economic sector in which money-owners directly hired significant numbers of wage earners was shipping. Merchant galleys and other trade ships had crews from 50 to 180 sailors. These sailors, themselves "equipped and experienced in their own kind of fighting" (Lane 1973: 49), along with a number of crossbowmen and other specialized armed men, were recruited in Venice before each voyage by being 'signed on' by a merchant or a taskmaster representing either a merchant or a fleet or the Commune. The merchant or taskmaster paid the sailors' wages for the entire voyage, which could last up to one year. During the voyage, seamen were also provided with daily rations (comprising biscuits, cheese, salt pork and wine).

However, once again, as with the seamen up until the end of the thirteenth century, no definitive capital–wage-labour relation existed, as wages were not the only, and in many cases not the most significant, source of remuneration for crew members. Even in the case of state-organized voyages or the unilateral *commenda* (*colleganza*), where labour was no longer considered as equivalent to 'money investment' (see Chapter 7), all salaried sailors were also 'partners' of their taskmaster in the trade venture. In other words, every sailor, in addition to being a wage earner, was simultaneously a 'trader'.

> The daily wage was only a part of what a seaman expected to gain from a voyage. On commercial voyages, all had rights to carry freight-free some merchandise with which to trade.
>
> (Lane 1973: 168)

Besides, in the historical period introduced by the First Crusade, every sailor, apart from being a 'shareholder' in the profits of a merchant expedition, was also a beneficiary of the booty from piracy, or from the sacking of enemy ships and towns, or from slave trade.[24] It is characteristic that before setting off on an outgoing merchant trip, during inspection at St Mark's Basin, crews

> [...] had to post bond that they would not attack friendly people [...]. The law provided that anyone refusing to attack an enemy ship when ordered should have his head cut off [...].
>
> (Lane 1973: 50)

Finally, not all sailors were 'free men' and therefore remunerated by wage and a part of the proceeds from trade or plunder: more than two out of ten seamen were generally either servants or slaves of other seamen, or debt slaves.

Debt slaves were divided into two categories: (i) convicted no-shows, that is, sailors who had signed up for a voyage, received wages beforehand and then failed to report at the ship's departure, hiding or pretending to be ill; many of them were charged a fine double the wages received, which they paid through forced recruitment as debt slaves;[25] (ii) sailors who borrowed money from a taskmaster or merchant in order to purchase merchandise for the trade expedition, anticipating related earnings that could cover the debt, but due to a poor outcome of the venture were unable to do so; in subsequent voyages, they were recruited as debt slaves to the borrower, merchant or taskmaster, until the debt was cleared.

Once again, in the case of Venice's maritime 'industry', full separation of the labourers from the means of production had not yet taken place. The money-owners, either isolated merchants or the Venetian Commune as a collective agent, bore once more the character of a *spurious bourgeoisie*: as money-begetting economic actors ('entrepreneurs'), they exploited a salaried labour force that was not fully separated from the means of production (contractual money-begetting mode of production). Maintaining a form of 'association' with money-owners and their taskmasters, salaried seamen anticipated a share, albeit a small one, from the proceeds accruing from commerce, plunder and slave trade.

At this point, it is worth mentioning that plunder and the trading of slaves, being warlike processes creating and disseminating 'profits' by exploiting foreign people and territories, forged strong ties of *consensus* among, and *submissiveness* of, the Venetian populace to the ruling class.

9.4 Concluding remarks

Venice remained a pre-capitalist economy and society under the economic, political and social rule of a class of patrician merchants, ship-owners and directors of state-owned enterprises until the end of the thirteenth century.

The money-begetting activities of the Venetian ruling class constituted an unsettled process of *original accumulation*, in Marx's context of the term. One pole of the process, the Venetian money-owners and their state, had already attained the clearly defined characteristics of a spurious bourgeoisie. The other pole, however, the *propertyless* proletarian, had not yet emerged, and this is precisely why the bourgeoisie remained *spurious*. The wage-remunerated poor still participated in the ownership of the means of production through forms of 'association' mediated by the very fact of their being wage earners.

A number of historical contingencies, chiefly related to economic antagonisms, war and crises that had been going on in the broader Mediterranean basin since the fourteenth century, ultimately led to the formation of a propertyless proletariat and the taking hold of its encounter with, and subsumption under, the state-organized Venetian capitalist class, as I will endeavour to analyze in Chapter 10.

Notes

1 Even Adam Smith, the 'father' of economic individualism, distances himself from the idea that the economic rise of the city states of the Italian peninsula may have been the outcome of the endeavours of some "typical self-made men", who "engendered and spread the entrepreneurial spirit". Smith writes:

> The cities of Italy seem to have been the first in Europe which were raised by commerce to any considerable degree of opulence. Italy lay in the center of what was at that time the improved and civilized part of the world. The cruzades too, though by the great waste of stock and destruction of inhabitants which they occasioned [...] were extremely favourable to that of some Italian cities. The great armies which marched from all parts to the conquest of the Holy Land, gave extraordinary encouragement to the shipping of Venice, Genoa, and Pisa, sometimes in transporting them thither, and always in supplying them with provisions. They were the commissaries, if one may say so, of those armies; and the most destructive frenzy that ever befel the European nations, was a source of opulence to those republicks.
>
> (Smith 2007: 406)

2 This form of piracy, closely connected with other state-backed money-begetting practices, was thus fully different from the kind of piracy developed in the Atlantic in the seventeenth and eighteenth centuries. As Peter Linebaugh and Marcus Rediker explain:

> A third phase, in 1650–1760, witnessed the consolidation and stabilization of Atlantic capitalism through the maritime state, a financial and nautical system designed to acquire and operate Atlantic markets. The sailing ship—the characteristic machine of this period of globalization—combined features of the factory and the prison. In opposition, pirates built an autonomous, democratic, multiracial social order at sea, but this alternative way of life endangered the slave trade and was exterminated.
>
> (Linebaugh and Rediker 2001: 328)

3 "Venice [...] inherited from the Byzantine Empire a tradition of unified allegiance to a sovereign state" (Lane 1973: 109).
4 As Daphne Penna writes,

> [a] first clear difference between East and West was the continuity of Roman law in Byzantium. [...] [F]rom the 8th century on, systems of feudal law began to develop in the West that were based on a personal bond between a lord and a vassal and were therefore important in the law of real property.
>
> (Penna 2012: 3)

[In Venice]

> the statute of 1195 consists of law of procedure, family law, law of succession and property law, as well as law of obligations and commercial law. In all these legal areas one can see a mixture of Roman, Byzantine, Germanic and Canon law; however, the strongest legal element remains Roman law.
>
> (op.cit.: 6)

5 "The exarchs or the governors general, first of all military officers, gradually concentrated in their hands the administrative and judicial functions and had the final word in the management of church affairs in the exarchate" (Vasiliev 1952: 575).
6 "[...] the clergy chanted *Te Deum Laudamus*, and the bells of the Campanile rang triumphantly" (Lane 1973: 91).

7 The only exceptions were the curators of St Mark, who served for life, managing the endowments of the church and caring for the upkeep of the building.

8 "The requirement that a man must serve when selected expressed the Commune's claim to unqualified allegiance" (Lane 1973: 109).

9 "The doge could command all the shipyard workers of the lagoons to come to work in the yards in which the government was building. When so conscripted, the carpenters and caulkers were paid" (Lane 1973: 48).

10 "The crews of the merchant marine and the navy were the same people, but the size of the crew was much larger on a vessel prepared to combat. [...] Venetian regulations distinguished between 'armed' and 'unarmed' ships by the size of their crews. Even a vessel built like a galley was not considered an 'armed ship' unless its crew numbered at least 60 men" (Lane 1973: 48).

11 "It would be difficult to decide which was in that age preferable economically: for the galleys to be owned by the managers of their mercantile voyages and to be rented to the government when military needs were dominant, as at Genoa; or, as at Venice, for the galleys to be owned by the state which wanted them for military purposes and to be rented for mercantile uses when they were not needed for war. But there was a political as well as an economic aspect to these alternatives. Genoa provided an example of how private ownership and private management in the military establishment made it easier for factions to tear the state apart. [...] Communal ownership of galleys expressed the solidarity of the Venetian nobility and strengthened that solidarity" (Lane 1966: 226).

12 "In the first commercial treaty between Venice and Byzantium, the Golden Bull of 992, Venetian ships in the Bosphoros were subject to an exit tax seven times the entry tax, reflecting in all likelihood a rough proportion of exports to imports [...] to the middle of the twelfth century – based on the commercial contracts of the Genoese notary Giovanni Scriba – exports to the Levant consisted almost exclusively of gold and silver in different forms (Muslim gold pieces, silver ingots, gold thread, and silverware)" (Day 2002: 809, 808–809).

13 "The resulting flow of trade through Venice raised most gratifyingly the tax receipts of the Commune" (Lane 1973: 125).

14 Although mainly navigators, Venetian merchants also travelled to the European north by land, mainly through the Brenner Pass in the Alps:

> [...] it is more than likely that by the time Frederic Barbarossa and Pope Alexander III met in Venice in 1177, trade links already existed between Germany and the city of Saint Mark, and that silver from the German mines was already playing an important role in Venice in competition with Byzantine gold.
>
> (Braudel 1984: 109)

The sea route through Gibraltar to Bruges and the English Channel was first introduced in 1277 by the Genoese.

15 "Venetians numbered at least 80,000 in 1200 and about 160,000 a century later in the lagoon area as a whole, with nearly 120,000 in the city. In western Europe in the Middle Ages, any place over 20,000 or 10,000 was considered a big city" (Lane 1973: 18).

16 The activities of these brotherhoods

> included not only devotions and orisons, but also every exercise of Christian charity, and therefore, above all things, mutual assistance [...] in every exigency, especially in old age, in sickness, in cases of impoverishment [...] and of wrongful imprisonment, in losses by fire, water or shipwreck, aid by loans, provision of work, and, lastly, the burial of the dead.
>
> (Brentano 1969: lxxxiv)

Within the framework of their religious ceremonies they also organized common meals for fraternity members. In Venice there existed at least fourteen religious brotherhoods, some of which (e.g. the Scuole Grandi) comprised 500–600 members each, including both rich and poor inhabitants of the city (Lane 1973: 105, 152).

17 "The guilds first recorded and officially regulated were the tailors, the jacket makers, the goldsmiths and jewelers, the dyers, the coopers, the cordage makers, and the barber-surgeons, which included the physicians" (Lane 1973: 106).

18 "[...] there was also no guild of mariners, neither of masters and mates, nor of ordinary seamen" (Lane 1973: 106).

19 "[...] some guilds felt strong enough [...] setting prices [...]. The Justices [...] forbade unilateral price-fixing and boycott by the tailors' guild. In 1219, they [...] laid down a series of basic regulation which all in the trade were bound by oath to obey" (Lane 1973: 106). In the 1260s,

> a law passed by the Great Council [...] strictly forbade, under threat of banishment or death, any craft to form any sworn association against the honor of the doge and his Council, or against the honor of the Commune, or against any other person – vague but sweeping language [...].
>
> (ibid.)

20 "The independent guild crafts, which had so dominated the economy of the towns in the late middle ages, gave way in the 16th and 17th centuries to the rapid rise of cottage industry (the so-called domestic system of capitalist industry). It made especially rapid headway in those branches of production, such as cloth manufacturing, which worked for specific markets or for export to other countries" (Rubin 1979: 24).

21 'Primordial' in the sense that the master–apprentice relationship did not allow the full-fledged development of the wage relation.

22 Buyer-up also controlled a large number of Venice's 'self-employed' labourers, that is, craftsmen who did not belong to guilds but worked at home.

23 Marx stresses that even in the case of masters hiring workers, the buyer-up is the one who appropriates the workers' surplus labour: "The merchant is the real capitalist and pockets the greater part of the surplus-value" (Marx 1991: 453). "It might be called a special kind of putting-out system because the craftsmen did not own the material on which they worked" (Lane 1973: 163).

24 As regards the cargo ships of slaves in the fourteenth century, "a 400 ton ship with a crew of 50 could carry 200 slaves" (Lane 1973: 133).

25 "[...] if they did not report [...] they were sought out by the policemen of the Nightwatch and either brought forceably on board or put in prison. [...] The thirteenth century laws had provided that whoever took wages and did not report must pay the double as penalty. Such a fine could be effective against persons who had property, but not against men who owned next to nothing [...] [they were] then put to work as debt slaves [...] so that they might work off what they owed" (Lane 1973: 168–169).

10 War economics and the ascent of capitalism in the fourteenth century

10.1 The Venetian colonial system: countering tendencies of disintegration after the Fourth Crusade

With the conquest of Constantinople by the crusaders in 1204 (see Chapter 8), Venice's doge Enrico Dandolo was proclaimed 'Lord of one quarter and one half [of a quarter] of the Empire of Romania'. The doge was the only one who was not obliged to take a feudal oath of allegiance to the Latin emperor.

This was a new, unprecedented situation for Venice and her rulers. Despite the fact that a sizeable part of the empire remained in the hands of Byzantine aristocrats, who, after the fall of Constantinople, had formed three new states, the Empire of Nicaea, the Empire of Trebizond and the Despotate of Epirus, enormous territories were being incorporated into the Latin Empire of Romania (Constantinople) and assigned as principalities and fiefs to Western nobles and knights, which included Venetians.

The allotment of such territories to Venice's ruling class of patricians, who until then had been engaged almost exclusively in maritime trade and other, therewith interconnected, money-begetting activities, produced a feudal tendency among them: they developed a predilection towards commissioning themselves as feudal lords and tribute appropriators overseas.

It is interesting that the doge himself, Enrico Dandolo, did not return to Venice after the end of the Fourth Crusade, but remained in Constantinople, essentially functioning as a powerful despot in the Latin Empire and as leader of the Venetian community in the city.

> The situation was without precedent in their political history. Their Doge showed no sign of coming home, though he sent back a large part of his fleet. His son Reniero continued to act as his regent in Venice while Dandolo plunged wholeheartedly into his new role as leader, defender and promoter of the Venetian cause in Byzantium. [...] Enrico Dandolo behaved like a Doge of an earlier age [...] under whose guidance the Venetians had been equally quick to appoint one of their own as patriarch.
>
> (Nicol 1988: 148–149)

When doge Enrico Dandolo died in May 1205 at the age of 98, the Venetians in Constantinople immediately elected a new leader, Marino Zeno, who was granted the titles of 'podestà' (an appellation bearing similar connotations with that of the doge: chief magistrate) and of 'Lord of one quarter and one half [of a quarter] of the Empire of Romania'. Boards of councillors were elected around him, imitating the structure of the respective boards in Venice. The Venetian community in Constantinople, as a self-reliant part of the new Latin Empire, seems to have felt strong enough and prepared to loosen its ties with Venice.

However, "Venice's lack of feudal institutions, as well as the continuation of Byzantine traditions" (Madden 2003: 23) simply meant that such initiatives deeply worried the majority of the Venetian ruling class at home. On August 1205, they elected a new doge, Pietro Ziani, who immediately demanded that all Romanian territories that had been ceded to Venetians would come under direct control of the Commune, and that the 'podestà' of Constantinople should be appointed by the Great Council.[1]

Nevertheless, the relation of forces between Venice and Constantinople was such that the doge in Venice conceded to the demands of certain powerful patricians, that they might appropriate for themselves any territory they wanted, and to hold it as a hereditary fief. Enrico Dandolo's nephew, Marco Sanudo, was among the first to benefit from this concession of the new doge; in 1207, he founded the Duchy of the Egeo Pelago (Archipelago), after he occupied the island of Naxos and several surrounding islands.

> To allow such private enterprise was in a sense an admission of weakness, an acknowledgment that the Doge of Venice could not hope to acquire or control such a multitude of scattered colonies.
>
> (Nicol 1988: 157)

All territories that had passed into the hands of Venetian patricians as feudal possessions were very soon detached from Venice's control and strategic calculations. This 'feudal tendency' among the Venetian aristocracy functioned as a process of disintegration of the 'empire' that doge Enrico Dandolo might well have envisaged. As Monique O'Connell points out, "[m]uch of the territory awarded in the partition of 1204 passed out of Venetian hands as quickly as it had passed in" (O'Connell 2009: 19).

The disintegrating 'feudal tendency' was kept in check only in the territories over which the state could take direct control. These were the island of Crete, the southern Peloponnesian cities of Modon and Coron, and Chalkis, the capital of the island of Negroponte (Euboea). All of them, especially Crete, occupied a very important strategic position in the Mediterranean, in addition to holding great economic significance for maritime trade routes and the supply of certain agricultural and manufactured products.

These territories became Venice's *colonies*, that is, they were directly subordinated under the state's rule and supervision.[2] Venice essentially imitated the 'pseudo-feudal' late Byzantine regime (see Chapter 8), granting land to military officials and nobles without the juridical and economic power or autonomy characteristic of actual feudal social relations; they were subjected to control by the local and Venetian central state apparatuses, and therefore obliged to fulfil certain economic or military obligations or commitments.[3] In this sense, through strict state control over her colonies that resembled the previous Byzantine economic and political order, Venice was insulated from the feudal tendencies that had developed among some of her patricians after the Fourth Crusade. The resident populations in the areas under Venetian rule faced only minor changes in terms of their economic and social conditions, as compared with their Byzantine past.

> [...] in Crete and a section of southern Messenia around Coron and Modon there was an almost direct transition from the empire's rule to that of Venice, a city governed by a non-feudal elite imbued with a firm sense of statehood. In these Venetian territories, therefore, the measure of continuity was likely to be much greater than in feudalized areas. Indeed, although using the feudal vocabulary, Venice upheld the supreme authority of the state and prevented any definitive privatization of Byzantine imperial prerogatives in judicial or fiscal matters. Venice [...] established a highly centralized bureaucratic system of government and supervision.
>
> (Jacoby 1989: 3)[4]

The Latin Empire of Romania proved to be short-lived. In July 1261, the leaders of the Empire of Nicaea conquered Constantinople and re-established Byzantium. Venice managed to keep her colonial possessions and naval bases in Crete, Negroponte, Modon, Coron and Cerigo (Kythira), but she had lost her privileged position in Constantinople.

10.2 Fighting for trade supremacy in the Mediterranean

10.2.1 The first period of wars (1257–1311) and the reform of Venice's polity

The restoration of the Byzantine Empire in 1261 did not succeed in or aim at re-constructing the level of state cohesiveness that had existed before the Fourth Crusade. The authority of provincial leaders and local lords was significantly increased, vis-à-vis that of the central state apparatus, as the process of feudalization of society, having been unfolding since the eleventh century (see Chapter 8), reached a point of no return in the years of Latin dominance.[5] According to Angeliki Laiou, this weakening of the central state, especially from the fourteenth century onwards, increased the significance of long-distance and maritime trade, which also forged ties of communication and cohesion between Byzantine territories.

[…] the Byzantine state no longer functioned as an efficient mechanism of integration. An integrating factor did exist in the fourteenth and fifteenth centuries: it was international trade, dominated and organized by the Italian city-states, Pisa for a while, but primarily Genoa and Venice. The needs and activities of the Italian merchants made of the eastern Mediterranean an integrated trade system, in which the various regions were drawn, each with its own relations with the Italians. As a result, there are regional economies – those of Macedonia and Thrace, Epiros, Thessaly, and the Peloponnese – with some contact with each other to be sure, but with the important factor being their relationship with the Italians and their role in the trading system of the eastern Mediterranean.

(Laiou 2002-a: 312; see also Arbel et al. 1989)

This new economic and social landscape in the Mediterranean boosted the economic roles of both Venice and Genoa, but also further fuelled the persistently lurking antagonism between them. After 1261, the Genoese were significantly favoured by the new Byzantine emperor, and they soon created a flourishing colony at Pera, just outside the Byzantine capital, Constantinople. Even before his accession to the Byzantine throne, in March 1261, at Nymphaeum, the new Emperor Michael VIII Paleologos signed a treaty with Genoa which granted tax-free trade to the Genoese throughout the empire (Vasiliev 1952: 537).

The rivalry between Venice and Genoa intensified after the Fourth Crusade, when the Genoese occupied the island of Chios and the city of Phocaea, which lay across from Chios on the coast of Asia Minor, and then proceeded to demand suzerainty over Crete instead of the Venetians. In the coming decades, the enmity between the two Italian city states would reach a peak and surpass the Venetian–Byzantine conflict in intensity,[6] inaugurating a long period of recurring wars.

The first Venetian–Genoese war broke out in 1256 at the crusader city of Acre, and lasted until 1270. The Venetian fleets achieved several noteworthy naval victories off Acre in 1258, off Monemvasia in 1263 and off Trapani in 1266 (Lane 1973: 73–79). However, throughout the whole period of hostilities, Venetian merchant fleets suffered a host of 'piratic' attacks by Genoese warships. The second Venetian–Genoese war erupted in 1294 in Cyprus and lasted until 1302. This time, the Genoese were in most cases victorious.[7] They organized large war fleets manned with crews of nearly 35,000 men, and twice destroyed or captured the Venetian fleets off Lajazzo (Ayas) at the Gulf of Alexandretta in 1295, and off Curzola (Korčula) on the Dalmatian coast in 1298. Throughout the whole period of war, the colonies of both parties suffered 'piratic' invasions of enemy ships (Lane 1973: 82–86). A few years after the second Genoese war, between 1308 and 1311, Venice unsuccessfully attempted to subjugate Ferrara, and suffered "large material losses" (Lane 1873: 65). Despite her defeat, Venice never lost her trade and naval supremacy in the Adriatic.

Despite adverse outcomes, neither the first nor the second Venetian–Genoese war, nor the war on Ferrara, was conclusive or even decisive with respect to the relation of forces on a military and economic level between the two rival city states. However, the wars, most notably the second Genoese war and the failure of Venice's attack on Ferrara, secured an advantageous situation for Genoa and triggered internal antagonisms in Venice; the wars also functioned as a catalyst for instigating crucial changes in the political and economic structures of the Venetian social formation.

In 1297, a significant expansion of the Great Council was decided upon by admitting many new members from rich families who, until then, had been regarded as 'commoners'. The Council now comprised more than 1,100 members, all descendants of about 200 families. Moreover, membership in the Council became permanent and hereditary. A new, enlarged class of nobles thence emerged, and the status of being 'noble' was identified with being a member of the Council, or better yet, belonging to a family who had a participating member in the Great Council. The Council was not only the pool from which higher administrative and military officers were recruited, but in essence replaced the General Assembly (Lane 1973: 112–114).

According to evidence, the expansion of the Great Council was initially seen as a process which was going to be periodically recycled in the future, i.e. as a method of incorporating the 'new rich' into the ruling political elite so that rivalries and antagonisms between 'old' families of patricians would be neutralized or counterbalanced. However, the consequences of the second Genoese war and the failed attempt to subjugate Ferrara, as well as the effects of the economic recession in Europe at the beginning of the fourteenth century,[8] resulted in the isolation of the Great Council and Venice's thereafter hereditary nobility by ruling out the possibility of any further expansion.[9]

To ease tensions among the 'new rich' who had not been admitted to the Great Council, and to control the influx of merchants and immigrants, the political status of 'native citizens' was granted to the members of Venice's upper middle class (see Chapter 9). The 'native citizens' among merchants or manufacturers enjoyed exactly the same privileges as the 'nobles', whose family members participated in the Great Council. Foreign merchants residing in Venice could acquire Venetian citizenship and its respective economic privileges after twenty-five years of permanent residence in the city.[10]

10.2.2 The plague and the second phase of wars (1348–1381)

In the aftermath of the second Genoese war and Venice's failed attempt to crush Ferrara, Genoa stabilized her position in merchant trade and her military presence in the Aegean and Black Seas, as well as in the straits connecting these seas. As a result, Venetian diplomacy tried to re-establish ties of alliance and reciprocal support with the Byzantine Empire, which was suffering, at the time, attacks by the Ottomans. In anticipation of a future military alliance against the Ottomans, a treaty between the two states was signed in 1324. The Venetians were allowed to trade corn from the Black Sea region of the Byzantine Empire without being taxed; they were not, however, allowed to export any corn grown within the Empire (Nicol 1988: 248 ff.). During that period, Venice was already facing difficulties manning merchant and war fleets, and authorities were increasingly turning to police and press gangs to 'force' recruitment.[11]

In 1347, the city was hit by the Black Death (i.e. the bubonic plague) "which killed in 1348 half of Venice's population and made similar ravages elsewhere" (Lane 1973: 169). The Venetian population was reduced to around 80,000 people.

As a result of the lack of labour brought about by the devastating effects of the plague, the Commune put forward policies encouraging immigration from the Italian mainland and the Mediterranean. Although these policies were, to a large degree, successful in attracting labourers into most economic sectors, they did not meet shortages in maritime activities, rendering it necessary to continuously recruit foreigners and forced labour from the colonies. The shortage of low-level crew members was even more acute in the war galleys. Venice had begun to depend more and more on mercenaries to carry out her wars.

Shortly after the plague had devastated Venice and most of Europe, in 1350, the third Venetian–Genoese war broke out, this time at Tana (Tanais), on the Black Sea. Not being able to man a fleet large enough for the war, the Venetians hired ships and crews from the King of Aragon and the Byzantine emperor, who had started having problems with the Genoese presence at Pera.[12] The war lasted until 1355, and its main battle, in 1352 in the Bosporus, resulted in extremely heavy losses on both sides, with the Venetian alliance unsuccessful in capturing Pera. The next important battle, in the harbour of Porto Longo near Modon in 1354, was a victory for the Genoese. The war ended, and after an acute internal schism among Genoa's ruling patricians had broken out in 1353, a peace treaty was signed in 1355, which served to avert the imminent threat for more war for a while.

In August 1363, Venice was confronted anew with serious problems. The majority of the Latin nobility of Crete, rallying against the imposition of a new tax by Venice, allied with the 'Greek' nobility of the island and, by granting new rights to the Orthodox Church, gained support from a large part of the local population. After imprisoning the duke, his councillors and the governors of the main cities in Crete, new officials were elected and independence from Venice as the 'Commune of Crete' was proclaimed, the figure of St Tito being adopted as the protector saint of the island.[13] Subsequently, support from Genoa was requested so as to sustain their power. Genoa, however, was unwilling to engage herself in another war with Venice. Venice organized an army of mostly mercenaries under Venetian command and succeeded in capturing Candia, the capital of Crete, in May 1364. Cretan resistance continued until 1368, when Venetian rule was re-established over the whole island.

The fourth Venetian–Genoese war, or, the War of Chioggia, erupted in 1377 close to Tenedos, and lasted until 1381. The Genoese signed an alliance with the King of Hungary and the Lord of Padua, and in 1378 were victorious at a battle of Pola in Istria. In the next year, 1379, the allied forces of Genoa and Padua conquered Chioggia at the southern entrance of the Venetian lagoons and besieged Venice. The situation in the besieged city was desperate, and the morale of the Venetian populace was in decline.[14]

Facing the danger of being conquered and sacked by the enemy forces, the doge and the nobility of Venice concentrated their efforts on reviving the people's morale, making "sweeping promises of political changes and of rewards" (Lane 1973: 193), and assigning military command to popular noblemen. Finally, the negative climate in Venice was reversed – and with the aid of Italian and English mercenaries, Chioggia was regained by the Venetians in June 1380, terminating the siege of Venice. With the Treaty of Turin signed the next year, Venice surrendered her claims on Tenedos, on Treviso and on special trade rights in Cyprus, but she succeeded in keeping her dominance in the Adriatic.

The War of Chioggia was the last threat to Venice's independence and integrity for nearly two centuries, until the Ottomans became a real peril; soon after the War of Chioggia, "the Genoese Commune was paralyzed by revolutions" (Lane 1973: 198). At this new conjuncture, and starting in 1386 with the conquest of Corfu, the Venetians nearly doubled their colonial territories within thirty years (see Chapter 11). During the same period, the city's population burgeoned, as immigrants came in from many parts of the Italian peninsula and the eastern Mediterranean.

The protracted period of war had given rise to state policies that paved the way for the transformation of Venice's economic and social landscape, with the emergence and subsequent prevalence of capitalist relations.

10.3 State power and the consolidation of the relation of capital

10.3.1 The 'point of no return' in overview: stabilization of wage labour and capitalist finance

As discussed in Chapter 9, since the twelfth century Venetian state had been developing a tendency towards the commanding over production processes and the ownership of assets, which were considered to be of cardinal significance, both from a military and an economic point of view. This was evident, for example, in shipbuilding, rope manufacture and commercial shipping. In the tempestuous times of the fourteenth century, these state-owned production sites were transformed into huge manufactures, organized on the basis of the capital–wage-labour relation. The encounter of the propertyless proletarian with the collective money-owner of the Venetian Commune, the latter personified by one or more higher state officials, took hold in these manufactures.

At the same time, concerning ships, strict state control, the rapid expansion of state ownership and the ever-increasing need for tax collection drastically restricted all non-salaried sources of income of the majority of seamen, creating a proletariat of wage-earning mariners. In this case as well, the merchants – money-owners auctioning off communal fleets, or shipowners commanding their private ships – became capitalists, as their coming "face to face and into contact" with the proletarians took hold.

Finally, in order to support the war, huge internal public debt was created, which nurtured both advanced budgetary management and fiscal policies, and capitalist finance.

10.3.2 Development of capitalist manufacture: the Arsenal, the Tana, the Zecca

During the Genoese wars, Venice's state-owned shipyard, the Arsenal, became the city's largest manufactury. In an effort to increase their merchant and war fleets, Venetian rulers had greatly enlarged the Arsenal in the wake of the second Venetian–Genoese war, bringing it under the command of an 'admiral', who served as general manager over several hundred workers. The whole plant had the structure of a big manufacture, with strict internal division of labour under the unified despotic authority and administration of the representatives of the Commune: a hierarchical structure was formed comprising directors, foremen, masters, skilled and unskilled workers and apprentices.[15]

After Dante Alighieri's visit to the Arsenal in 1320, "the biggest and busiest spectacle of industrial activity that Dante ever saw, or could have seen, the biggest of the time" (Lane 1973: 163), he depicted hell in his *Divine Comedy* as a place similar to the crowded and oppressive landscape of the Arsenal. He wrote:

> As in the Arsenal of the Venetians
> Boils in the winter the tenacious pitch
> To smear their unsound vessels o'er again,
>
> For sail they cannot; and instead thereof
> One makes his vessel new, and one recaulks
> The ribs of that which many a voyage has made;
>
> One hammers at the prow, one at the stern,
> This one makes oars, and that one cordage twists,
> Another mends the mainsail and the mizzen[16];

Such a manufacturing organization was unparalleled at the time. It is interesting to note that both in Byzantium and Genoa, shipyards were still organized on an artisanal level.[17] The majority of the Arsenal workers, about 75%, belonged to three guilds, those of shipwrights, caulkers and oarmakers; the rest belonged to smaller guilds (Davis 2009: 7). All these guilds "spoke for employees – and to that extent resembled labor unions" (Lane 1973: 106). The Arsenal workers, the *arsenalloti*, although receiving low wages – no higher than those of low-level crew members of a ship – were notable for their increased 'patriotism', for their eagerness to take up arms to protect the Commune from external or internal threats. This stance was rooted, among parameters mostly ideological in character (see also Chapter 12), in the guaranteed employment and pay system provided to them by the state.[18]

The loyalty of the arsenalotti and their 'political' engagement in favour of Venice's social order is interpreted by Robert C. Davis as being a manifestation of their not belonging to the working class. He writes:

> The arsenalotti never became a working class. Rather than experience a sense of alienation from their workplace, they ran it themselves; far from being marginalized, they became thoroughly integrated into the ruling order of the Republic, to the extent of gaining a stake in the well-being of its patrician regime. This study has operated on the assumption that these shipbuilders derived their distinctive character as much from their civil role as from their workplace, and that they thus cannot be approached in isolation from the larger context of Venetian society.
>
> (Davis 2009: 7)

However, as already discussed in Chapter 7, it is not any subjective "sense of alienation", but the objective incorporation of labourers into a set of social relations that defines a class (see also Milios 2000; Milios and Economakis 2011). As Marx demonstrates, manufacture is a form of capitalist production which entails on the one hand capitalist authority and management, and on the other the "collective" worker, that is, the working class, but also wage-earners belonging to the new petty bourgeoisie – of "officers (managers), and sergeants (foremen, overseers)" (Marx 1887: 232).

> In manufacture [...] the collective working organism is a form of existence of capital. The mechanism that is made up of numerous individual detail labourers belongs to the capitalist. Hence, the productive power resulting from a combination of labours appears to be the productive power of capital. Manufacture proper [...] creates a hierarchic gradation of the workmen themselves.
>
> (Marx 1887: 248)

The 'admiral' of the Arsenal, as "personified capital, functioning in the production process simply as the bearer of capital" (Marx 1991: 958), headed the rank of managers that appropriated the surplus value produced by the collective worker.

The Arsenal was not the only large Venetian manufacture in the fourteenth century. Next to it stood the Tana, the state-owned cordage manufacture which "received for sortage and taxation all the hemp or cordage brought to Venice" (Lane 1966: 269). In the fourteenth century, three qualities of cordage were produced in the Tana, each for different types of ships, under the strict supervision of commissioned state officials.[19] As in the case of the Arsenal,

> Many laborers worked together there in co-operation under centralized direction and an imposed discipline.
>
> (Lane 1966: 270)

The workers were paid by piece wages. Masters were not accompanied by family members as they were in their workshops, and if they brought in their apprentices, the latter remained under the supervision of Tana officials and foremen, and not under that of their own masters. As a measure of 'social policy', unskilled workers were selected by rotation from a list of people interested in working, subject to approval by the heads of the Tana. To inspect and contain inappropriate behaviour of workers, a special body of officers was formed.[20]

Even before the development and expansion of the Arsenal, another large state-owned manufacture, having been in operation with over a hundred workers since the thirteenth century, was the mint, which was called the Zecca. As with the Tana, it was hierarchically organized, divided into several departments according to the coins being produced, each department having its own workers, weighers and inspectors. The head of the mint, acting as general manager, was responsible for safeguarding the materials used in the production process and for the quality of the coins. He was assisted by a number of accountants and other officials. Prior to 1284, only silver coins were minted, as the Byzantine golden hyperpyra were likely still in use (Braudel 1979: 132). Thereafter, golden Venetian ducati were produced.

Apart from the large, state-owned manufactures, a number of private artisan workshops were progressively enlarged, attaining the character of small or medium manufacturing establishments, as, for example, in printing,[21] metal processing or glass and mirror production in the area of Murano. By the late fourteenth century, a steadily growing part of Venice's middle bourgeoisie and spurious bourgeoisie were being transformed into capitalists.

10.3.3 The proletarianization of seamen

As discussed in Chapter 9, until the end of the thirteenth century, salary-remunerated seamen could not be regarded as wage labourers in the sense that they also participated in merchant expeditions as 'partners' of their taskmasters, shipowners or captains (being thus 'fellow merchants' or stakeholders in piratic booty as well).

This situation changed rapidly after the second Genoese war[22] and the plague. As already mentioned, the building of the new Arsenal during this period brought the vast majority of Venetian merchant ships not only under state regulation and control, but also gradually under state ownership:

> By 1330 the government was no longer interested in having galleys privately built.
>
> (Lane 1966: 224)

> [...] in the first part of the fifteenth century [...] the merchant galleys were almost all owned by the commune and chartered by annual auctions for private operation.
>
> (op.cit.: 199)

This gradual 'nationalization' of Venice's merchant fleet was not associated with a conflict between state authority and 'private enterprise'. As explained, the very configuration of the Venetian ruling class entailed a close intertwining of money-begetting private activities with state power and state control.

> [...] in Venice there was no separation between a class of business executives and a class of government bureaucrats. The same individuals operated the fleets whether they did so separately [...] or by common action [...], on behalf of private partnerships or on behalf of the commune.
>
> (Lane 1966: 216)

As maritime trade was Venice's main economic activity, with "cargoes often worth 100,000 ducats per galley" (Lane 1973: 338), seamen were the largest group of Venetian labourers, comprising around one-fourth of the city's labour. In the mid-fourteenth century, a typical galley had a crew of 200 men, 175 of whom were oarsmen. A state-chartered merchant convoy to the Levant or to Flanders utilized a crew of nearly 3,500 seamen, out of whom around 3,000 were oarsmen.[23]

At the end of the thirteenth century, major innovations were introduced in shipping. The portolan chart, introduced in the 1270s probably by Pisans, and the compass, also invented at the end of the thirteenth century, both opened up new possibilities in maritime travel. Early in the fourteenth century, Venetian artisans became the most famous producers of portolan charts. To the innovations of the period belonged double-entry bookkeeping, introduced at the beginning of the fourteenth century, which greatly improved the management of maritime ventures. "Bookkeeping and arithmetic [...] were taught in Venice by pedagogues called 'masters of the abacus'" (Lane 1973: 141).

State ownership of merchant ships, which were auctioned off to money-owners for private operation, enabled the shaping of state policies aimed at reducing protection costs (see Chapter 9), the subsidizing of Venetian maritime travel,[24] the implementation of measures of 'social policy' in favour of impoverished members of the Venetian nobility,[25] and, above all, the management of the state budget by increasing state revenues via the setting of freight rates,[26] customs duties and tax farming, as well as via the reduction of expenses through numerous cost-saving regulations and practices.

State policies aimed at raising state revenues and balancing the communal budget were of vital importance for the Venetian state due to the enormous war expenditures of the period, which were temporarily compensated for by forced loans paid by the Venetian rich (see the next section).

Soon after the Second Genoese War, and especially after the devastating consequences of the plague, the Venetian Senate, in an effort to farm taxes and duties from all maritime commercial activities, forbade oarsmen and other low- and medium-level crew members to trade their own merchandise, thus leaving wages as their only source of revenue. Protests by seamen in the early fifteenth century, in the midst of a new phase of wars (see Chapter 11), resulted in an exception from this prohibition, but to a level hardly approaching a few months' wages.

> When customs officials began seizing cottons brought to Venice by seamen among their clothes, the Senate allayed protest by decreeing in 1414 that each sailor could have a customs exemption of 10 ducats.
>
> (Lane 1973: 342)

Such exceptions did not hinder the transition from 'profit sailing' to 'wage sailing' – the creation of a maritime proletariat.

By the fourteenth century,

> Venice had long ago left behind the egalitarian and non specialized organization of commerce that was typical of Europe in the early medieval period and was one of the first to move beyond profit sailing – where all on board shared in the profits of a successful voyage – to wage sailing, where sailors received a fixed wage. The professionalization of commerce was under way as early as the fourteenth century when the declining use of the commenda went hand in hand with the decline in the role of the part-time investor. As the role of the occasional investor diminished, a clearer line developed between merchant and nonmerchant.
>
> (Greene 2000: 169)

The *commenda*, a financial form appropriate for the contractual money-begetting mode of production, faded away. New financial instruments emerged, suitable for large-scale trade and capitalist entrepreneurship (such as the *maona*, deposit banking system, etc., see below); the *commenda* was restricted to a role of small-scale domestic finance:

> Having been ousted from its great role in international trade, [...] most contracts of *colleganze* in the fourteenth century were loans to shopkeepers

and craftsmen or to banks for use "in Rialto", as the expression went. [...]
In practice the loans were generally renewed at some standard rate, 8% in
1330 and 5% after 1340.

(Lane 1966: 60)

The social condition of the vast majority of seamen was reduced to that of
low-paid workers, parallel to the fast diversification of categories of labour on
ships and the polarization of salaries between officers and specialized seamen
on the one hand, and the mass of oarsmen and other 'inferior' forms of labour
on the other.

To be an oarsman, a *galeotto*, as a regular means of livelihood became a sign
of inferiority, but it was this low kind of labor that was most in demand.
When the state was chartering merchant galleys for voyages to Flanders,
the Black Sea, and Cyprus-Armenia, a half-dozen or more for each voyage, these ships required nearly 3,000 oarsmen [...]. With the industrial
opportunities within the city expanding, the rewards and working conditions on the galley bench were not such as to attract that many Venetians.

(Lane 1973: 167–168)

The wage of an ordinary oarsman in the fourteenth century was less than 25
ducats a year, comparable to that of unskilled hewers of stone, whereas that
of ordinary bowmen approached 30 ducats a year. Mates (*nauclerii*) were paid
45–50, and galley masters 90–100 ducats a year. One hundred ducats a year
was also the average pay of a foreman ship carpenter in Venice's Arsenal (Lane
1966: 267; Lane 1973: 333).[27]

Policy measures and other changes in the fourteenth century thus led to
the formation of a large proletariat on ships. The capitalist mode of production became the dominant exploitation form on Venetian ships and the spurious bourgeoisie of shipowners and merchants was transformed into a (fraction
of the) capitalist class.

A major consequence of the proletarianization of oarsmen and ordinary
seamen was, as already mentioned, a reduced supply of maritime labour.
To cope with the increasing need of enlisting low-level crew members, the
Venetian state resorted to various methods of recruiting forced labour: press
gangs organized by local Venetian authorities brought in forced wage labour
from Crete and Dalmatia; at the same time, prisoners of war were enlisted
as galley slaves on the rowers' benches, along with slaves imported from the
Black Sea. Alongside capitalist exploitation, the money-begetting slave mode
of production was being revived on Venetian ships.

As discussed in Chapter 7, the emergence of capitalism coincides with "the
'inclusion' of direct personal coercion into the economic relation as such";
coercion then acquires the form of 'free labour'. In all instances where a lack
of 'free labour' exists, forms of coerced labour, and above all the money-
begetting slave mode of production, reappear as a 'necessary' manifestation
of 'entrepreneurship'.

10.3.4 *Public debt and capitalist finance*

The Venetian–Genoese wars generated huge military expenditures for the Venetian state, which could not be financed by ordinary means of revenue raising (indirect taxes, customs duties, fines, etc.). Starting in the midst of the first Genoese war, in 1262, the Venetian Commune resorted to forcing Venice's richest inhabitants to finance military expenses by way of forced loans.

According to the system introduced, the wealth of each inhabitant was assessed by state authorities and the 'rich' or well-off, that is, those with property valued at more than 300 ducats, were called to subscribe as lenders to the state. People who were obliged to subscribe contributed 24% of their wealth to the public debt. However, properties were assessed "at about one third of real value" (Lane 1973: 184), meaning that well-off inhabitants contributed only about 8% of their known wealth to the public debt. The only wealth assessment that survives, one from 1379, gives us a picture of those Venetians who were 'rich' or well-off in the second half of the fourteenth century: of the 2,128 people assessed that year, one-eighth of all heads of Venice's households, 1,211 were nobles and 917 commoners.

> Outstanding rich were 91 nobles and 26 commoners, with assessments indicating that their real wealth ranged from 10,000 to 150,000 ducats.
> (Lane 1973: 151)

By introducing the system of forced loans, the state created a Bond Office (Camera degli Imprestiti) to administer the funded public debt, later known as the Monte Vecchio, which paid all lenders an interest of 5% per year in two tranches. At the same time, a secondary market was created to allow holders of state bonds to sell them to other 'investors'.

A financial market thus emerged, as the bonds of the Monte Vecchio became an 'investment option' for many money-owners. In parallel, speculation with state bonds flourished, as their price fluctuated with changing economic and geopolitical conjunctures. As Marx stresses, a system of state debt paves the way for the ascent of capitalism, and Venice's ruling class of money begetters was the first to introduce this system:

> The system of public credit, i.e., of national debts, whose origin we discover in Genoa and Venice as early as the Middle Ages, took possession of Europe generally during the manufacturing period. [...] The public debt becomes one of the most powerful levers of primitive accumulation. As with the stroke of an enchanter's wand, it endows barren money with the power of breeding and thus turns it into capital [...]. The state creditors actually give nothing away, for the sum lent is transformed into public bonds, easily negotiable, which go on functioning in their hands just as so much hard cash would. But further, [...] the national debt has given rise to joint-stock companies, to dealings in negotiable effects of all kinds, and to agiotage, in a word to stock-exchange gambling and the modern bankocracy.
> (Marx 1887: 535–536)

The Venetian system of public debt functioned nearly without friction for more than a century, attracting money from abroad, with the state always being able to pay fixed interest to bondholders and keep the overall debt level within manageable limits. In practice, Venice had created a reliable and stable system of 'national debt' more than three centuries before the British, and on this basis developed a private financial market as well (see below).[28]

The size of the Venetian funded debt rose from 5,770 ducats in 1255 (before the introduction of the system of forced loans) to 154 thousand ducats in 1279, following the first Genoese war. It increased to 1.1 million ducats in 1313, in the aftermath of the second Genoese war, but then went down to 423 thousand ducats in 1343, as the government was rebuying bonds, especially in times when prices were falling.[29] During the fourth Genoese war, the public debt surged to 3.27 million in 1379, and to 4.73 million ducats in 1381 (Lane 1966: 88).

The fourth Genoese war and the siege of Venice by enemy forces in the years 1379–1380 created a major financial crisis in Venice. The state introduced levies of 107% of the assessed wealth of its well-off inhabitants; however, not being able to pay interest, it defaulted to its bondholders for the first time since the foundation of the Monte Vecchio; in the secondary market, bond prices crashed and interest rates soared.

> The system of forced loans which had worked well in the past turned into a disaster for those families with large holdings of government bonds. In a couple of years, the Monte Vecchio burgeoned from about 3 million to about 5 million ducats. The forced levies were 107 percent of assessments, which meant one quarter to one third percent of known wealth. Family accumulations of government bonds and even real estate were dumped in the market in order to have the cash to pay these levies. For the first time, there was a catastrophic drop in the market price. From 92.5 in 1375, it fell to 18 in 1381, when interest was suspended. Real estate prices also fell drastically, as the government condemned the property of defaulters.
> (Lane 1973: 196)

Amidst the major economic and political turmoil, speculation reached unprecedented levels. Money holders, even among Venice's inhabitants with property valued at below the assessment limit, and who were thus not obliged to contribute to the public debt, enriched themselves when the financial crisis began softening after 1382 by buying large quantities of cheap state bonds with high yields,[30] in anticipation of rising bond prices. The same scenario was repeated fifty years later, when Venice waged invasive wars on Lombardy (see Chapter 11).

The Venetian public debt and financial markets gradually recovered after the end of the fourth Genoese war. Interest payment to bondholders "was resumed in 1382 but made subject to withholding taxes that gave 4 per cent to some categories of taxpayers and 3 per cent to others" (Lane 1966: 87).

In their investigation of major financial disasters in historical perspective, Hoffman et al. reach the conclusion that crucial to "surviving large losses" and re-establishing financial balance is the existence of numerous middle classes who can borrow money against collateral (real estate or business), and who are also in a position to participate in the public debt market by purchasing bonds. This was definitely the case with Venice in the late fourteenth century, when a mass of medium- and high-level state officials, well-off artisans and manufacturers, small- and medium-sized merchants, foremen, shopkeepers, etc. speculated on the public debt in the months following the fourth Genoese war, thereby contributing to its recovery. By 1402, the outstanding public debt went down to 3.6 million ducats and bond prices had increased to 66% of their face value (Lane 1966: 87).[31]

> It is no surprise that the earliest financial centers (Venice and Genoa in the Middle Ages, Antwerp and Amsterdam in the sixteenth and seventeenth centuries) were cities in which members of what we would call the middle class – merchants – exercised considerable political influence. Financial intermediaries such as bankers were influential too, but their concern was serving the middle-class merchants. The middle class in the early financial centers thus wielded enough power to get the government to support financial markets.
>
> (Hoffman et al. 2007: 183)

Trade revived,[32] as did private finance, which had already been boosted by the early introduction of funded public debt in Venice. Private banking establishments accepting deposits and providing loans were developed at the turn of the thirteenth to the fourteenth century, mainly by the numerous dealers in foreign money sited in the Rialto area.[33] In the fourteenth century, Venetian private banks introduced the practice of giro-banking, "an ingenious way to economize on coin" (Hoffman et al. 2007: 143) that allowed payments and offered credit by transferring deposits from one account (that of a client or of the bank itself) to another.[34] Consumer credit also developed in the same period: "loans to consumers were at a fixed rate and secured by collateral" (Lane 1966: 67).

Other forms of credit which had been rapidly developing since the early fourteenth century were bills of exchange (Lane 1973: 147 ff.), and *maonas*, which were the first forms of joint stock companies, initially developed by Genoese adventurers[35] in the fourteenth century, and soon after imitated by the Venetians in an effort to achieve monopolistic conditions in the maritime trade of certain commodities or trade on certain routes (Lane 1966: 50 ff.). Dealing in futures is also reported to have existed in the fourteenth century, whereas in the 1350s, "true insurance contracts began to appear, with premiums ranging between 15 and 20 per cent of the sum insured" (Ferguson 2008: 185). In the late fourteenth century, Venice's financial sphere had developed supreme, even compared to other economically advanced Italian city states of the period.

Italian commercial centres like [...] Pisa or nearby Florence proved to be fertile soil for [...] financial seeds. But it was above all Venice, more exposed than the others to Oriental influences, that became Europe's great lending laboratory. It is not coincidental that the most famous moneylender in Western literature was based in Venice.

(Ferguson 2008: 33)

The Venetian state repeatedly attempted to regulate private banking and finance, imposing and policing interest rate limits,[36] or in some cases restricting certain financial activities, even at times pretending to comply with papal decretals against 'usury';[37] however, these attempts were only partially effective. The expansion of private finance was only reversed by financial meltdowns, most of which were related to political events such as the fourth Venetian–Genoese war, which led to the collapse of the public debt market between 1379 and 1381.

***

By the end of the fourteenth century, a crucial transformation of Venetian society had taken place, and capitalist social relations of wage-earning proletarians subsumed under capitalist rule prevailed in the major branches of the economy: the sectors of fabricating material goods, on the one hand, with the creation of gigantic – for the (historical) period – state-owned capitalist manufactures, and the transformation of a contingent of masters' workshops into medium-scale capitalist enterprises; the sector of maritime trade on the other, with the proletarianization of the majority of seamen. Capitalist finance, boosted by the funded public debt, completed the picture of a society governed by the capital relation.

It was not a process of "transition from feudalism to capitalism", but rather the taking hold of an aleatory encounter between a state-organized precapitalist ruling class of money-owners and a proletariat rapidly emerging among the city's poor.

Notes

1 A new podestà of Constantinople, Ottaviano Quirino, was appointed by Venetian authorities in 1207.

2 State officials of various ranks and authorities constituted the colonial administration of Crete. At the top stood the Duke of Crete, who was elected by the Venetian Great Council for a limited period of time:

> the Duke and two consiliarii were at the top of the hierarchy and formed the local administration (regimen). The overall military administration was entrusted to the capitano of Candia, higher functionaries, the rectores, took charge of military and civil justice, while at the lowest administrative level were the castellani.
>
> (Maltezou 2006: 20)

The pre-existing Byzantine nobility of landowners succeeded in being incorporated into the Venetian system of administration after instigating a series of revolts of the local population:

> the local archondes, ignored by the Venetians at the beginning of their occupation, succeeded, thanks to the various rebellions, in obtaining recognition of their landholdings and their former privileges, and, moreover, secured their integration in the Venetian system and equal economic status with the foreign feudatories.
>
> (ibid.: 22)

3 Allaire Stallsmith aptly illustrates the nonfeudal character of agrarian relations in the Venetian colony of Crete:

> Whether the farm was called a feudum or a timar, the impact of the system on the peasant was much the same. The Venetians may have called the landholders feudatarii but, strictly speaking, their regime on Crete was not feudal, as the Venetian state did not delegate judicial and financial authority to the feudatories. Likewise, even though the classical Ottoman system in theory regarded all land as the possession of the sultan, who granted its use to his sipahis, these cavalrymen were not feudal lords, nor were their dependents serfs.
>
> (Stallsmith 2007: 151–152)

An opposing, and in my view unfounded, approach is formulated by Lujo Brentano: "The need to keep Crete and Corfu by war means, led the capitalists of Venice to introduce a feudal economic and social order in the above mentioned islands" (Brentano 1916: 46).

4 See also Vasiliev 1952: 569: "Another document of the same period testifies that the western conquerors continued to maintain the conquered population as formerly, exacting from them nothing more than they had been used to under the Greek emperors".

5 In the Latin Empire of Romania,

> [t]he importation of western feudalism implied a marked departure from Byzantine tradition, as it involved the disappearance of the state and the transfer of its authority and prerogatives to private hands. Privatization was one of the most fundamental expressions of the process of feudalization, and had important, long-lasting social implications.
>
> (Jacoby 1989: 3)

6 In 1276, a truce was signed in Constantinople between Venice and the Byzantine Empire (Nicol 1989: 198).

7 In 1284, Genoa conquered and sacked Pisa, clearly establishing her supremacy over the northwestern coasts of the Italian peninsula.

8 "At the end of the thirteenth century, after a long period of growth, western Europe entered a period of economic stagnation, and the era in which significant numbers of new men were able to become rich came to an end. Statistics for this economic crisis are difficult to come by, but Italy's coastal cities must have felt it immediately. What we can trace in this period is a change in the trade policy of Venice, which from 1315 on assumed an increasingly hostile attitude toward foreigners. Although Venice had relied on foreign capital to finance its war effort as recently as the Second Genoese War, it now rejected foreign influences. The provveditori di comun, a newly established authority, now required every merchant to prove his Venetian citizenship" (Bösch 2002: 82). On the European economic crisis of the period, see also Braudel (1979: 112).

9 An exception to this 'rule' was made in September 1381, just after the end of the fourth Genoese war (see below), when thirty additional families were granted hereditary membership in the Great Council (Lane 1979: 196).

10 "In 1305, the Great Council declared that those who had lived in the city for twenty-five years should receive citizenship and those who had been there for ten years should be permitted to stay. However, since only full citizens with the right de intus et extra were entitled to the city's trade privileges, the nobility had basically secured its commercial interests against competitors" (Bösch 2002: 83).

11 "[...] in 1322, the police were offered 2 grossi for each galeotto they could round up" (Lane 1973: 168).

12 "But what a reversal since the twelfth century when Venice supplied the men to defend the Byzantine Empire [...]. Now Venice was acting as paymaster and was depending heavily on Greeks and Catalans to fight Venice's battles" (Lane 1973: 177).

13 "The Revolt of St Tito differed from all previous revolts in one fundamental respect. For the first time, the Latin colonists initiated the uprising, and allied themselves with the Greeks of the island. Nowhere in the territories controlled by Venice had such an event occurred up to that time" (McKee 1994: 176).

14 "When draftees were ordered to man 16 galleys by signing on for the galleys of their choice, only enough for 6 galleys reported. The rest refused to go to the Naval Office to enroll" (Lane 1973: 192).

15 "[...] the central direction [...] of the Arsenal concentrated on keeping track of materials and testing the quality of the end product. [...] A group of masters totaling about thirty, with a separate foreman shipwright for each type, was considered not too big to be supervised by craft foremen [...]" (Lane 1973: 164).

16 Dante Alighieri (2008: 136). In Bertolt Brecht's *Life of Galileo*, Galilei Galileo says:

> My work in the great arsenal of Venice brought me into daily contact with draftsmen, architects and instrument makers. Those people taught me many new ways of doing things. They don't read books but they trust the testimony of their five senses, most of them without fear as to where it will lead them.
>
> (Brecht 2008: 24)

17 "One fact that argues against the existence of manufacturing enterprises in shipbuilding is that the small number of late Byzantine arsenals did not operate continuously and with the same level of quality; rather, craftsmen skilled in shipbuilding were only occasionally enlisted for modest fleet building programs. If funds flowed into urban production processes, it was probably only to maintain them at a given level, not to expand them to any significant extent" (Matschke 2002: 493). In Genoa, "[a] variety of specialized craftsmen transformed fabrics, iron, wood, and other material into sails, anchors, nails, and rope with which to build and equip ships" (van Doosselaere 2009: 89). One century later, in the 1470s, the Venetian Arsenal "became twice as large as it had been when its bustling crowds and dirt impressed Dante Alighieri" (Lane 1973: 362), numbering thousands of workers.

18 "[...] once enrolled in the [...] workforce pay roster, they could find paying work in the Arsenal whenever they should choose to do so. Even if they were too old, sick, or incompetent to do anything useful, the state guaranteed them their daily pay [...], as long as they managed to show up at the shipyards in the morning" (Davis 2009: 8).

19 In a declaration by the Venetian Senate in the 1330s, it is stated that "the manufacture of cordage in our house of the Tana [...] is the security of our galleys and ships and similarly of our sailors and capital" (cited in Lane 1966: 270).

20 "Moreover, here, as in the adjoining Arsenal, the congregation of so many workers in one place created a special police problem where economic rancor might be added to the normal incentives to stealing, quarrelling, and wilful destruction" (Lane 1966: 279).

21 "Heading a shop with perhaps as many as ten to fifteen persons [...] such master printers belonged to the class which I have called craftsmen-managers and which had always been relatively important in Venice" (Lane 1973: 317).

22 "Military demands or threats explain nearly all the instances of communal operation [...]" (Lane 1966: 215).

23 To each ship's crew belonged "20 to 30 'bowmen' among whom were included after 1460 cannoneers and then some arquebusiers" (Lane 1973: 338).

24 "In 1317 and 1318 private operators of Flanders were given a new form of subsidy, the use of state-owned galleys, rent free" (Lane 1966: 209).

25 "[...] the Senate created the institution 'bowman of the quarterdeck' [...] to assist poorer members of the nobility to recoup their fortunes. Adding to their salaries what they made on their ventures, a noble bowman could gain 100 to 200 ducats on a voyage" (Lane 1973: 344).

26 "The rates set by the Senate for the voyages to the east were sufficiently high so that auctioning galleys for those voyages yielded the government more than enough to pay the cost of building and outfitting the galleys" (Lane 1973: 339).

27 "For comparison it may be noted that writers who boasted of Venice's wealth considered nobles as well off only if they had income of 1,000 ducats a year and counted as really rich those with 10,000 a year" (Lane 1973: 333).

28 "Much of the innovation in western Europe has taken place in a small number of urban financial centers: Venice and Genoa in the Middle Ages; Antwerp and Amsterdam in the sixteenth and seventeenth centuries; and London, Paris, and Berlin in the 1700s and 1800s" (Hoffman et al. 2007: 129).

29 "By their system of forced loans, they could raise the money to hire fleets without straining the resources of the rich" (Lane 1973: 177). "Instead of making any repayments of old issues, the government provided for a sinking fund to buy in bonds when prices were low" (Lane 1973: 184).

30 "Now, if you buy a government bond while war is raging you are obviously taking a risk, the risk that the state in question may not pay your interest. On the other hand, remember that the interest is paid on the face value of the bond, so if you can buy a 5 per cent bond at just 10 per cent of its face value you can earn a handsome yield of 50 per cent. In essence, you expect a return proportional to the risk you are prepared to take. [...] It is no coincidence that the year 1499, when Venice was fighting both on land in Lombardy and at sea against the Ottoman Empire, saw a severe financial crisis as bonds crashed in value and interest rates soared" (Ferguson 2008: 73).

31 "But there had occurred in the meantime a big turnover in the ownerships of bonds and of real estate" (Lane 1973: 197).

32 "The main concern was to set in motion the currents of trade [...] special attention was paid to the transport of the precious merchandise yielding high profits and customs duties, and for this purpose merchant galleys were again sent to Romania, to Beirut, to Alexandria, and to Flanders" (op.cit.).

33 "It is tolerably clear that private banking in Venice began as an adjunct of the business of the campsores, or dealers in foreign moneys. In a city having a great and varied trade with many countries, these dealers necessarily held an important place, close to the stream of payments which was constantly in motion. [...] In an act of September 24, 1318, however, [...] the receipt of deposits by the campsores is recognized as an existing practice, and provision is made for better security for the benefit of depositors. [...] [S]omewhere between 1270 and 1318

the money-changers of Venice were becoming bankers, by a method similar to that by which the same class of men in Amsterdam a couple of centuries later, and later still the London goldsmiths, became bankers" (Dunbar 1892: 10–11).

> Dealing in money, therefore, i.e. trade in the money commodity, first develops out of international trade. As soon as various national coinages exist, merchants [...] convert coins of various kinds into uncoined pure silver or gold as world money. Hence the exchange business, which should be viewed as one of the spontaneous bases of the modern money trade. From this there developed exchange banks, in which silver (or gold) functions as world money – known as bank or commercial money - as distinct from currency [...]. In England, goldsmiths still functioned as bankers for the greater part of the seventeenth century.
> (Marx 1991: 433–434)

34 "[T]heir main function was to write transfers and thus to rotate (girate) credits from one account to the other" (Lane 1973: 147).

35 The island of Chios had been held since 1346 by "a commercial trading company of Genoese, the Maona of the Justiniani. [...] It is the first example we find recorded in history [...] of a mercantile company of shareholders [...] exercising all the duties of a sovereign" (Finlay 2013: 70–71). The Maona of the Justiniani (or Giustiniani) on Chios comprised a capital of 2,300 shares, each of which had a value of 100 genuini or Genoese liras (Zolotas 1924: 329).

36 "In the 1380s and 1390s Jewish bankers in Venice were rumoured to be falsifying the records by claiming to have parted with twice as much money as they had really lent, so that interest rates were double as they appeared to be" (Pullan 2001: 68).

37 "A legal basis for these interest-paying deposits was laid in 1301 when a commission drew up regulations to prevent four kinds of illicit deals in money: in selling exchange, in buying or selling goods on credit, in dealing in futures, and in placing money at interest (ad presam). In all four cases the exceptions were important [...]. Money could be placed at interest only with a bank, or other establishment which was well known as generally accepting money at interest [...] No doubt these rules only sanctioned and perhaps restricted practices already current in the thirteenth century. Many contracts and court records show that these practices continued in the next century" (Lane 1966: 65).

Part III

After the encounter took hold

The reproduction of capitalism on an expanded scale

11 Venice alongside the new capitalist powers

11.1 Venice and capitalism in historiography and Marxist literature

As stated in the Introduction, the question of the genesis of a social system concerns the emergence and consolidation of a specific social structure, and the taking hold of its constituent elements in a historically unique configuration of class domination and exploitation. In Part II (especially Chapters 9 and 10), I have illustrated how capitalism as a social system emerged and dominated Venetian society in the late fourteenth century. The entire process evolved through a number of historical contingencies that transformed the pre-existing monetized, pre-capitalist society into one where the capitalist mode of production *prevailed*, by converting on the one hand a mass of labourers into wage-earning proletarians, and on the other the money-begetting taskmasters and holders of wealth into capitalist manufacturers, merchants and ship-owners. To my knowledge and understanding, this transformation of labourers into proletarians, and thus of money begetters into capitalists, took place in Venice before anywhere else, in the midst of a crisis inflicted by war.[1]

Within this very same process of transformation, all other fundamental constituent elements of capitalism as a social system took shape (see also Chapter 1): the monetization of the economy and society; formation of big businesses in all major sectors of the economy through the concentration of capital, with the subsequent dissociation of the capitalist from the labour process as such; capitalist competition within the social formation, eventually leading to recurrent redistributions of capital and wealth among major economic actors, despite measures of protectionism and monopolistic regulations against rival states; the development of a capitalist financial sphere on the foundations laid by the expanding public debt and the secondary bond market that accompanied it; the shaping of a state capable of expressing the interests of the Venetian aggregate social capital and a corresponding 'laic' ('republican') ideological framework promoting popular consensus to power and thus social cohesion (see also Chapter 12).

Venice prevailed as an independent state in spite of all kinds of threats until 1797, when she was subjugated to Napoleon's armies. As I will argue in this chapter, Venice remained a capitalist social formation until the very last days of her existence, despite the fact that her prominence in European economy and politics had been losing ground since the sixteenth century, as capitalist social relations spread throughout Western Europe and new economic and military powers emerged.

It is clear, of course, that Venetian capitalism at the end of the eighteenth century was in many aspects different from its earlier form at the end of the fourteenth century, and, by the same token, different from present-day capitalism. However, now as then, it is and was a *capitalist social system* that we are referring to, a system possessing identical structural features shaped around the capital–labour relationship.

What differentiates my analysis from other approaches that stress the early development of capitalism in Venice is my distinction between capitalist and non-capitalist forms of money-begetting 'entrepreneurial' activities (as, for example, the money-begetting slave mode of production – see Chapter 7 – or the contractual money-begetting mode of production, endeavours of the Venetian spurious bourgeoisie – see Chapter 10 – the latter being common in other Italian city states as well). The most pronounced difference between capitalist and non-capitalist money-begetting activities is the "taking hold" of the wage relationship as the main form of remuneration of labourers subjected to the rule of money-owners, or, in other words, the incorporation of "personal coercion into the economic relation as such" (see Chapter 10). The authors to whom I refer conflate all forms of money-begetting 'entrepreneurship' and identify them with capitalist activity. As a result, they detect the emergence of capitalism in the twelfth or thirteenth centuries (or even earlier) in nearly all 'commercial' city states on the Italian peninsula.

An example of this is the case with Fernand Braudel, who diagnoses the existence of capitalism in the thirteenth century despite the fact that he himself traces the difference between the "enterprise [which] might be on the way to being capitalist, but it was not capitalist in the proper sense" (Braudel 1982: 251, see Chapter 7). In his famous oeuvre *Civilization and Capitalism, 15th–18th Century*, he writes:

> There is no doubt in my mind: on this point Sombart is right. Thirteenth century and a fortiori fourteenth-century Florence was a capitalist city, whatever meaning one attaches to the word. [...] What is less understandable is his basing his entire analysis on a single city: Florence (Oliver C. Cox has put up an equally convincing case for Venice[2] [...]).
>
> (Braudel 1982: 578)[3]

Frederic C. Lane, in his numerous works on Venetian history, argues that on the one hand Venice "was the first to become capitalistic",[4] and on the other that capitalism had been dominant in the states of the Italian peninsula since "the twelfth and thirteenth centuries". His argument derives from his 'broad' conceptualization of capitalism as a money-begetting activity based on a prior advanced investment.

> A more vigorous, more general growth in population and trade occurred [...] during the so-called Age of Faith in the twelfth and thirteenth centuries. For the Italian city-states the so-called Age of Faith was in fact also an age of capitalism, if we mean by capitalism a society so organized that men can make money by investing their capital.
>
> (Lane 1966: 521)

Jairus Banaji (2010) bases his analysis on the concepts of Marxian analysis (see Chapter 7). There are points where he seems to reach conclusions similar to mine:

> By the fourteenth century, Venice was an economy *dominated* by capital, with the same families controlling trade, transport, finance, and industry. More or less the same was true of Genoa in the fifteenth century.
>
> (Banaji 2010: 260)

However, on other points, he adopts a more ambiguous approach, similar to that of the authors already mentioned in this chapter, seemingly identifying capitalism with other money-begetting economic activities in existence since the twelfth century:

> As a broad periodisation, I would suggest that we see the twelfth to fifteenth centuries as the period of the growth of capitalism in Europe ('Mediterranean capitalism') and the sixteenth to eighteenth centuries as the period of Company-capitalism, marked by more brutal methods of accumulation and competition.
>
> (Banaji 2010: 257–58)[5]

The merit of Banaji's approach is, among other considerations, that it critically distances itself from a long Marxist tradition that identifies mercantile capitalism with 'feudalism'.

> And it seems logically absurd to me to imagine that a history of capitalism can be written using a notion of commercial capital that was developed by Marx for the kind of capitalist economy that evolved only in the nineteenth century. In practice, of course, this is largely what has tended to happen. The most striking case of this is Maurice Dobb, who [...] sought to understand origins [of capitalism] in terms of factors peculiar to England. There is a methodological impasse at work here, a staggering confusion of history and logic that accounts for the singular inability of Marxists influenced by Dobb to confront the past of capitalism beyond

such manifestly untenable assertions as: "The capitalist system was born in England. Only in England did capitalism emerge, in the early modern period, as an indigenous national economy".

((Wood 1991: 1); Banaji 2010: 256)

I have explicitly dealt with this Marxist tradition, which Banaji, among others,[6] aptly criticizes, in Chapter 5. At this point, I will not reiterate those arguments but will briefly and critically refer to some conclusions of this tradition in respect to Venice and the other maritime republics of the Italian peninsula.

Perry Anderson, when discussing the role of the absolutist state in the process of 'transition from feudalism to capitalism', introduces the idea of the 'failure' of the Italian states to be part of this transition: despite the fact that they introduced state structures and policies pertaining to absolutism, they could not produce the 'feudal national' state indispensable for the transition due to the 'premature development' of their 'mercantile capital'.

> The Absolutist State arose in the era of the Renaissance. A great many of its essential techniques – both administrative and diplomatic – were pioneered in Italy. It is therefore necessary to ask: why did Italy itself never achieve a national Absolutism? [...] The critical determinant of the failure to produce a national Absolutism should be sought elsewhere. It lies precisely in the premature development of *mercantile capital* in the North Italian cities, which prevented the emergence of a powerful re-organized *feudal* State at the national level. It was the wealth and vitality of the Lombard and Tuscan Communes which defeated the most serious effort to establish a unified feudal monarchy which could have provided the basis for a later Absolutism.
>
> (Anderson 1974-b: 143)

In Chapter 5, I criticized the idea of the 'feudal' foundations of the absolutist state. In the subsequent chapter, I will review the notions of 'national feudalism' and 'premature mercantile capital' that Anderson introduces. At this point, I will focus on the persistence of these ideas and, above all, their conclusion that capitalism on the Italian peninsula 'failed', a conclusion often reiterated in more recent Marxist literature.

Louis Althusser formulates the 'failure of capitalism' thesis on the basis of Marx's theoretical scheme of the encounter ([coming] "face to face and into contact", in Marx's words) between the money-owner and the proletarian, arguing that this encounter never took hold:

> We can go even further, and suppose *that this encounter occurred several times in history before taking hold in the West*, but for lack of an element or a suitable arrangement of the elements, failed to 'take'. Witness the thirteenth-century and fourteenth-century Italian states of the Po valley, where there were certainly men who owned money, technology and

energy (machines driven by the hydraulic power of the river) as well as manpower (unemployed artisans), but where the phenomenon nevertheless failed to 'take hold'. What was lacking here was doubtless (perhaps – this is a hypothesis) that which Machiavelli was desperately seeking in the form of his appeal for a national state: *a domestic market* capable of absorbing what might have been produced.

(Althusser 2006: 198)

Althusser essentially reintroduces an extreme version of the traditional under-consumptionist 'home market question', which constituted the basic tenet of Narodnik Marxism in the late nineteenth century, and which Lenin so fiercely criticized (see Chapter 3).

The same under-consumptionist approach is formulated by Robert Brenner:

Correlatively, the backward, largely peasant agriculture appears to have largely cut off the possibility of developing a significant home market in Italy itself.

(Brenner 1976: 67)[7]

Henry Heller, in the spirit of Anderson, also seems to believe in a "political failure" of 'merchant capitalists', substantiated in relation to a supposedly already-existing 'Italy'!

Ultimately Anderson's suggestion that the failure of Italian capitalism was political seems conclusive. The *inability of Italy to unify itself* into an early modern territorial state set the limits to the development of its capitalism. No doubt this failure was connected to the entrenched localized power of these same merchant capitalists. Successive attempts to carry out such a unifying revolution from above by emperors or despots during the late medieval period were defeated. Failure blocked the emergence of a national market and of a national political entity that could *defend Italy militarily* and economically against foreign invasion.

(Heller 2011: 60, emphasis added)

The most zealous proponent of the non-productive and non-capitalist character of the Venetian and other economies of the Italian peninsula is, of course, Ellen Meiksins Wood.

In a non-capitalist market, where trade was not driven by price competition and competitive production but depended on direct extra-economic command of markets and success in extra-economic – particularly military – rivalry, commerce was more of a zero-sum game, where one city's gain was another's loss.

(Wood 2003: 59; see also Wood 2002: 48;
Wood 2003: 54, 56–57, 65–66)

The authors that I have cited above overlook the tens of thousands of seamen on Venetian (and also Genoese, Pisan, etc.) ships, and so do not wonder about the class domination and exploitation relations to which they were subjected; they equally do not consider the thousands of wage labourers in the Arsenal, the mint and the large private printing, weaving, glassmaking and other enterprises in Venice, Florence, etc.; it is only on this basis that they can argue that capitalism appeared as an exclusive phenomenon of the 'English countryside', neglecting the fact that since the end of the sixteenth century, the Venetian economy had been dominated by manufacturing, and not maritime trade, as was the case in the preceding centuries. It is even more erroneous, however, for a Marxist to resurrect the ancient mercantilist doctrine that trade be "a zero-sum game, where one city's gain was another's loss".[8] Historical evidence shows that the major city states of the Italian peninsula all got richer during the High Middle Ages and the Renaissance!

11.2 Venice's supremacy in the fifteenth century

In the late fourteenth and the first three decades of the fifteenth centuries, Venice took advantage of Genoa's internal split and aggressively increased its colonial territory in the eastern Mediterranean and the Aegean Seas, Dalmatia and Istria (the *Stato da Màr*), and on the Italian mainland (the *Domini di Terraferma*).[9]

Both the *Stato da Màr* and the *Domini di Terraferma* were ruled by Venetian officials as colonial territories that safeguarded Venice's military and economic pre-eminence (see also Chapter 10).[10] "Only occasionally did Venice see its terraferma subjects other than as foreigners" (Law 1992: 166). However, as time passed, the Venetian rule in both regions attained a more "confederate" rather than "colonial" character (O'Connell 2009, see also Chapter 12; for Crete, see Holton 2006).

It is characteristic that in the Navigation Act passed by the Venetian Senate in 1602 (fifty-nine years before the first English Navigation Act), Greek-speaking sailors from the *Stato da Màr* are considered to be Venetians, so that the requirement of having no less than two-thirds of each ship's crew manned by Venetians could be maintained.

Up until the mid-fifteenth century, "the world-economy centred on Venice" (Braudel 1984: 124). The total Venetian budget in the 1420s (if one takes into consideration the territories of *Stato da Màr* and the *Terraferma*) was equal to or even larger than that of the emerging territorial states of England, Spain or France, despite the fact that the new territorial states comprised a population more than ten times that of the Venetian Empire. Fernand Braudel formulates his comparison of the Venetian and French state budgets of the period as follows:

> To the revenue of the Signoria (750,000 ducats) we should add those of the Terraferma (464,000) and of the empire – the Mar or sea as it was

called (376,000). The total (1,615,000 ducats) sets the Venetian budget in the front rank of budgets in Europe – and even this is not quite the whole story. For if the population of the entire Venetian complex (city, Terraferma and empire) is estimated at about one and a half million maximum, and that of France under Charles VI as fifteen million (for the purposes of a very rough and ready calculation), then the latter, with ten times as many inhabitants, ought to have had a budget ten times that of Venice – viz. 16 million ducats. The paltry size of the French budget, one million, serves to underline the overwhelming superiority of the city-states compared to the 'territorial' economies and allows one to imagine what this early concentration of capital must have signified for a single city.

(Braudel 1984: 120)

The picture started to change some time in the mid-fifteenth century. The conquest of Constantinople by the Ottomans in 1453, the end of the Hundred Years' War in the same year and the resulting political and military consolidation of France and England as territorial states, the inauguration of the Tudor period in England in 1485, the rise of Portugal and Spain and the colonization of the Americas, all established a new military, political and economic landscape in Europe, shifting political-military power relations in favour of the new absolutist states of the Atlantic (Portugal, Spain, France and England), while the centre of capitalist economic production gradually moved to the North (Bruges, Antwerp, Amsterdam, London, etc.). From the late sixteenth century, as Venetian commercial supremacy was challenged by new competitors, a restructuring of the Venetian economy took place based on the rapid growth of the manufacturing and financial spheres. It was the Ottomans, however, who remained the real threat to Venice and her empire.

11.3 The Ottoman peril

The Ottoman Empire should not be regarded as an absolutist state. It was a pre-capitalist state dominated by the Asiatic mode of production (Milios 1988, see also Chapter 7). It did, however, encourage and protect trade and all other money-begetting activities within its territory in order to collect tributes from it. In other words, "absorption into the Ottoman Empire did not ring desolation, as many Western Christian writers have implied" (Lane 1973: 299).[11] The main strategy of the Ottomans, up until the decline of their empire in the eighteenth century and after, was the expansion of its territory. They conquered a large part of southern and central Europe, and twice sieged Vienna (in 1529 and 1683).

With the conquest of Negroponte in 1470, the Ottomans started annexing Venetian colonial territories up into the early eighteenth century: they conquered Montenegro in 1479, Coron and Modon in 1500, Durazzo (Dyrrachion) in 1501, Naxos and the surrounding Aegean islands in 1566, Cyprus in 1571, Kefalonia (Cephalonia) in 1572 and Crete in 1669. However, the Venetians succeeded in re-establishing their rule over Morea (the Peloponnese) in 1688, only to lose it again to the Ottomans in 1712.

Until the final subjection of all its territories to the French army in 1797, Venice succeeded in keeping under her rule the *Domini di Terraferma* – her colonies on the Italian peninsula – her Istrian, Dalmatian and Albanian possessions, Corfu and all the other Ionian islands except for Kefalonia (Cephalonia).

Crucial to the survival of Venice and several of her colonial dominions was the victorious naval Battle of Lepanto in 1571, which was between the Christian Holy League formed by Spain, Malta, Venice, Genoa and the Papal States, and the Ottoman Empire. In the battle, Venice provided 110 out of the League's total 208 warships, and her admirals practically commanded the manoeuvres of the Christian fleet.

By the end of the sixteenth century, Venice continued to be a leading naval power in the Mediterranean. She was also a leading economic and political power, as I will discuss in the next sections.

11.4 The spread of capitalism in Europe and Venice's economic restructuring

As already mentioned, money-begetting economic forms led to capitalism in parts of the Italian Peninsula, Antwerp and Flanders, Amsterdam and Portugal, Spain, France, England, etc. The process of the taking hold and reproduction of capitalism in Europe does not fall within the scope of this book. From a methodological point of view, the study of the introduction or birth of capitalism in one region or another, and the subsequent expanded reproduction of capitalist exploitation and domination relations of class power in these regions, would call for a concrete and concentrated analysis of each concrete historical process, and not just general assumptions about the 'transition from feudalism to capitalism'. Nevertheless, two conclusions of Fernand Braudel seem worth mentioning at this point.

1   International trade created a 'domino effect', or, in other words, played the role of catalyst in the emergence of new poles of capitalism in different parts of Europe; it transplanted money-begetting activities, merchandise, production and financial techniques, capitalists and proletarians to these blossoming centres:

> The establishment of a regular maritime link between the Mediterranean and the North Sea ushered in a decisive invasion by the southerners [...]. For Bruges this could be described both as an annexation and as a new departure. It was an annexation because the southerners effectively captured a development which Bruges might conceivably have been able to manage singlehanded. But it was also a new departure in the sense that the arrival of the sailors, ships and merchants of

the Mediterranean brought in a wealth of goods, capital, and commercial and financial techniques. Rich Italian merchants came to live
in the city [...]. Thus Bruges came to be the centre of a huge trading
area, covering no less than the Mediterranean, Portugal, France, England, the Rhineland, and the Hansa. The town grew in size: 35,000
inhabitants in 1340, and possibly 100,000 by 1500.

(Braudel 1984: 99)[12]

2   Despite the formation of dominant absolutist states, which reshuffled
    political and military power relations on the continent and created the
    presuppositions for the consolidation and the expanded reproduction of
    capitalism, capitalist economic relations continued to be centred around
    a number of important cities for centuries:

> It must be pointed out that until about 1750 the dominant centers
> were always cities, city-states. For Amsterdam, which still dominated
> the economic world in the mid-eighteenth century, can justifiably
> be called the last of the city-states, the last polis of history. Behind
> her, the United Provinces were but a shadow government. [...] Until
> 1750, therefore, Europe rotated about a series of important cities that
> had been given stardom as a result of the role they played: Venice,
> Antwerp, Genoa, and Amsterdam.
>
> (Braudel 1979: 95–96)

With the new economic, military and political picture that was being shaped
in Europe from the end of the fifteenth century, Venice and the other cities
of the Italian peninsula lost ground to the European North.[13] Venice never
ceased to constitute an important centre of European capitalism, nevertheless.

Frederic C. Lane thus summarizes Venice's economic and social structure
in the sixteenth century:

> The development of such cities as Lisbon, Seville, Antwerp, and London
> made the commercial pre-eminence of Venice less outstanding than
> it had been, but it also provided markets for Venetian merchants and
> craftsmen, so that Venice was certainly more populous – reaching nearly
> 190,000 inhabitants – and probably wealthier in the sixteenth century
> than it had been in the fifteenth [...] [T]he Venetians [...] seemed strange
> in an almost entirely agrarian Europe because they did not sow or reap.
> They obtained their food in exchange for transport services and salt.
>
> (Lane 1973: 305)

Losing her pre-eminence in international trade designated not the 'failure' of
Venetian capitalism, but rather the shift of production towards manufacture
and finance. In the period of 1560–1660, the size of the Venetian commercial
fleet was halved (Fusaro 2015: 135); in the same period, however, manufacture took the lead.

At the end of the sixteenth century, "growth in some segments and decline in others had made structural changes [...]. The marine industries were less important relatively at the later date" (Lane 1973: 334). The silk industry flourished,[14] as well as other sectors like printing,[15] glass and cloth production,[16] lace making, furniture, leather work, jewellery, etc. In all these sectors, the capitalistically organized enterprises that employed a significant number of wage labourers were in the lead. Concentration of capital developed rapidly, as certain state-owned and private enterprises were growing significantly.

In the second half of the sixteenth century, the Arsenal employed 2,000–3,000 workers depending on the circumstances, and developed the first assembly lines in history that were based on the production of standardized, interchangeable ship parts (Lane 1973: 363). The Tana and the Zecca (the mint) endured as enormous enterprises for the historical period, while new, huge private enterprises sprung up. Even when crises temporarily crippled the Arsenal and other state enterprises, big private capitalists continued to dominate all branches of manufacture in Venice, even in the shipbuilding sector until the collapse of the republic in 1797.

> For manufacture of cloth of the new 'Dutch type', a certain Isaaco Gentile received privileges in 1763. He had spinning machinery, thirty two looms, and a thousand employees on a location with fifteen rooms [...]. Industrial as well as agricultural products from the Mainland were important in giving Venetian trade as high a total value in 1797 as it had had three hundred years earlier.
>
> (Lane 1973: 424)

The putting-out system had attained clear capitalist features since the sixteenth century, as labourers became fully dependent on capitalists – buyer-up (see Chapters 3 and 10). Through the putting-out system, women were also increasingly incorporated into the labour market.[17]

The financial sector also grew in importance. After 1526, five new banks were created. In 1587, after a dramatic bank failure, the state-owned Banco della Piazza di Rialto was created, to be followed by a second public bank, the Banco del Giro in 1619. Wars were often financed by the issue of bank money, and "bank deposits did in fact circulate as a kind of money" (Lane 1973: 330). Despite increasing public debt, especially during periods of war, the Venetian state always succeeded in overcoming recurring financial crises, as it managed to collect enough money from transaction and consumption taxes, as well as from direct taxes, which had been introduced in the fifteenth century. However, on average, bondholders of Venetian public debt earned more money from interest receipts than they paid in direct taxes. After the war in Cyprus (1570–1573), voluntary perpetual annuities and life annuities began to be issued, and these guaranteed a stable income to those who were well off.

Venice had become the main centre of maritime insurance in Europe in the fifteenth century, and in the 1560s, when "the total tonnage of the Venetian merchant marine reached its peak" (Lane 1973: 381), foreign brokers were also numerous in the city, with their offices in the *Calle della Sicurtà* (Insurance Street).

As the Venetian economy turned from maritime trade to manufacture, the problem of sufficient grain stores was dealt with in an alternative way: a state project of land reclamation in the *terraferma* that had begun in the late sixteenth century enabled substitution of grain imports and "made the Venetian domains very nearly self-sufficient in the seventeenth century and reduced the extent to which the wealth of the Serenissima depended on the sea" (Lane 1973: 307). The Venetian 'home market' was expanding.

Being an important capitalist economic centre in Europe, Venice regularly attracted immigrant populations from the Mediterranean, from the Italian peninsula and from other regions as well. Joanne Ferraro describes the brilliance of Venice at the end of the sixteenth century as follows:

> The thriving industrial base attracted droves of foreign peoples searching for employment in the merchant fleet and the navy [...]; in port services; and in the crafts. Luxury industries, including lead crystal and plate glass, soap, silks, and jewelry, attracted a global market. Nearly 10,000 people labored in the wool and silk industries; others were stonemasons, glass-makers, sugar refiners, leather workers, coppersmiths, blacksmiths, goldsmiths, and printers. The wool industry flourished, specializing in medium-quality Spanish and Neapolitan wool. [...] Urban finance complemented trade and manufacture.
>
> (Ferraro 2012: 106–107)

The maturing of Venetian capitalism created a growing polarization between rich and poor, as it often happens with capitalism and its 'development'. Wages of ordinary sailors and craftsmen fell significantly at the beginning of the fifteenth century, to about 20 ducats a year, most likely due to a relative abundance of seamen. As discussed in Section 10.3.3 of Chapter 10, seamen had been earning additional income by being permitted to carry tax-free merchandise with them on the ships. In the fifteenth century, however, this permission or measure benefitted high-ranking crew members rather than ordinary seamen, the latter being confined to the status of wage-earning proletarians; ordinary seamen were given permission to trade merchandise valued at no more than half their yearly wage, thus earning only a little extra money in addition to their wages.[18] Rising wages at the beginning of the sixteenth century were tolerated only in certain manufacturing branches, and were suppressed in shipping by government decrees that fixed base wages for sailors, keeping them at the same level for over a century, with nominal increases never meeting surging prices.[19] Under certain circumstances, however, when there was a dearth of seamen from the late sixteenth century onwards, wage increments were arranged through bonuses by the *capitani* themselves, who were eager to compile competent crews, and were willing to provide extra pay to their seamen out of their own pockets. Parallel to that, beginning in the 1540s, when fraternities and guilds were ordered by the state to furnish conscripts to the Venetian fleet, bonuses up to half the base wage were paid by guilds and fraternities to all stand-ins, who would substitute their conscripted members as oarsmen or ordinary seamen. In periods of shortage of crews, therefore, wages of ordinary seamen would rise significantly, despite rates of base wages fixed by decree. At the end of the sixteenth century, price inflation was followed by a comparable but lower rise in nominal wages.[20]

In the mid-sixteenth century, ordinary labourers earned a wage of about 20 ducats per year, similar to that of oarsmen and ordinary seamen. Skilled craftsmen or master seamen earned more than double than ordinary labourers, about 50 ducats a year. Even higher were the wages of a ship's master, at about 100 ducats per year, and of higher level Arsenal cadres and civil servants such as accountants, lawyers, etc., who earned 180–200 ducats a year. By way of comparison, wages of *capitani* and other high officials belonging to the class of patricians ranged between 750 and 1500 ducats a year, allowing them to offer bonuses to their crews during times of shortage of maritime labour.

Naturally, at the top of the social scale stood the big capitalists, whose profits allowed them to live in luxury or extravagance, whereas at the bottom of the social scale, besides beggars and paupers, were slaves and some servants. According to the census of 1563, servants and slaves made up 7–8% of Venice's population.

Generally speaking, it may be stated that although the income, or rather the purchasing power, of the lower proletarian wage-earning classes fluctuated in correspondence with shortages or surpluses of labour in the labour market, remaining on average at quite a stagnant level for long periods of time, the wages of high-level employees or commanders, and generally the income of those who were well off, were rising. At a significantly faster pace was, of course, the accumulation of riches by the capitalist class.

Convicts and slaves had been increasingly used as oarsmen since the end of the sixteenth century, as Venice's role in international maritime trade gradually lost ground to the Portuguese, Spanish, Dutch and English, and as her economy was rapidly turning from maritime travel to manufacture. In the big, new Venetian galleasses of the seventeenth century, with crews up to 500 seamen, it was not unusual for about 40% of crewmembers to be convicts and slaves.

In the seventeenth century, the rapid growth of Venetian manufacture attracted the majority of the available workforce, resulting in a shift of labour skills needed from seamen to craftsmen. The city's maritime trade depended not only on foreign seamen, but also on foreign (English or French) ships. However, a crisis in Venice's textile production in the eighteenth century reversed this tendency in the 1760s and again "shifted the proportion of craftsmen to seamen in favour of the latter" (Lane 1973: 424). Venetian capitalists – merchants, shipowners, financiers – once again expanded business in the Mediterranean, as they found profitable outlets for their activities there. In the eighteenth century, "in the Levant trade generally, Venetians were in second place behind the French" (ibid.: 425).

By adapting to the shifting circumstances of economic upsurge, stagnation or crisis, and moving from one economic sector to another, Venice's capitalists followed the immanent 'laws of capital': the anticipation of and search for increased profitability. In this sense, they simply acted as capitalists:

> [T]he very nature of private ownership of capital and capitalist competition, through the mediation of each capitalist firm searching to maximize its own profit [...], creates the mechanisms through which the general laws of motion of the system impose themselves.
>
> (Marx 1991: 75)

11.5 Crises and recoveries

In the centuries of her existence as an independent capitalist social formation, Venice came up against a number of severe, at times devastating, crises, followed by periods of recovery and growth. From the point of view of the capitalist economy, this is an expected 'regularity': economic crises are inherent in the capitalist system; however, "permanent crises do not exist" (Marx 1968: 497). Crises are conjunctural suspensions of the conditions for unimpeded reproduction of aggregate social capital. They constitute transitory manifestations of the internal contradictions of capitalism and not permanently operative causal relationships that inherently govern capitalist relations (Milios et al. 2002: 182). However, it is worth stressing at this point that some of the severest crises are sometimes driven by causes exogenous to the economy, such as plagues and wars.

Within fifty years since the late sixteenth century, Venice was devastated by two plague epidemics: the first, in the years 1576–1577, reduced the city's population from 190,000 to 125,000, and the second, in 1630–1633, equally destructive, hacked Venice's population from 150,000 to 100,000 inhabitants. At the end of the eighteenth century, Venice's population was again 140,000, clearly below the 1575 pre-plague level. The plague proved to be an important factor in curtailing Venice's economic and political prominence.

Wars have always played a significant role in restructuring economic relations, increasing the public debt and wreaking havoc on financial markets. Soon after the outbreak of the Ottoman–Venetian War of 1499–1503, three out of the four major Venetian banks collapsed in 1499–1500; the War of the League of Cambrai, in which Venice fought against France, triggered "a catastrophe for Venetian bondholders" in 1509, as "[i]nterest on both Monte Nuovo and Monte Vecchio were suspended and their prices plummeted"

(Lane 1973: 324–325). Crises and financial turmoil have always been a starting point for the introduction of economic and social policy measures. For example, the grain famine of 1527–1529 brought about by the combination of bad weather and the effects of the Habsburg (Hapsburg)–Valois War of 1521–1526, in which Venice allied with France against Spain, England, The Holy Roman Empire and the Papal States, was the occasion for the introduction of poor hostels,[21] which were later used as institutions for the supervision and control of pauperism.

The restructuring of the Venetian economy, which we allusively described in the foregoing section of this chapter, was also connected with phenomena of economic crisis. A drop in freight rates in the 1460s and 1470s was the backdrop for a crisis in the shipbuilding sector and the Arsenal, and for the introduction of protectionist policies, which eventually proved ineffective. The Ottoman–Venetian war of 1499–1503 revived the Arsenal, however. Another crisis at the Arsenal in 1617–1619 led the Venetians to hire foreign ships; production in the Arsenal recovered only after 1667. In 1721, in the wake of a peace treaty with the Ottoman Empire, production in the Arsenal fell again to low levels; after 1763, when Venetian maritime and financial activity in the Mediterranean surged again, the shipbuilding sector and the Arsenal flourished anew. The Venetian merchant fleet numbered 60–70 ships in 1763, 238 in 1775 and 309 ships in 1794 (Lane 1973: 419).

Maria Fusaro conceptualizes the restructuring of the Venetian economy from maritime trade to manufacture and finance at the turn of the sixteenth century as being a result of a major crisis and decline of the Venetian *empire*, which had lost its global leadership to a new hegemonic empire, the English. According to the author, the realm for gaining global hegemony was at the time not the Atlantic, but still the Mediterranean.

> The rise of England and the crisis of Venice are always mentioned in the same breath by historians; as Richard Rapp put it, 'it was the invasion of the Mediterranean, not the exploitation of the Atlantic, that produced the Golden Ages of Amsterdam and London'. Before that, Venice dominated the Mediterranean and was rightly considered an international trading power to be reckoned with. Afterwards the situation in the Mediterranean changed drastically, and Venice's influence had to be profoundly re-evaluated.
>
> (Fusaro 2015: ix)

Oliver Cromwell Cox put forward a similar idea several decades earlier. He argued that after every shift in global economic and political leadership, the former hegemon, who loses predominance on the international level, gets trapped in a temporary stagnation.

> Barring business maladjustments, capitalism may thus be said to have had a continuous era of prosperity from its beginning to the First World War.

[...] And yet, localized capitalist stagnation resulted, in every instance, when there was a change in leadership. The displaced leader suffered at least relative retrogression; and it lost its dynamic initiative in the system. That was the fate of Venice, Lübeck, Holland, and Britain.

(Cox 1959-a: 207)

Despite 'relative retrogression', crises and recovery, and restructuring and changes in the prominence of her various economic sectors, Venice remained a capitalist social formation until her collapse in 1797. In the next chapter, I will deal with the political and ideological aspects of Venetian society in its capitalist era.

Notes

1 This 'localized' first emergence of capitalism justifies Marx's intuitive grasp: "we come across the first beginnings of capitalist production as early as the 14th and 15th century, sporadically, in certain towns of the Mediterranean" (Marx 1887: 508). As Marcus Rediker, commenting on Sean T. Cadigan, aptly stresses: "Yes, capitalism 'arrived in some parts of the production process much earlier than in others,' and I do not see how Cadigan can argue otherwise, unless he believes that modes of production burst upon the historical scene Minerva-like, fully-formed" (Rediker 1989: 341).

2 To my understanding, Oliver C. Cox, in the book mentioned by Braudel (Cox 1965b), as well as in other books of his, probably refers to Venice rather as a historical example, not as an exclusive case. Cox writes: "We do not know, of course, when capitalism originated" (Cox 1959-a: 144).

3 In the third volume of his major work, Braudel interprets the formation of the Venetian and Genoese colonial systems after the Fourth Crusade (1204) as evidence of an already "advanced" capitalism in both social formations: "Genoa and Venice, [...] merchant and colonial powers (and the *colonial* tells us that they had already reached an advanced stage of capitalism)" (Braudel 1984: 118). Following the same line of thought, Luciano Pellicani connects Venice's "full-fledged colonial empire" (Pellicani 1994: 156) with "the Venetian capitalist bourgeoisie [which] was not only the dominant class, but also held direct political power. [...] Venice was not an isolated phenomenon. All the market cities of the Low Middle Ages were dominated by the bourgeoisie" (ibid.).

4 "Among the cities of medieval Europe, Venice was the first to become capitalistic in the sense that its ruling class made its livelihood by employing wealth in the form of commercial capital – cash, ships and commodities – and used their control of government to increase their profits" (Lane 1966: 57).

5 As do Braudel (1984), Pellicani (1984), etc., Banaji correlates Venetian (and Genoese) colonialism after 1204 with capitalism: "The 'Fourth' Crusade (1204) secured Venetian dominance over the East Mediterranean and consolidated *the hold of the purely capitalist element in the ruling oligarchy*" (Banaji 2010: 268, emphasis added).

6 Marcus Rediker, investigating the formation of the maritime proletariat, writes:

I suggested [...] that some portion of merchant capital, traditionally conceived as capital that operated only in the sphere of circulation, did in itself necessarily create value by setting in motion and exploiting wage labour, much of which belonged to merchant seamen. Seeing 'production' as the process by which value is created (which includes, therefore, the transportation of commodities), I argued that seamen were value-producing proletarians in the period of manufacture (not machinofacture), and hence part of a working class that has long been held to be non-existent under 'merchant capital'.

(Rediker 1989: 341)

And he concludes: "Seamen were among the earliest of workers to depend entirely upon the wage for their subsistence" (ibid.: 338).

7 When the Narodniks argued that the poverty of the peasants ruled out the possibility of the development of a significant home market, and thus of capitalism in Russia, Lenin replied: "the problem of the home market as *a separate, self-sufficient problem* not depending on that of the degree of capitalist development does not exist at all" (Lenin 1977 Vol. 3: 69, emphasis added; see also Chapter 3).

8 The doctrine of trade as a 'zero-sum game' conceptualizes profit as being 'profit upon alienation': an 'unequal exchange' takes place, in which the one party achieves a *gain* 'upon alienation' of an owned commodity, whereas the other party suffers a *loss* equal in magnitude to the first party's gain:

> The idea that profit is created within the process of circulation is encountered in almost all mercantilist writing [...]. From a theoretical point of view, the doctrine of 'profit upon alienation' signified a complete repudiation of any solution to the problem of profit and surplus value in general.

(Rubin 1979: 368)

As explained in Section 5.6, capitalist trade constitutes a productive process, creating value and surplus value for the owner of the means of production (e.g. the capitalist ship-owner). Despite his ambivalences (see Chapter 5) Marx writes: "[...] the transport industry, storage and the dispersal of goods in a distributable form should be viewed as production processes that continue within the process of circulation" (Marx 1991: 379).

9 "In the forty years between 1380 and 1420, Venice more than doubled its territory and population. Venice extended its rule to Corfu and the mainland city of Butrinto in 1386; Argos, Nauplion, and Andros in 1388; Tinos, Mykonos, and Negroponte in 1390; Durazzo in 1392; Alessio in 1393; Scutari and Drivasto in 1396; Lepanto and Patras in 1407; Zara, Ossero, Arbe, Cherso, and Nona in 1409; Sebenico in 1412; Zonchio in 1417; and Spalato, Traù, Curzola, Brazza, Lesina, Pago, and Cattaro in 1420. [...] Venice extended its mainland dominions dramatically during the same period: Vicenza, Feltre, and Belluno in 1404, Rovigo, Verona, and Padova in 1405, Udine in 1420, Brescia in 1426, and Bergamo in 1428. By the late fifteenth century, Venetian territory stretched from central Italy to the Peloponnesus and beyond, to the islands of Crete and Cyprus, a distance of 29,694 square miles" (O'Connell 2009: 22). Venetian conquests culminated in the takeover of Cyprus in 1489, and of the Ionian Islands in 1500.

10 "The Senate in 1441 stated that 'our agenda in the maritime parts considers our state and the conservation of our city and commerce,' suggesting that by the mid-fifteenth century, the defense of Venetian security and prosperity was tied into the maintenance of its maritime domains. [...] The Venetians imposed a system of standard weights and measures in their territories, controlled the currency, and carefully regulated local markets to the advantage of Venetian merchants. In the case of key commodities, such as wheat or salt, Venice demanded that local producers sell only to the city at a fixed rate. Venice also drew on the human resources of its subject cities, demanding that its territories provide sailors for its fleet or workers for its fortifications" (O'Connell 2009: 22–23).

11 The Serbian-born American historian Traian Stoianovich draws the following conclusion in connection with the economic protection that Ottoman authorities granted to their subjects: "The victory of the Ottoman Empire symbolized,

in the sphere of economics, a victory of Greeks, Turks, renegade Christians, Armenians, Ragusans, and Jews over the two-century-old commercial hegemony of Venice and Genoa" (cited by Lane 1973: 300).

12 The British 'East India Company', and later the Dutch East India Company, both emulated the structure and functions of the Genoese *maona* (see Chapter 10):

> It was not until the 17th century that the northern Europeans became important imperialists. Their favourite organization was an East Indies company that combined imperialism with private enterprise. Typically, these firms were highly capitalized joint stock companies that traded in Asia or the Americas, maintained military and naval forces, and established fortified trading posts abroad. All of the northern powers had them. The English East India Company was chartered in 1600 and its Dutch counterpart two years later.
>
> (Allen 2011: 19)

13 "The definitive shift at the end of the sixteenth century from the Mediterranean to the North Sea represented the victory of a new region over an old one. It also represented a vast change of scale. Aided by the new rise of the Atlantic, the general economy, trade, and even the monetary supply expanded. And once again the rapid growth of the market economy – which faithfully kept its appointment at Amsterdam – supported on its broad back the expanded constructions of capitalism" (Braudel 1979: 67).

14 "[…] at the end of the century, there were more silk weavers than shipwrights or caulkers in Venice" (Lane 1973: 310).

15 "Out of a total of 1,821 publications known to have been issued in the years 1495–97 from all presses existing, 447 were printed at Venice, whereas Paris, then next in importance, printed only 181" (Lane 1973: 311).

16 The output of cloth production increased from 2,000 pieces in 1516 to 20,000 in 1565 (see Lane 1973: 309).

17 "The spinning women remained unorganized, and they were so numerous in surrounding villages that special rules were made to enable them to pass customs barriers when they came to Venice to get wool and bring back thread" (Lane 1973: 313).

18 A similar regime allowing for additional income from the trading of goods was also common in the English merchant fleet in the seventeenth century:

> In 1621 the Trinity House of Deptford produced a certificate 'that the following portage, outward and homeward, free of custom, is appropriate': on an eastern Mediterranean voyage, £100 in goods for the master, £10 for officers, and £5 for seamen.
>
> (Blakemore 2017: 1174)

The yearly wage of an ordinary English seaman was at the time approximately £12.

19 "In 1519 the Senate cut the rate of base pay for oarsmen from 12 lire a month [23.2 ducats a year, JM] to 8 lire [15.5 ducats a year, JM] […] the rate was raised to 10 lire [19.5 ducats per year, JM] in 1524. It stayed there for the rest of the century, while prices and other wages mounted" (Lane 1973: 366). Karl Marx illustrates the "forcing down of wages by act of Parliament" in sixteenth-century England in Chapter 28 of Volume 1 of *Capital*.

20 "These nominally higher salaries could still not keep up with the heavily inflated prices of foodstuffs and manufactured goods. Indeed, a rise in a worker's daily rate of pay did not imply an increase in earnings" (Iordanou 2016: 806).

21 "To assuage the flood of beggars within the city, the government built temporary shelters and, while forbidding begging, arranged to provide food in these 'hospitals' until the next harvest" (Lane 1973: 332).

12 Political power and social cohesion

12.1 The Venetian state as a capitalist state

In Chapters 8–10, I demonstrated the crucial role of the state in the consolidation of class power relations in the Venetian social formation and in the final transformation of pre-capitalist money-begetting economic relations into capitalist relations of class domination and exploitation.

The Venetian state functioned from its inception as a collective apparatus of patrician money-owners who also manned its higher ranks and ruled over all other classes of society. The state produced multiple packages of rules and regulations, not only for maritime trade, but also for every sector of economic activity; they policed markets, production and people, restraining every practice that could oppose the money-begetting activities of Venice's noble class and all other financially prominent owners of wealth. It also functioned as a collective 'entrepreneur', in founding such enormous, for the age, manufactures, such as the Arsenal, the Tana and the mint (the Zecca), or in bringing under legal state ownership nearly the totality of Venice's merchant ships, which it then auctioned off to individual merchants or other money-owners.[1] The comparatively large state budget bolstered many forms of money-begetting activities, including banking. In the aftermath of the Venetian–Genoese wars, and especially after the War of Chioggia, the state greatly expanded the financial sphere by creating a huge public debt through forced loans from the rich, and a well-organized secondary market of government bonds.

Finally, in the late fourteenth century, the state decisively facilitated the generalization and stabilization of wage relations by suppressing the surviving forms of 'association' between money-owners and labourers, thus ultimately transforming the former into capitalists and the majority of the latter into proletarians. As a result, Venice was the first to take steps towards capitalist relations of class domination and exploitation, only to be followed by other city states on the Italian peninsula, and subsequently in Northern Europe and in the Atlantic. The Venetian state had acquired the fundamental characteristics of a capitalist state: it embodied the interests of the entire social capital of the polity. At the level of the economy, the state contributed decisively to creating the general material conditions for the reproduction of capitalist relations. This included political management of the workforce, interventions for boosting the profitability of overall social capital, state management of money and the institutional and legal framework underwriting the 'freedom' of the market. At the political and ideological–cultural level, the state legitimated the exercise of bourgeois political power as being in the 'common interest'.

My analysis thus corroborates the following conclusions of Giovanni Arrighi, despite our differences of opinion on other issues regarding the rise and nature of capitalism (see Chapter 5):

> The most powerful and leading state [...] (Venice) is the true prototype of the capitalist state, in the double sense of 'perfect example' and 'model for future instances' of such a state. [...] *Pace* Sombart, if there has ever been a state whose executive met the *Communist Manifesto*'s standards of the capitalist state ('but a committee for managing the common affairs of the whole bourgeoisie'), it was fifteenth-century Venice. From this standpoint, the leading capitalist states of future epochs (the United Provinces, the United Kingdom, the United States) appear as increasingly 'diluted' versions of the ideo-typical standards realised by Venice centuries earlier.
> (Arrighi 1993: 153)

However, this thesis about the capitalist character of the Venetian state presupposes that one gives *an affirmative answer* to the following two questions, which have been repeated in order to stress the supposedly obsolete, and therefore pre-capitalist, character of the Venetian state:

a   Can a state and polity form structured on the segregation between the aristocracy, citizens and commoners be considered as a form of capitalist state? As Martin and Romano (2000b: 3 ff.) show, a considerable number of historians since the nineteenth century have depicted the Venetian state and its ability to represent those living under its authority as a "decadent, oligarchic and unable to reform" type of polity.
b   Can a state not representing (or based on) a *nation*, or differently put, not affiliated with a *national territory*, be a 'modern', i.e. capitalist, state? As we saw in Chapter 11, this is precisely the issue raised by Anderson, Althusser, Heller, etc., who gave a negative answer to the implicated question, claiming that Venice and the other city states of the Italian peninsula 'failed' to become actual capitalist social formations because they could not develop a 'national political entity'.

I will not endeavour to embark upon a detailed analysis of Venetian society and its state. The scope of this book is to deal with Venice's history only to the extent that it illustrates the process of evolution and consolidation of capitalism. Thus, in the next two sections, I will confine myself to presenting the Venetian state from the point of view of its capitalist features.

12.2 State apparatuses and forms of representation

The Venetian state had acquired two basic characteristics of a capitalist type of state in the fourteenth century, at the time of transformation of the spurious bourgeoisie into a capitalist class:

a   Impersonal functioning of state apparatuses based on the 'rule of law' and 'equal justice' for all inhabitants of Venetian territory, regardless of their special status (patricians, citizens by birth, 'popolari', immigrants or slaves).[2]

> The central organs of government formed a pyramid [...]. Distrust of individual power made the Venetians depend on committees and councils. Even in their judicial system, sentences were not imposed by an individual judge but by several judges acting together. Each committee or council was checked by some other committee or council so as to assure the rule of law.
>
> (Lane 1973: 95)

b   A system of selecting high-level state officials, who rotated from one office to another, which, combined with the structure of the government pyramid, guaranteed the 'relative autonomy' of the state and its political and economic functions or interventions from all fractions of the ruling class (either patrician families[3] or fractions of entrepreneurs according to the branch of their economic activity, etc. – see Chapter 9).[4]

As Nicos Poulantzas extensively argues:

> [T]he capitalist state, while predominantly representing the interests of the hegemonic class or fraction [...], enjoys a relative autonomy with respect to that class and fraction as well as to the other classes and fractions of the power bloc.
>
> (Poulantzas 1975: 97)

Both elements played a decisive role in creating consensus for political power by Venice's population.

Although the Venetian government and the doge were elected by the Great Council, a closed body of male patricians aged 25 years and older, it constituted one of the most 'representative' state forms in Europe until the French Revolution. In the sixteenth century, Venetian male patricians participating in the state's Great Council comprised between 4% and 5% of the city's male population of the given age group. By comparison, two and a half centuries later, the electorate in England was around 3%, and in Scotland, below 0.2% of the population (The National Archives 2017).[5]

This is one of the reasons why the Venetian polity system was praised by many radical thinkers and political philosophers before the French Revolution.

The English political theorist of republicanism, James Harrington, in his influential book *The Commonwealth of Oceana* (published in 1656 and dedicated to Oliver Cromwell, "His Highness The Lord Protector of The Commonwealth of England, Scotland and Ireland"), considers Venice as a 'model' for the British Commonwealth, stressing that "Venice, though she do not take in the people, never excluded them" (Harrington 1992 [1656]: 17). Going even further, he argues:

> The commonwealth of Venice, being that of which all others is the most equal in the constitution, is that wherein there never happened any strife between the senate and the people [...]. I have not stood upon a more particular description of this ballot, because that of Venice, exemplified in the model, is of all others the most perfect.
>
> (Harrington 1992 [1656]: 33, 34)[6]

Harrington's idea that Venice "never excluded the people" refers, on the one hand, to the fact that the Venetian government always addressed 'the Venetian people' as a whole,[7] and on the other, that a political regime (as a manifestation of class power) shall always strive to achieve consensus and acceptance, or at least tolerance, of the ruled populations (classes), something that Venice's rulers seem more or less to have achieved.

A similar concern as regards the representation of subaltern classes by the state is expressed by Baruch Spinoza, especially in his last unfinished work, the *Political Treatise* (1676–1677), where he argues that state power shall be rooted in the "right of the people".[8]

Spinoza names "absolute" the government that expresses "freedom" and the "right" of the people (the multitude) and, comparing different forms of state, argues that democracy, is, in this respect, the best form of polity (see also Israel 2001). However, an "aristocratic" regime like that of Venice, he argues, is always more advantageous as compared to an absolute monarchy.[9] Finally, he concludes:

> To ensure that all patricians stand on equal terms in making decisions and in electing ministers of state and that all business is speedily dispatched, *the system observed by the Venetians deserves our full approval*. To nominate ministers of state, they appoint some members of the council by lot, and when these have nominated in due order the candidates for office, every patrician votes for or against the candidate by secret ballot [...]. Through this procedure not only do all patricians stand on equal terms in making decisions and business is speedily dispatched, but also each is absolutely free to cast his vote.
>
> (Spinoza 2002: 732, emphasis added)

Frederic C. Lane uses the term *republicanism* to describe the type of political regime to which Venice's state belonged.[10] The lack of hereditary assignment of the highest political post (the doge), the restricted periods of service held by patricians in each office, the inspection and auditing of all committees and officials, the settling of conflicts by voting processes in bodies with broad participation and at the same time measures for the 'common good' or for 'equal justice', like the procuration of adequate grain, employment policies in state-owned enterprises, the conscription of crews for the war fleets by lot and rotation, etc. (see Chapter 10), all created the image of an impersonal state authority comprising 'impartial' state apparatuses, and thus legitimizing state policies and decisions in the eyes of Venice's inhabitants, in spite of the fact that privileges enjoyed by the nobility and citizens by birth were inaccessible to Venice's commoners.

We see, therefore, that social segregation between patricians and commoners does not necessarily involve a non-capitalist or by definition 'less representative' state as compared, for example, with the English constitutional monarchy of the seventeenth century or later, but simply a more clear-cut shutting-out of upward social mobility of commoners through the state (e.g. education and state bureaucracy). In other words, upward social mobility of non-patricians was rendered possible not by becoming a state official, but only by economic means and processes, that is, by financial success as a capitalist or middle bourgeoisie.

Venetian economy and society were socially more polarized than present-day capitalist economies. In spite of social and income polarization between, on the one hand, capitalists, high-ranking state officials and wealthy master artisans, and, on the other, proletarians and mere shopkeepers of meagre means, Venice's political and legal framework generated images of collective belonging. Institutions such as fraternities, schools[11] and parishes, as well as institutionalized practices like the worshipping of the republic's patron saint, St Mark, as a form of exclusive state cult and identity, public ceremonies and meals regularly organized by the state authorities[12] or the church, festivals and charities,[13] all played the role of Ideological State Apparatuses, whose main function was to inscribe ideas and practices into all social classes and groups pertaining to capitalist interests and the ruling ideology.

> [...] professional particularism was the means by which more men gained a part in framing the rules that regulated their activities as members of an occupational group and in choosing its officials. [...] Guildsmen as such were only second-class citizens, yet they had citizenship of a kind. Thus consolidated, the Venetian Republic gained a high reputation for the success with which it solved many problems in state building [...] namely, upholding public law over private privilege and vengeance, curbing the Church's political influence, and inventing mercantilist measures to increase wealth.
>
> (Lane 1966: 525–526)

From the fifteenth century onwards, the Venetian state systematically directed the production of an official 'Venetian history' as a means of imprinting forms of 'patriotism' into the minds of the city's and the empire's inhabitants: that is, loyalty to the state and consensus on its policies. In a way reminiscent of nineteenth-century processes of nation-building in Europe (see below), we encounter here an earlier version of a state strategy of constructing the "*historicity of a territory and [the] territorialisation of a history*", where "the markings of a territory become indicators of history that are written into the State" (Poulantzas 1980: 114).

In 1486, the Senate rejected the versions of Venetian history written by some prominent scholars and approved the *Rerum Venetarum* (*Of Venetian Matters*) composed "by a second-rate professional humanist called Sabellico" (Lane 1973: 220).

> The decree of the Venetian Senate on September 1, 1486 granted to Marcantonio Sabellico the permission to print the 33 books of *Rerum Venetarum*, and in the very next year the work was already published [...] 32 of the 33 books of the work had been written in no more than 15 months, more precisely in the period between January 1485 and March 1486.
>
> (Marin 2013: 136–137)

Focusing on the forms of representation of Venetian subjects by the state, we should not forget, of course, that the centre and kernel of the Venetian state, as with every state, was always the *repressive state apparatus*, comprising the government, the Inquisitors, the secret police and all other repressive bodies, the judiciary and the jails, the administrative councils, the war fleet and the mercenaries, the spies and the hangmen, etc.

> The social defense system was especially important for protecting the monopoly of power and for providing a climate of peace and stability essential for trade. In the fourteenth century this system was considerably enlarged and strengthened with police patrols eventually reaching a proportion of one patroller to every 250 inhabitants. At the same time, much of the judicial system was streamlined and rationalized.
>
> (Ruggiero 1978: 243)

Venetian criminal law was compiled and codified on the basis of the *Promissione Maleficorum*, an early legal document produced during the time of Doge Jacopo Tiepolo (1229–1249), which also contained an appendix for punishments corresponding to respective breaches of law or crimes. It is remarkable that crimes concerning the economic and political status quo, that is, violations of property relations or of owed allegiance to state authorities, in Venice or in her colonies, were ranked among the crimes carrying the most severe penalties. More specifically, "robbery was the crime of greatest concern to the ruling class which wrote and applied the law",[14] as was the case with any recalcitrance to state policies that could be interpreted as insurgency.[15]

The subaltern classes of Venetian society repeatedly advanced different forms of resistance to class exploitation and oppression. Such issues, while of interest, lie beyond the scope of this book.

In concluding this section, if I could stress one point distilled from my analysis, it would be this: capitalism prevailed as a dominant mode of production, simultaneously shaping its pertinent economic and political forms, without a preceding social revolution.[16]

This conclusion is, of course, not an original one, as most capitalist countries, in Europe and beyond, do not have a record of a 'bourgeoisie revolution' in their respective histories. Besides, as Marx clearly states in *Capital*, in Western Europe "the capitalist era dates from the 16th century" (Marx 1887: 508), despite remnants of degenerated feudal relations, and despite poverty and the decline in production (and in peasant consumption!) in the agrarian sector of countries like seventeenth- and eighteenth-century France (Rubin 1979: 91–105). This clearly means that the French Revolution, for example, broke out at least two centuries after capitalism had prevailed in (non-agrarian sectors of) the French and other European economies and societies. So-called bourgeois revolutions, like the English of the seventeenth, or the French of the eighteenth century, were first and foremost mass movements that shook the relation of forces between the ruling and the ruled classes, and in this manner, by definition, also reshuffled the balance of power between the different fractions comprising the ruling class, and also created new balances of power between state apparatuses. At the same time, these movements also contained anti-capitalist trends, expressing a tendency towards direct democracy and communism, which is immanent in the practices of the proletarian classes (initially utilized and subsequently oppressed by the emerging new political regimes), as Eduard Bernstein (1895, 1980) has shown in the case of the English Revolution.[17]

As classes primarily constitute social relations and practices (see Chapter 7), the ruling class, comprising different fractions, is primarily a strategy of class exploitation and domination over the ruled classes. This ruling strategy is constantly modified in accordance with developments and turning points of class struggle, which reshuffle power relations between the ruling and the ruled, but also between the fractions of the ruling class. The American or French Revolutions in the late eighteenth century did not signify the 'transition from feudalism to capitalism', but a major reshuffling of class relation of forces within a capitalist social formation and a relevant restructuring of capitalist state apparatuses, bringing to the fore new forms of oppression, governance and consensus. As Oliver Cromwell Cox stresses, when speaking about the French Revolution:

> The revolution removed all intermediary political loyalties between the individual and the state. This, then, was the supreme organizational triumph of capitalism: the shattering of the social estates and the ascendance of individualism.
>
> (Cox 1959-a: 147)

The transformations of capitalist power brought about by the French Revolution established and subsequently disseminated across the rest of Europe a new form of cohesion of existing capitalist social formations: nationalism!

12.3 The 'national question', Venice's state and its colonial territories

We now come to the main argument of the previously described narrative(s) advocating the notion of the 'failure' of Venetian capitalism (see Chapter 11). Did the Venetian capitalist state 'fail' because it did not succeed in uniting the Italian nation? The answer is categorically No! The (Italian) nation did not exist until the nineteenth century, centuries after the prevalence of capitalism in Venice, Genoa, Florence and the rest of Western Europe. *The Venetian–Genoese wars were not civil wars!*

Eric Hobsbawm situates the beginning of the age of nations and nationalism in Europe in and around the nineteenth century (with the first steps having been taken in the late eighteenth century). More specifically, concerning Italy, he writes:

> In the days of Mazzini [...] for the great bulk of Italians, the Risorgimento did not exist so that, as Massimo d'Azeglio admitted in the famous phrase: 'We have made Italy, now we have to make Italians.'
>
> (Hobsbawm 1992: 44)

> If French had at least a state whose 'national language' it could be, the only basis for Italian unification was the Italian language, which united the educated elite of the peninsula as readers and writers, even though it has calculated that at the moment of unification (1860) only 2,5% of the population used the language for everyday purposes.
>
> (Hobsbawm 1992: 60–61)

Sporadic references to 'Italy' before the 'age of nationalism' shall not be perceived in the framework of contemporary national ideologies. For political leaders and intellectuals of existing states on the Italian peninsula before the nineteenth century, 'Italy' was a 'vision' or a "cultural consciousness" (Gramsci 2007: 60) to a degree similar to the way 'Europe' was for European states in the early twentieth century.

> When Petrarch made an appeal for peace between Venice and Genoa, calling for both to recognize that they were parts of a larger whole, Italy [...] neither city was any more moved by the appeal than England and Germany would have been in 1915 by an appeal in the name of European nationality.
>
> (Lane 1973: 180)[18]

While it is true that Niccolò Machiavelli in *The Prince* [1513] envisaged that "Italy [...] may behold its saviour", so that "our native country may be ennobled" (Machiavelli 1981: 138), as Hobsbawm's analysis documents, the nation emerges only when nationalism and the 'national idea' become a mass movement, or at least are recognized as an ideological,[19] sentimental and political

stance by a considerable part of a population. Despite visions of isolated intellectuals, the development of a 'national cause' did not take shape in Italy
or Europe before the eighteenth or nineteenth century, a process actually
empowered by the French Revolution.

Let me reiterate some points I have already made, building upon both what
has ensued and (some) reference to Marxist theory, as regards the correlation
between the capitalist state and the nation.

The capitalist state 'condenses' the overall rule of capital in a social formation, at the same time presenting it as being in the 'common interest' of
society. In other words, the capitalist state must always homogenize every
community within its political territory into an *indigenous population* supposedly possessing *common interests*, and distinguish it from the 'other' (the populations of other states or territories). This means that the strategic interests
of the capitalist class that are being 'condensed' by the state always entail a
compromise with the indigenous subaltern classes. Modern nation-building
and nationalism have played an important role in the homogenization of a
capitalist state's indigenous populations: the nation constitutes the historically shaped and specifically capitalist unity (cohesion) of the antagonistic
classes of a social formation, tending to unify the 'internal', and demarcate
and distinguish it from the 'external', i.e. the 'non-national'. The process of
nation-building was initiated in Europe centuries after capitalism had established its rule in many social formations and parts of the continent. Nationalism and national identity emerged in the late eighteenth and nineteenth
centuries, roughly in the wake of the French Revolution.

More concretely, the Venetian state had been a capitalist state since the
fourteenth century, long before the 'age of nationalism'; through the functions of its apparatuses, the strategic interests of the Venetian bourgeoisie
were established as 'common interests' of the republic. In other words, allegiance to the state by the subaltern classes was safeguarded without the
mediation of a national or racial identity, but rather by a feeling of common
belonging to a polity, combined with a nearly religious sense of common
belonging.[20] This political element, itself possessing strong economic foundations, played a decisive role in creating consensus for political power by the
subaltern classes, and also by colonial populations and immigrants settling in
Venice from other parts of the Mediterranean and the Italian peninsula.

> Welcomed for their skills and attracted by the city's reputation for rela-
> tively plentiful food and equal justice, immigrants replenished its popu-
> lation after each visitation of war and plague.
>
> (Lane 1973: 201)

The 'other', and even more so, the 'enemy', was not the 'ethnic' alien or immigrant settling in Venice, but the subject of a foreign state. As Venice's relation with foreign states frequently alternated between a condition of alliance
to one of hostility (if one does not take into consideration 'eternal enemies',

as in the case of the Genoese),[21] Venetian crews were obliged to take an oath before leaving Venice "that they would not attack friendly people" (Lane 1973: 50), that is, those 'alien' or 'other' people whom the Venetian state, at any given moment, defined as 'allies'.

We shall not forget that Venice was not a mere city state, but an empire, and this empire did not extend solely or even primarily to the Italian peninsula, the *terraferma*, but also to the Mediterranean, the *Stato da Màr*, with Crete being one of the most important Venetian colonial territories up until 1669.

Throughout her colonial territories, Venice established the same form of administration and the same type of institutions, which mirrored the Venetian polity and granted expanded powers to local elites, as long as these local powers were incorporated into Venice's strategic priorities, and the republic's legal, economic and institutional frameworks.

> Venetian rule in each locality was carefully adjusted to local circumstances, creating a "composite" or "federal" state structure. There are significant similarities between Venice's rule in its mainland and its maritime territories – notably its jurisdictional complexity, institutional structure, and reliance on negotiation, contestation, and accommodation in the day-to-day practice of rule. As was the case on the mainland, Venetian maritime administrators worked in concert with civic councils composed of local elites. In both the mainland and maritime cases, these councils provided a structure for regional self-government, but recently Papadia-Lala's important work on councils in Greek-speaking Venetian territories has highlighted the degree to which maritime civic councils also channelled religious and ethnic identities into stable social categories through the inclusion or exclusion of various groups from civic life.
>
> (O'Connell 2009: 9)

Cities and other communities in the Mediterranean were incorporated into the Venetian imperial system in exactly the same way as cities and regions on the Italian peninsula were, despite differences in religion.[22] Each region of the *Stato da Màr*, just as with the regions of the *terraferma*, possessed their own institutions of local governance and an appreciable degree of autonomy in relation to Venice. In this context, each and every region developed its own variants of social cohesion and communal identity.

The empire was thus shaped as a hybrid sovereignty, somewhere between a colonial realm and a confederation of dominions, each possessing a commensurate, but also distinct, 'local' identity.[23]

In Crete, the Catholic or Latin (mostly of Venetian origin) minority had been speaking the local Greek–Cretan dialect since the fourteenth century,[24] the division between Orthodox and Catholic dogmas had become fragile among the island's inhabitants,[25] Cretan elites developed close economic and political ties with Venetian patricians[26] and Renaissance art in Candia and the other main Cretan cities flourished almost to the same extent as in the cities on the Italian peninsula. In this context, a new identity of collective belonging was shaped, which was neither Venetian nor Byzantine (nor 'Greek'), but *Cretan*. The Cretan 'multitude' gradually shaped its own unique sense of community, as partition lines based on religion, language, culture, etc., began losing significance, and local institutions and forms of governance uniformly organized everyday life and negotiated appeals. Despite the fact that official modern Greek historiography refers to the Venetian period of Crete in terms of a national yoke (*Venetokratia*), there existed not a 'Greek people' subjected to 'Venetian occupation', but rather a Cretan 'multitude' (of both aristocrats and commoners) comprising different social classes and groups. The demarcation lines between social classes divided Cretan society as a whole, not nations.

Commenting on the repercussions of the Revolt of St Tito (see Chapter 10), Sally McKee writes:

> Here today's vocabulary fails most tellingly, for it is difficult to describe the significance of the 1363 revolt without recourse to modern, anachronistic terminology. [...] Does the term 'national' adequately describe the sentiment shared by Latin Cretans and Venetians of the metropolis, or does it more accurately describe the sentiment which prompted Latin Cretans to secede from Venice and join forces with Greek Cretans? Short-lived though the revolt may ultimately have been, the raising of the St Tito standard displayed a flash of imaginative political will which sought to redefine the people of this colony as neither Greek nor Latin, but as Cretan.
>
> (McKee 1994: 204)

This local identity of collective belonging was, of course, imprinted on the aristocracy but also on parts of the populace as a 'Venetian value' system. Large segments of the populations of the *Stato da Màr* forged ties with the Venetian high rule for accessibility to Venice's judicial and institutional system.[27] After the surrender of Crete to the Ottomans in 1669, most inhabitants from Candia, the capital of the island, emigrated to Venice or Greek-speaking dominions of the *Stato da Màr*.[28]

Despite existing processes of an early building of 'patriotism' (allegiance to the state related to the incorporation of the state's and empire's subjects into the framework of state apparatuses, the inscription of 'Venetian values' and 'official history', ceremonies, charities and forms of education, cultural and artistic production, etc.), we cannot yet speak of an actual process of nation-building comparable to the one that took place in many parts of Europe following the French Revolution.

Venice, not having been a nation state (see also Bowd 2010: 235), but a capitalist polity encompassing a population with supposed 'common interests', was always ready to exploit the advantages of accepting 'foreigners' into their state or colonial territory.[29]

The Greeks lived in a well-defined community in Castello; the Germans, most of them merchants, resided at Rialto in the Fondaco dei Tedeschi; and Turks lived in a somewhat more loosely knit community in the parish of San Giacomo dall'Orio. The Jews, themselves a multi-ethnic community of German, Italian, Iberian, and Levantine origins, were confined to the Ghetto from 1516 on. [...] the Florentines and the Lucchesi both chose to reside in the parishes nearest the Rialto.

(Martin and Romano 2000b: 21)[30]

At the same time, as Venice never ceased to constitute a maritime republic, communities of Venetians, often quite numerous, were established all over the Mediterranean and beyond (Ferraro 2012: 108).

The Venetian state and society, having existed in the historical period prior to 'the age of nationalism' from the fifteenth century onwards, had successfully created forms of economic and social interaction,[31] and republican representation and loyalty to state authorities that facilitated the expanded reproduction of capitalist relations of exploitation and domination, while simultaneously preserving a multicultural society and an empire extending both to the Mediterranean East and the Mainland West. Venice remained a capitalist society and a colonial power until her decline.

To formulate this final result in a different way, I would say that for centuries, Venice constituted a capitalist *society* and a capitalist *state* (the latter as a material–political condensation of capitalist domination and exploitation), without the society being a *national* society and without the capitalist state being a *national* state.

The Greeks, Dalmatians, Friulians, and Lombards subject to the city in the lagoons were all vital elements in the Venetian state, so that the lion of St. Mark never planted all four feet firmly on Italian soil.

(Lane 1973: 431)

Was this lack of a 'national element' a sign of backwardness? I could posit the same question in more current terms: was the outcome of the two referendums in the Italian regions of Lombardy (Milan) and Veneto (Venice) on 22 October 2017, where more than 90% of the voters in each region voted in favour of autonomy from Italy, a sign of backwardness? Given the fact that, from an ethnic point of view, neither Lombardy nor Veneto are regions nationally differentiated from the rest of Italy, the referendums expressed aspirations for new, *non-national* capitalist polities!

The parallelism between the two historical examples, the Venetian social formation from the late fourteenth to the eighteenth centuries on the one hand, and parts of contemporary northern Italy on the other, may at first glance seem puzzling. Nevertheless, there is a common element in both cases: the significance of forms of governmentality *beyond national politics, beyond national rhetoric, beyond national cohesion* or *national territorialization*. In other words,

I am referring to the significance of forms of governmentality based on technologies of power deriving from internationalized (or 'globalized') monetary and financial processes and regulatory norms (Emmanouilidis 2016). In a recently published book that I co-authored, we stressed the following:

> [...] contemporary capitalism comprises a historically specific form of the organization of capitalist power wherein governmentality through financial markets acquires a crucial role.
>
> (Sotiropoulos et al. 2013: 4)

> There are three key abstract elements that characterize this process of regulation: 1. It has a heterogeneous population as its target [...] 2. It deals with collective phenomena [...] 3. Collective phenomena are grasped in statistical terms.
>
> (ibid: 164–165)

From the financing of the public debt through forced loans from the wealthy inhabitants of Venice, to the conscription of crews for war fleets by lot and rotation, while allowing any conscript to pay for a stand-in to substitute for him in the fleet service, the three abstract elements we identify were present in Venice and her empire: a *heterogeneous* population was dealt with in *collective* and *statistical–impersonal* terms.

Gilles Deleuze and Felix Guattari connect the ascension of territorial states, and later of national states, not with the emergence of capitalism but with the need to territorialize, as a means of facilitating capitalist reproduction on an expanded scale. They write:

> capitalism started out from city-towns, but these pushed deterritorialization so far that immanent modern States had to temper their madness, to recapture and invest them so as to carry out necessary reterritorializations in the form of new internal limits.
>
> (Deleuze-Guattari 1994: 98)

The importance of territorialization seems again, in the era of neoliberal financialization, to be losing ground: non-national forms of governmentality based on market rules have once again been playing a decisive role. In this sense, Venice's capitalism may be seen as less obsolete; on the contrary, it may have been a return to the future.

Notes

1   The following pertinent proposition by Louis Althusser is worth remembering at this point:

> The distinction between the public and the private is a distinction internal to bourgeois law, and valid in the (subordinate) domains in which bourgeoisie law exercises its 'authority' [...]: the State, which is the State *of* the ruling class,

is neither 'public' nor 'private'; on the contrary, it is the precondition for any distinction between public and private.

(Althusser 1984-a: 18)

2 As Guido Ruggiero stresses:

While much of the rest of Europe was still under the rule of the households of hereditary kings or local nobles, Venice lived and traded under a rule of written law interpreted by elected councils and judges and enforced by an elaborate bureaucracy.

(Ruggiero 1978: 243)

In one case, in 1355, the doge himself, Marin Falier, was sentenced to death and beheaded (Lane 1973: 181–182).

3 "Venice avoided the dominance of any single family and perfected a system of checks and balances within its ruling class" (Lane 1966: 530).

4 "In a sense the Venetian patriciate, while also directing policy, making laws and commanding warships, actually was itself a bureaucracy, its members being prepared to perform supervisory, executive and accounting functions elsewhere deputed to men outside the traditional ruling caste" (Mallett and Hale 1984: 493).

5 According to *The National Archives*,

in early-19th-century Britain very few people had the right to vote. A survey conducted in 1780 revealed that the electorate in England and Wales consisted of just 214,000 people – less than 3% of the total population of approximately 8 million. In Scotland the electorate was even smaller: in 1831 a mere 4,500 men, out of a population of more than 2.6 million people, were entitled to vote in parliamentary elections.(www.nationalarchives.gov.uk/pathways/citizenship/struggle_democracy/getting_vote.htm)

6 "When Englishmen, having executed Charles I, engaged in vigorous debate over desirable forms of government, many pointed out to Venice to show a republic's good possibilities. Their arguments were echoed a century later in the rhetoric of the revolution which created a new republic in America" (Lane 1973: 405).

7 "[...] by 1148 the new duke tells us in a document that he has made an oath at his accession to cuncto communi Venetico populo, 'the whole common Venetian people'. The commune thus crystallised quickly here, but without changing the governmental system of the city at all" (Wickham 2015: 180).

8 "This right [that men hold in common], which is defined by the power of a people, is usually called sovereignty, and is possessed absolutely by whoever has charge of affairs of state" (Spinoza 2002: 687).

9 "[...] an aristocracy should consist of a large number of patricians [...] it comes closer than monarchy to an absolute form of government, and is therefore more suitable for the preservation of freedom" (Spinoza 2002: 723).

10 "[...] republicanism gave to the civilization of Italy from the thirteenth through the sixteenth century its distinctive quality" (Lane 1966: 520).

11 "Venice provided subsidies for some ducal notaries to enable them to attend school in 1336, and tax exemptions for scholars were also common" (Denley 1990: 106).

12 "Clearly, the consumption patterns of Venetians mirrored the hierarchy of class and financial means, and there were stark differences. Perhaps none was more important than food, humans' most basic necessity. It thus became an important social and political tool for Venetian magistrates in order to cement civic loyalty" (Ferraro 2012: 115–116).

13 "On the whole, in sixteenth-century Venice charity was the 'moral duty' of the government and the wealthy. [...] Venetian authorities were interested in social

order and control, hence their systematic support of the work of the charitable organizations in the city. [...] [F]rom the sixteenth century every public notary was ordered to formally ask testators whether they wished to make donations to specific charitable institutions" (Iordanou 2016: 813).

14 "The *Promissione* began with a long section on robbery. That section, unlike other sections dealing with violent crimes, included a detailed scheme of penalties. Its position at the beginning of the criminal code, in addition to the detailed penalties, indicates that robbery was the crime of greatest concern to the ruling class which wrote and applied the law. Moreover, robbery was evaluated by the *Promissione* without reference to violence, but rather on the basis of the quantity of property taken. Penalties were carefully graded into several levels of severity, according to the value of the loss. [...] Hanging was the penalty for anyone who stole more than forty lire. For repeaters, however, the law contained no gradations: hanging was the penalty. [...] Much more brief were the subsequent sections on assault and murder. [...] Penalties for assault that drew blood [...]were left to the discretion of the judge [...]. The contrast in the eyes of the law between robbery and assault was clear. [...]There was judicial discretion in penalties for violence, but carefully codified penalties for property crimes" (Ruggiero 1978: 245). See also Davis 2009: 104.

15 "There was a tax riot in 1265 of such violence that the doge, Ranieri Zeno, a leader in the wars for the lordship of the Gulf and promulgator of the maritime code of 1255, pretended to give in to the rioters, although later he hunted out and hung their leaders" (Lane 1973: 106–107).

16 In Venice, "[t]he lower classes were never incited to revolt, or given the opportunity to revolt, by vengeful nobles offering to be their leaders" (Lane 1973: 271).

17 "Communism is for us not a *state of affairs* which is to be established, an *ideal* to which reality [will] have to adjust itself. We call communism the *real* movement which abolishes the present state of things. The conditions of this movement result from the premises now in existence" (Marx and Engels 1998: 57).

18 Petrarch wrote to Venice's doge Andrea Dandolo around 1350:

> I beseech you not to let the flourishing Republic committed to your care, and all this rich and lovely part of Italy which lies between Alps and Apennines, become the prey of hungry foreign wolves, from whom wise Nature, as I constantly repeat, has separated us by ridges of the Alps themselves.
>
> (cited by Whitfield 1966: 31)

By way of comparison, Antonio Gramsci wrote in his *Prison Notebooks* in the early 1930s:

> There is today a European cultural consciousness, and there exists a long list of public statements by intellectuals and politicians who maintain that a European union is necessary. It is fair to say that the course of history is heading toward this union and that there are many material forces that will only be able to develop within this union. If this union were to come into existence in x years, the word 'nationalism' will have the same archaeological value as 'municipalism' has today.
>
> (Gramsci 2007: 60–61)

Less than a decade after these lines were written, in 1939, history's most terrible massacre between European nations was set in motion.

19 Analysing the notion of ideology, Antonio Gramsci makes the following apt remark:

> One must not think of 'ideology' or doctrine as something artificial and mechanically superimposed (like a garment over the skin, as opposed to the skin,

which is organically produced by a creature's entire biological organism) but rather as something historically produced, as a ceaseless struggle.

(Gramsci 1996: 56–57)

20 The importance of St Mark as Venice's protector saint did not suffice to differentiate the Venetian populace from that of the enemy's, as, e.g., the populace of Genoa, who were under the protection of St George. The schism between the two states was political (rooted of course in economic antagonisms), and political rivalries were only marginally determined by religious criteria. We shall not forget that both Venice and Genoa very frequently allied alternately with "the schismatic Greeks", in their effort to dominate over one another. When in 1261 the Genoese assisted Michael VIII Paleologos in conquering Constantinople, Pope "Innocent III [...] excommunicated the Genoese for taking the side of the schismatic Greeks" (Nicol 1988: 179).

21 Mrs. Oliphant, trying to imagine Marco Polo's sentiments when, as a prisoner of war, he arrived in Genoa around 1298, accepts the historical evidence that a Venetian was "born to hate the Genoese":

> But now what a revelation to him must have been the wild passion and savage delight of those near neighbours with but the width of a European peninsula between them and so much hatred, rancour, and fierce antagonism! Probably however Marco having born to hate the Genoese, was occupied by none of these sentimental reflections.

(Oliphant 1889: 155)

22 "[...] representatives from the community of Nauplion presented themselves to the Senate in 1445 and asked for a number of local offices to be eliminated, claiming that the offices were useless and a burden on the local treasury. The Senate complied, but several months later, the *podestà* of Nauplion wrote to the Senate denouncing the representatives as false. The false representatives were Greek, he said, and all the offices eliminated had been for Latins" (O'Connell 2009: 112).

23 These identities are, of course, very difficult to be apprehended by all those who adhere to the ideology of 'national identity' and perceive the *Stato da Màr* as primarily Greek, and the *terraferma* as Italian. As Frederic C. Lane points out,

> [w]e should not wait for Italian historians to take the lead in emphasizing this republican element in their history. Like contemporary members of the historical profession in other lands, [...] they are largely concerned with the nationalism of their own nation. Many of them are preoccupied by the problem of national unity, even in describing a period in which such unity was conspicuous by its absence.

(Lane 1973: 536)

24 "[...] the common language of Crete was Greek, that is Cretan dialect, and by the end of our period the use of Italian was more or less restricted to the realms of administration and culture. Educated men would of course be bilingual, but it is clear from documents of the sixteenth century that women, even from noble Venetian families, would usually know only Greek. Greek was written in both the Greek and Latin alphabets, and a number of manuscripts of literary works survives in Latin script" (Holton 2006: 14). It is of interest that Vitsentzos Kornaros, the most important Cretan romantic poet, author of *Erotokritos* in the local Cretan dialect, was of Venetian ancestry, of the famous patrician Cornaro (or Corner) family. As David Holton points out, in reviewing works by Stylianos Alexiou, Giannis Mavromatis and Peter Warren, "most scholars now accept the identification of the poet with Vicenzo Cornaro, son of Giacomo and brother of Andrea, who lived from 1553 to 1613/1614" (Holton 2006: 298).

25 "On religious or secular festivals grand processions attracted large audiences of Orthodox and Catholics alike" (Maltezou 2006: 44).

26 "Residents of Crete were the most frequent recipients of special favors in the maritime empire, receiving well over half of the total number of *grazie* recorded for the *stato da mar*. Since the Veneto-Cretan elite was closely tied to the Venetian patriciate through relationships of marriage or business partnerships, it had more access to the necessary connections to introduce a petition into the labyrinth of the Venetian councils and ensure that it received a favorable hearing" (O'Connell 2009: 101).

27 "[…] conflicts over property and inheritance between the maritime state's wealthiest inhabitants often ended up before Venetian courts" (O'Connell 2009: 88).

28 "Large numbers of Cretans found refuge in the Ionian Isles, where they transplanted their culture and traditions and played a major part in the intellectual awakening and general cultural development of the Heptanese in the succeeding centuries" (Maltezou 2006: 19).

29 By contrast, the emergence of a nation manifests itself as a totalitarian tendency of ethnic purity and ethnic cleansing: the incorporation of the populations of the state into the main body of the nation, negative discrimination against 'minorities' and whomever does not become part of the nation, sometimes to the point of violently expelling them from the main body of the nation. As Nicos Poulantzas puts it:

> The enclosures implicit in the constitution of the modern people-nation are only so awesome because they are also fragments of a history that is totalised and capitalised by the state. Genocide is the elimination of what become 'foreign bodies' of the national history and territory: it expels them beyond space and time […]. Concentration camps are a modern invention in the additional sense that the frontier-gates close on 'anti-nationals' for whom time and national historicity are *in suspense*.
>
> (Poulantzas, 1980: 114–115)

30 "By 1478 it is estimated that there were already some 4,000 Greeks living in Venice" (Holton 2006: 4).

31 "A wide range of social affiliation linked people of different stations together in more than one way, starting within the household and extending to the workplace, the tavern, the market, the parish church, the neighborhood faction, guilds, confraternities, ethnic communities, and sexual relations. Baptisms, godparenting, guardianships, marriages, marital dissolution, business relations, legal disputes, funerals, feasts, charity, religious events, ceremonies, games, and brawls brought families, parishioners, and neighbors […] together with foreign subjects, refugees, and tourists, again producing *hybrid mixes of cultures that came to be known as 'Venetian'*" (Ferraro 2012: 77–78, emphasis added).

Bibliography

Abulafia, David (1977) *The Two Italies: Economic Relations between the Norman Kingdom of Sicily and the Northern Communes*, Cambridge: Cambridge University Press.

Abulafia, David (2012) *The Great Sea: A Human History of the Mediterranean*, London: Penguin Books.

Allen, Robert C. (2011) *Global Economic History: A Very Short Introduction*, Cambridge: Cambridge University Press.

Althusser, Louis (1976) *Essays in Self-Criticism*, London: Verso.

Althusser, Louis (1984a) "Ideology and Ideological State Apparatuses (Notes towards an Investigation)", in Althusser, Louis, *Essays on Ideology*, London: Verso: 1–60.

Althusser, Louis (1984b) "Reply to John Lewis", *Essays on Ideology*, London: Verso: 61–139.

Althusser, Louis (1990) *For Marx*, London: Verso.

Althusser, Louis (2006) *Philosophy of the Encounter: Later writings 1978–87*, London: Verso.

Althusser, Louis, Étienne Balibar (1997) *Reading Capital*, London: Verso.

Althusser, Louis, Étienne Balibar, Roger Establet, Pierre Macherey, and Jacques Rancière (2015) *Reading Capital*, London: Verso.

Amin, Samir (1974) *Accumulation on a World Scale*, New York: Monthly Review Press.

Amin, Samir (1976) *Unequal Development: An Essay on the Social Formations of Peripheral Capitalism*, New York: Monthly Review Press.

Amin, Samir (1996) "The Ancient World-Systems versus the Modern Capitalist World System", in Frank, Andre G. and Barry K. Gills (eds.) *The World System: Five Hundred Years or Five Thousand?*, London and New York: Routledge.

Anderson, Perry (1974a) *Passages from Antiquity to Feudalism*, London: New Left Books.

Anderson, Perry (1974b) *Lineages of the Absolutist State*, London: New Left Books.

Arbel, Benjamin, Bernard Hamilton and David Jacoby (eds.) (1989) *Latins and Greeks in the Eastern Mediterranean after 1204*, London and New York: Routledge.

Arrighi, Giovanni (1993) "The Three Hegemonies of Historical Materialism", in Gill, Stephen (ed.) *Gramsci, Historical Materialism and International Relations*, Cambridge: Cambridge University Press: 148–185.

Arrighi, Giovanni (1996) *The Long Twentieth Century*, London and New York: Verso.

Arrighi, Giovanni (1999) "Globalization, State Sovereignty, and the 'Endless' Accumulation of Capital", in Smith, D. A., D. J. Solinger and S. C. Topik (eds.) *States and Sovereignty in the Global Economy*, London and New York: Routledge.

Aston, Trevor Henry and Charles H. E. Philin (eds.) (1985) *The Brenner Debate: Agrarian Class Struggle and Economic Development in Pre-Industrial Europe*, Cambridge: Cambridge University Press.

Bakker, J. I. (Hans) (2003) "The Weber-Rachfahl Debate: Calvinism and Capitalism in Holland? (Part One)", *Michigan Sociological Review*, Vol. 17, (Fall): 119–148.

Balibar, Étienne (1983) "Sur le concept marxiste de la 'division du travail manuel et du travail intellectuel' et la lutte des classes", in Belkhir, Jean (ed.) *L'Intellectuel: L'intelligentsia et les manuels*, Paris: Anthropos, 97–117.

Balibar, Étienne (1984) "Marx et l' Entreprise", *Politique Aujourd'hui*, No. 5: 24–32.

Balibar, Étienne (1986) "Klassen/Klassenkampf", in Labica, G. and G. Bensussan (eds.) *Kritisches Wörterbuch des Marxismus*, Vol. 4, Berlin: Argument: 615–636.

Balibar, Étienne (1997) "On the Basic Concepts of Historical Materialism", in Althusser, Louis and Etienne Balibar (eds.) *Reading Capital*, London: Verso: 199–308.

Banaji, Jairus (1977) "Modes of Production in a Materialist Conception of History", *Capital & Class*, Vol. 3, No. 3: 1–43.

Banaji, Jairus (2003) "The Fictions of Free Labour: Contract, Coercion, and So-Called Unfree Labour", *Historical Materialism*, Vol. 11, No. 3: 69–95.

Banaji, Jairus (2010) *Theory as History: Essays on Modes of Production and Exploitation*, Leiden and Boston: Brill.

von Below, Georg (1926) *Probleme der Wirtschaftsgeschichte*, Berlin: Verlag von J.E.B. Mohr.

Bernstein, Eduard (1895) *Kommunistische und demokratisch-sozialistische Strömungen während der englischen Revolution*, Stuttgart: J.H.W. Dietz.

Bernstein, Eduard (1980) *Cromwell and Communism: Socialism and Democracy in the Great English Revolution*, London: Spokesman Books.

Bettelheim, Charles (1968) *La Transition vers l'économie socialiste*, Paris: Maspero.

Bettelheim, Charles (1974) *Cultural Revolution and Industrial Organisation in China*, New York: Monthly Review Press.

Bettelheim, Charles (1975) *Economic Calculation and Forms of Property: An Essay on the Transition Between Capitalism and Socialism*, New York: Monthly Review Press.

Blakemore, Richard J. (2017) "Pieces of eight, pieces of eight: seamen's earnings and the venture economy of early modern seafaring", *Economic History Review*, Vol. 70, No. 4: 1153–1184.

Bonefeld, Werner (2001) "The Permanence of Primitive Accumulation: Commodity Fetishism and Social Constitution", *The Commoner*, No. 2, September, www.commoner.org.uk

Bösch, Gerhard (2002) "The Serrata of the Great Council and Venetian Society", in Martin, John and Dennis Romano (eds.) *Venice Reconsidered: The History and Civilization of an Italian City State, 1297–1797*, Baltimore: The John Hopkins University Press: 67–88.

Bowd, Stephen D. (2010) *Venice's most Loyal City: Civic Identity in Renaissance Brescia*, Cambridge, MA and London: Harvard University Press.

Brass, Tom (2011) *Labour Regime Change in the Twenty-First Century. Unfreedom, Capitalism and Primitive Accumulation*, Leiden and Boston: Brill.

Braudel, Fernand (1972) *The Mediterranean and the Mediterranean World in the Age of Philip II*, London: Fontana/Collins.

Braudel, Fernand (1979) *Afterthoughts on Material Civilization and Capitalism*, Baltimore and London: The John Hopkins University Press.

Braudel, Fernand (1981) *Civilization & Capitalism 15th-18th Century. Vol. 1: The Structures of Everyday Life*, New York: Harper & Row.

Braudel, Fernand (1982) *Civilization & Capitalism 15th-18th Century. Vol. 2: The Wheels of Commerce*, New York: Harper & Row.

Braudel, Fernand (1984) *Civilization & Capitalism 15th-18th Century. Vol. 3: The Perspective of the World*, New York: Harper & Row.

Brecht, Bertolt (2008) *Life of Galileo*, London: Bloomsbury Publishing.

Brenner, Robert (1976) "Agrarian Structure and Economic Development in Pre-Industrial Europe", *Past and Present*, Vol. 70, No. 1: 30–75.

Brenner, Robert (1978) "Dobb on the Transition from Feudalism to Capitalism", *Cambridge Journal of Economics*, Vol. 2, No. 2: 121–140.

Brenner, Robert (1982) "The Agrarian Roots of European Capitalism", *Past and Present*, Vol. 97, No. 1: 16–113.

Brenner, Robert (1985) "The Agrarian Roots of European Capitalism", in Aston, Trevor Henry and Charles H. E. Philin (eds.) *The Brenner Debate. Agrarian Class Struggle and Economic Development in Pre-Industrial Europe*, Cambridge: Cambridge University Press: 213–327.

Brenner, Robert (2001) "The Low Countries in the Transition to Capitalism", *Journal of Agrarian Change*, Vol. 1, No. 2: 169–241.

Brenner, Robert (2003) *Merchants and Revolution: Commercial Change, Political Conflict and London's Overseas Traders 1550–1653*, London and New York: Verso.

Brenner, Robert (2006) "What is, and what is not, imperialism? *Historical Materialism*, Vol. 14, No. 4: 79–105.

Brentano, Lujo (1916) *Die Anfänge des modernen Kapitalismus*, München: Verlag der K. B. Akademie der Wissenschaften.

Brentano, Lujo (1969 [1870]) *On the History and Development of Gilds and the Origin of Trade Unions*, New York: Burt Franklin.

Bresson, Alain (2016) *The Making of the Ancient Greek Economy: Institutions, Markets and Growth in the City-States*, Princeton and Oxford: Princeton University Press.

Brook, Timothy (ed.) (1989) *The Asiatic Mode of Production in China*, New York: M.E. Sharpe.

Callinicos, Alex (2007) "Does Capitalism Need the State System", *Cambridge Review of International Affairs*, Vol. 20, No. 4: 533–549.

Callinicos, Alex (2010) *Bonfire of Illusions: The Twin Crises of the Liberal World*, Cambridge: Polity Press.

Carchedi, Guglielmo (1977) *On the Economic Identification of Social Classes*, London: Routledge & Kegan Paul.

Chisholm, Hugh (ed.) (1911) "Comacchio", in *Encyclopædia Britannica*, Vol. 6, 11th ed., Cambridge: Cambridge University Press: 749.

Cohen, Gerald A. (1989) *History, Labour and Freedom: Themes from Marx*, Cambridge: Cambridge University Press.

Cohen, Edward E. (1992) *Athenian Economy and Society: A Banking Perspective*, Princeton: Princeton University Press.

Cox, Oliver Cromwell (1959a) *Caste, Class and Race: A Study in Social Dynamics*, New York: Monthly Review Press.

Cox, Oliver Cromwell (1959b) *The Foundations of Capitalism*, London: Peter Owen Ltd.

Cox, Oliver Cromwell (1964) *Capitalism as a System*, New York: Monthly Review Press.

Crone, Patricia (2003) *Pre-industrial Societies: Anatomy of the Pre-Modern World*, London: Oneworld Publications.

Dante, Alighieri (2008) *The Divine Comedy: Inferno*, tr. Henry Wadsworth Longfellow, Digitalized version of the 1870 edition, Boston: Fields, Osgood, & Co., www.gutenberg.org/cache/epub/1004/pg1004-images.html (accessed February 5, 2018).

Davis, Robert, C. (2009) *Shipbuilders of the Venetian Arsenal: Workers and Workplace in the Preindustrial City*, Baltimore: The John Hopkins University Press.

Day, John (2002) "The Levant Trade in the Middle Ages", in Laiou, A. (ed.) *The Economic History of Byzantium: From the Seventh through the Fifteenth Century*, Washington DC: Dumbarton Oaks Research Library and Collection: 807–814.

Dean, Trevor and Chris Wickham (eds.) (1990) *City and countryside in Late Medieval and Renaissance Italy: Essays Presented to Philip Jones*, London and Ronceverte: The Hambledon Press.

De Angelis, Massimo (2007) *The Beginning of History: Value Struggles and Global Capital*, London: Pluto Press.

Deleuze, Gilles and Felix Guattari (1983) *Anti-Oedipus. Capitalism and Schizophrenia*, Minneapolis: University of Minnesota Press.

Deleuze, Gilles and Felix Guattari (1987) *A Thousand Plateaus: Capitalism and Schizophrenia*, Minneapolis: University of Minnesota Press.

Deleuze, Gilles and Felix Guattari (1994) *What is Philosophy?*, New York: Columbia University Press.

Denley, Peter (1990) "Governments and Schools in Late Medieval Italy", in Dean, Trevor and Chris Wickham (eds.) *City and Countryside in Late Medieval and Renaissance Italy: Essays Presented to Philip Jones*, London and Ronceverte: The Hambledon Press: 93–107.

Dobb, Maurice (1975) *Studies in the Development of Capitalism*, New York: International Publishers.

Dobb, Maurice (2006) "A Reply", in Hilton, R. (ed.) *The Transition from Feudalism to Capitalism*, Delhi: Aakar Books: 57–67.

Van Doosselaere, Quentin (2009) *Commercial Agreements and Social Dynamics in Medieval Genoa*, Cambridge: Cambridge University Press.

Dunbar, Charles F. (1892) "The Bank of Venice", *The Quarterly Journal of Economics*, Vol. 6, No. 3: 308–335.

Dutschke, Rudi (1974) *Versuch, Lenin auf die Füsse zu stellen*, Berlin: Wagenbach.

Ebner, Alexander (2000) "Schumpeter and the 'Schmollerprogramm': Integrating Theory and History in the Analysis of Economic Development", *Journal of Evolutionary Economics*, Vol. 10, No. 3: 355–372.

Economakis, George (2001) "Land Reform", in Barry Jones, R. J. (ed.) *Encyclopedia of International Political Economy*, Vol. 2, London and New York: Routledge: 901–902.

Economakis, George (2005) "Definition of the Capitalist Mode of Production: A Re-examination (with Application to Non-capitalist Modes of Production)", *History of Economics Review*, Vol. 42, No. 1: 12–28.

Economakis, George and John Milios (2001) "Historical School. German", in Barry Jones, R. J. (ed.) *Encyclopedia of International Political Economy*, Vol. 2, London and New York: Routledge: 686–687.

Emmanouilidis, Marios (2016) "Urban Panics and Black Holes. Ambiguities and Deceleration in the Time of Financialization", in Geheimagentur, Schäfer, Martin Jörg, and Vassilis S. Tsianos (eds.) *The Art of Being Many. Towards a New Theory and Practice of Gathering*, Bielefeld: transcript Verlag: 233–250.

Engels, Friedrich (1961) "Letter to Werner Sombart March 11 1895", in *Beitrage zur Geschichte der deutscher Arbeiterbewegung No. 3*. Reprint: Marx and Engels, Selected Works, Vol. 3: 504–506, www.marxists.org/archive/marx/works/1895/letters/95_03_11.htm

Engels, Friedrich (2010) *Origins of the Family, Private Property, and the State*, London: Penguin Classics.

Ferguson, Niall (1999) *The House of Rothschild: Money's Prophets 1798–1848*, London: Penguin Books.

Ferguson, Niall (2008) *The Ascent of Money: A Financial History of the World*, London: Penguin Books.

Ferraro, Joanne M. (2012) *Venice: History of the Floating City*, Cambridge: Cambridge University Press.

Finlay, George (2013) *A History of Greece, Vol. 5: Greece Under Ottoman and Venetian Domination*, Oxford: Oxford University Press.

Foreign Office, Miscellaneous series (1892) *No 217. Report on the Condition of Labour in Russia*, Athens: Historical Archive of the National Bank of Greece.

Fourtounis, George (2013) "'An Immense Aspiration to Being': The Causality and Temporality of the Aleatory", in Diefenbach, Katja, Sara R. Farris, Gal Kirn and Peter D. Thomas (eds.) *Encountering Althusser. Politics and Materialism in Contemporary Radical Thought*, London and New York: Bloomsbury: 43–60.

Frank, Andre Gunter (1969) *Kapitalismus und Unterentwicklung in Lateinamerika*, Frankfurt/M.: Europäische Verlagsanstalt.

Frank, Andre Gunter and Barry K. Gills (eds.) (1996) *The World System: Five Hundred Years or Five Thousand?*, London and New York: Routledge.

Fusaro, Maria (2015) *Political Economies of Empire in the Early Modern Mediterranean: The Decline of Venice and the Rise of England, 1450–1700*, Cambridge: Cambridge University Press.

Gerstein, Ira (1989) "(Re)Structuring Structural Marxism", *Rethinking Marxism*, Vol. 2, No. 1: 104–133.

Godelier, Maurice (1978) *Sur les sociétés précapitalistes*, Paris: Maspero.

Gramsci, Antonio (2007) *Prison Notebooks, Vol. III*, New York: Columbia University Press.

Greene, Molly (2000) *A Shared World: Christians and Muslims in the Early Modern Mediterranean*, Princeton: Princeton University Press.

Haldon, John (1993) *The State and the Tributary Mode of Production*, London and New York: Verso.

Haldon, John (ed.) (2009) *A Social History of Byzantium*, Oxford: Blackwell.

Harman, Chris (2004) "The Rise of Capitalism", *International Socialism*, No. 102. www.isj.org.uk/?id=21 (accessed June 1, 2017).

Harman, Chris (2006) "Origins of Capitalism", *International Socialism*, No. 111. www.isj.org.uk/index.php4?id=219&issue=111 (accessed June 2, 2017).

Harnecker, Marta (2000) *Conceptos Elementales del Materialismo Historico*, Havana: Siglo Veintiuno.

Harrington, James (1992 [1656]) *The Commonwealth of Oceana*, Cambridge: Cambridge University Press.

Harvey, Alan (1989) *Economic Expansion in the Byzantine Empire, 900–1200*, Cambridge: Cambridge University Press.

Heck, Gene W. (2006) *Charlemagne, Muhammad, and the Arab Roots of Capitalism*, Berlin and New York: Walter de Gruyter.

Heinrich, Michael (2012) *An Introduction to the Three Volumes of Karl Marx's Capital*, New York: Monthly Review Press.

Heinsohn, Gunnar and Otto Steiger (1989) "The Veil of Barter", in Kregel, Jan A. (ed.) *Inflation and Income Distribution in Capitalist Crisis*, London: Macmillan: 175 ff.

Heller, Henry (2011) *The Birth of Capitalism: A Twenty-First-Century Perspective*, London: Pluto Press.

Hendy, Michael F. (1985) *Studies in the Byzantine Monetary Economy c. 300–1450*, Cambridge: Cambridge University Press.

Hilton, Rodney (1952) "Capitalism – What's in a Name?", *Past & Present*, Vol. 1, No. 1: 32–43.

Hilton, Rodney (1975) *The English Peasantry in the Later Middle Ages*, Oxford: Clarendon Press.

Hilton, Rodney, (ed.) (2006a) *The Transition from Feudalism to Capitalism*, Delhi: Aakar Books.

Hilton, Rodney (2006b) "Introduction", in Hilton, R. (ed.) *The Transition from Feudalism to Capitalism*, Delhi: Aakar Books: 9–30.

Hilton, Rodney (2006c) "A Comment", in Hilton, Rodney (ed.) *The Transition from Feudalism to Capitalism*, Delhi: Aakar Books: 109–117.

Hobsbawm, Eric (1992) *Nations and Nationalism since 1780: Programme, Myth, Reality*, Cambridge: Cambridge University Press.

Hoffman, Philip T., Gilles Postel-Vinay and Jean-Laurent Rosenthal (2007) *Surviving Large Losses: Financial Crises, the Middle Class, and the Development of Capital Markets*, Cambridge, MA and London: Harvard University Press.

Holton, Robert J. (1985) *The Transition from Feudalism to Capitalism*, London: Macmillan Education.

Holton, David (ed.) (2006) *Literature and Society in Renaissance Crete*, Cambridge: Cambridge University Press.

Hopkins, T. K. and I. Wallerstein (1979) "Grundzüge der Entwicklung des modernen Weltsystems", in Senghaas, D. (ed.) *Von Europa lernen. Entwicklungsgeschichtliche Betrachtungen*, Frankfurt/M.: Suhrkamp: 280 ff.

Howgego, Christopher (1995) *Ancient History from Coins*, London and New York: Routledge.

Hung, Hsueh-ping (1969) "The Essence of the 'Theory of Productive Forces' is to Oppose Proletarian Revolution", *Peking Review*, No. 38: 5–8.

Hung, Kao (1969) "From Bernstein to Liu Shao-chi", *Peking Review*, No. 38: 8–9.

Iordanou, Ioanna (2016) "Pestilence, Poverty, and Provision: Re-evaluating the Role of the *popolani* in Early Modern Venice", *The Economic History Review*, Vol. 69, No. 3: 801–822.

Israel, Jonathan I. (2001) *Radical Enlightenment: Philosophy and the Making of Modernity 1650–1750*, Oxford: Oxford University Press.

Jacoby, David (1989) *Latins and Greeks in the Eastern Mediterranean after 1204*, London and New York: Routledge.

Jacoby, David (2001) *Byzantium, Latin Romania and the Mediterranean*, Aldershot: Ashgate.

Jessop, Bob (1985) *Nicos Poulantzas - Marxist Theory and Political Strategy*, London and Basingstoke: Macmillan Publishers LTD.

Kaplan, Michael (2009) "The Producing Population", in Haldon, John (ed.) *A Social History of Byzantium*, Oxford: Blackwell: 143–167.

Katz, Claudio J. (1993) "Karl Marx on the Transition from Feudalism to Capitalism", *Theory and Society*, Vol. 22, No. 3: 363–389.

Kautsky, Karl (1988) *The Agrarian Question*, London: Zwan Publications.

Keynes, John Maynard (2013) *The Collected Writings of John Maynard Keynes, Vol. XX-VIII, Social, Political and Literary Writings*, Cambridge: Cambridge University Press for the Royal Economic Society: 253–54.

Kyrtatas, Dimitris (2002) "Domination and Exploitation", in Cartledge, Paul, Edward E. Cohen and Lin Foxhall (eds.) *Money, Labour and Land: Approaches to the Economies of Ancient Greece*, London and New York: Routledge: 140–155.

Kyrtatas, Dimitris (2011) "Slavery and Economy in the Greek World", in Bradley, Keith and Paul Cartledge (eds.) *The Cambridge World History of Slavery*, Cambridge: Cambridge University Press: 91–111.

Lacher, Hannes (2005) "International Transformation and the Persistence of Territoriality: Toward a New Political Geography of Capitalism", *Review of International Political Economy*, Vol. 12: No. 1: 26–52.

Laibman, David (2007) *Deep History: A Study of Social Evolution and Human Potential*, New York: SUNY Series in Radical Social and Political Theory.

Laiou, Angeliki E. (ed.) (2002a) *The Economic History of Byzantium: From the Seventh through the Fifteenth Century*, Washington DC: Dumbarton Oaks Research Library and Collection.

Laiou, Angeliki E. (2002b) "The Agrarian Economy, Thirteenth–Fifteenth Centuries", in Laiou, Angeliki (ed.) *The Economic History of Byzantium: From the Seventh through the Fifteenth Century*, Washington DC: Dumbarton Oaks Research Library and Collection: 311–375.

Laiou, Angeliki E. (2002c) "The Byzantine Economy: An Overview", in Angeliki, Laiou (ed.) *The Economic History of Byzantium: From the Seventh through the Fifteenth Century*, Washington DC: Dumbarton Oaks Research Library and Collection: 1145–1164.

Lane, Frederic C. (1966) *Venice and History: The Collected Papers of Frederic C. Lane*, Baltimore: The John Hopkins University Press.

Lane, Frederic C. (1973) *Venice, a Maritime Republic*, Baltimore and London: The John Hopkins University Press.

Lane, Frederic C. (1979) *Profits from Power: Readings in Protection Rent and Violence-Controlling Enterprises*, Albany: State University of New York.

Law, John E. (1992) "The Venetian Mainland State in the Fifteenth Century", *Transactions of the Royal Historical Society*, Vol. 2: 153–174.

Le Goff, Jacques (1980) *Time, Work and Culture in the Middle Ages*, Chicago and London: The University of Chicago Press.

Lenin, Vladimir I. (1917) *Letters from Afar*, www.marxists.org/archive/lenin/works/1917/lfafar/first.htm, (accessed October 2, 2017).

Lenin, Vladimir I. (1977) *Collected Works*, Vols. 1–4, Moscow: Progress Publishers.

Lilie, Ralph-Johannes (1994) *Byzantium and the Crusader States 1096–1204*, Cambridge: Clarendon Press.

Linebaugh, Peter and Marcus, Rediker (2001) *The Many-Headed Hydra. Sailors, Slaves, Commoners, and the Hidden History of the Revolutionary Atlantic*, Boston: Beacon Press.

Lukács, Georg (2009) *Lenin: A Study on the Unity of his Thought*, London and New York: Verso.

Luxemburg, Rosa (1971) *The Accumulation of Capital*, London: Routledge and Kegan Paul.

Machiavelli, Niccolò (1981) *The Prince*, London: Penguin classics.

Madden, Thomas F. (2003) *Enrico Dandolo and the Rise of Venice*, Baltimore: The John Hopkins University Press.

Mallet, Michael E. and John R. Hale (1984) *The Military Organisation of a Renaissance State. Venice c. 1400 to 1617*, Cambridge: Cambridge University Press.

Maltezou, Chryssa (2006) "The Historical and Social Context", in Holton, David (ed.) *Literature and society in Renaissance Crete*, Cambridge: Cambridge University Press: 17–48.

Mandel, Ernest (1968) *Marxist Economic Theory*, Vol. 2, London: Merlin.

Mandel, Ernest (1971) *The Formation of the Economic Thought of Karl Marx*, New York and London: Monthly Review Press: 9–90.

Mandel, Ernest (1991) "Introduction", in Marx, Karl *Capital. A Critique of Political Economy*, Vol. 3, London: Penguin Classics.

Mao, Tsetung (1977) *A Critique of Soviet Economics*, London and New York: Monthly Review Press.

Maridaki-Karatza, Olga (2002) "Legal Aspects of the Financing of Trade", in Laiou, Angeliki (ed.) *The Economic History of Byzantium: From the Seventh through the Fifteenth Century*, Washington DC: Dumbarton Oaks Research Library and Collection: 1105–1120.

Marin, Şerban V. (2013) "Marcantonio Sabellico's *Rerum Venetarum* and 'the Definitive History of Venice'. The Beginnings of the Official Historiography in Venice?", *Revista Arhivelor*, Vol. XC/2013, No. 1–2: 134–177.

Martin, John and Dennis Romano (eds.) (2000a) *Venice reconsidered: the history and civilization of an Italian city state, 1297–1797*, Baltimore: The John Hopkins University Press.

Martin, John and Dennis Romano (2000b) "Reconsidering Venice", in Martin, John and Dennis Romano, (eds.) *Venice Reconsidered: The History and Civilization of an Italian City State*, 1297–1797, Baltimore: The John Hopkins University Press: 1–35.

Marx-Engels-Werke (MEW) (1976), Karl Marx Friedrich Engels Werke, Institut für Marxismus-Leninismus beim ZK der SED, vols. 8–38, Berlin: Dietz Verlag.

Marx, Karl (1864) *Results of the Direct Production Process*, Draft Chapter 6 of Vol. 1 of Capital, tr. Ben Fowkes, www.marxists.org/archive/marx/works/1864/economic/ (accessed December 14, 2017).

Marx, Karl (1887) *Capital. A Critique of Political Economy*, Vol. 1 www.marxists.org/archive/marx/works/download/pdf/Capital-Volume-I.pdf (accessed December 2, 2017).

Marx, Karl (1968) *Theories of Surplus Value, Part II*, Moscow: Progress Publishers.

Marx, Karl (1976) "Notizen zur Reform von 1861 in Russland", *MEW*, Vol. 19, Berlin: Dietz Verlag: 407–424.

Marx, Karl (1987) A Contribution to the Critique of Political Economy, in Marx, Karl and Friedrich Engels (eds.) *Collected Works*, Moscow: Progress Publishers: 257–417.

Marx, Karl (1989) "Circular letter to August Bebel, Wilhelm Liebknecht, Wilhelm Bracke and Others", in Marx, Karl and Friedrich Engels (eds.) *Collected Works*, Vol. 24, Moscow: Progress Publishers: 253–269.

Marx, Karl (1991) *Capital. A Critique of Political Economy*, Vol. 3, London: Penguin Classics.

Marx, Karl (1992) *Capital, A Critique of Political Economy*, Vol. 2, London: Penguin Classics.

Marx, Karl (1993) *Grundrisse*, London: Penguin Classics.

Marx, Karl (2010) "*Economic Manuscript of 1861–63 (Continuation)*", in Marx, Karl and Friedrich Engels (eds.) *Collected Works*, Vol. 33, Chadwell Heath: Lawrence and Wishart.

Marx, Karl and Friedrich Engels (1985) *The Communist Manifesto*, London: Penguin Classics.

Marx, Karl and Friedrich Engels (1989) *Marx-Engels Collected Works (MECW)*, Vol. 24, New York: International Publishers.

Marx, Karl and Friedrich Engels (1998) *The German Ideology including Theses on Feuerbach and Introduction to the Critique of Political Economy*, Amherst, NY: Prometheus Books.

Matschke, Klaus-Peter (2002) "Commerce, Trade, Markets, and Money: Thirteenth–Fifteenth Centuries" in Angeliki, Laiou (ed.) *The Economic History of Byzantium: From the Seventh through the Fifteenth Century*, Washington DC: Dumbarton Oaks Research Library and Collection: 771–806.

McKee, Sally (1994) "The Revolt of St Tito in Fourteenth-Century Venetian Crete: A Reassessment", *Mediterranean Historical Review*, Vol. 9, No. 2: 173–204.

McKee, Sally (2004) "Inherited Status and Slavery in Late Mediterranean Italy and Venetian Crete", *Past and Present*, No. 182: 31–53.

McKee, Sally (2008) "Domestic Slavery in Renaissance Italy", *Slavery and Abolition*, Vol. 29, No. 3: 305–326.

Meikle, Scott (1995) *Aristotle's Economic Thought*, Oxford: Clarendon Press.

Merrington, John (2006) "Town and Country in the Transition to Capitalism", in Hilton, Rodney (ed.) *The Transition from Feudalism to Capitalism*, Delhi: Aakar Books: 170–195.

Milios, Jean (1988) *Kapitalistische Entwicklung, Nationalstaat und Imperialismus. Der Fall Griechenland*, Athens: Kritiki.

Milios, John (1989) "The Problem of Capitalist Development: Theoretical Considerations in View of the Industrial Countries and the New Industrial Countries", in Gottdiener, M. and N. Komninos (eds.) *Capitalist Development and Crisis Theory*, London: Macmillan.

Milios, John (1997) "Der Marxsche Begriff der asiatischen Produktionsweise und die theoretische Unmöglichkeit einer Geschichtsphilosophie", *Beiträge zur Marx-Engels-Forschung. Neue Folge*, Berlin: Argument Verlag.

Milios, John (1999) "Preindustrial Capitalist Forms: Lenin's Contribution to a Marxist Theory of Economic Development", *Rethinking Marxism*, Vol. 11, No. 4 (Winter): 38–56.

Milios, John (2000) "Social Classes in Classical and Marxist Political Economy", *American Journal of Economics and Sociology*, Vol. 59, No. 2 (April): 283–302.

Milios, John (2002) "Theory of Value and Money. In Defence of the Endogeneity of Money"; in Sixth International Conference in Economics – Economic Research Center, METU, Ankara, September 11–14.

Milios, John, Dimitri Dimoulis and George Economakis (2002) *Karl Marx and the Classics, an Essay on Value, Crises and the Capitalist Mode of Production*, Aldershot: Ashgate.

Milios, John and Dimitris P. Sotiropoulos (2009) *Rethinking Imperialism: A Study of Capitalist Rule*, London: Palgrave Macmillan.

Milios, John and George Economakis (2011) "The Middle Classes, Class Places, and Class Positions: A Critical Approach to Nicos Poulantzas's Theory", *Rethinking Marxism*, Vol. 23, No. 2: 226–245.

Millett, Paul (1991) *Lending and Borrowing in Ancient Athens*, Cambridge: Cambridge University Press.

Mommsen, Wolfgang J. and Jürgen Osterhammel (eds.) (1987) *Max Weber and His Contemporaries*, New York: HarperCollins.

Montag, Warren (2003) *Althusser*, Houndmills and New York: Palgrave Macmillan.

Morfino, Vittorio (2005), "An Althusserian Lexicon", *Borderlands e-journal*, Vol. 4, No. 2, www.borderlands.net.au/vol4no2_2005/morfino_lexicon.htm, (accessed October 2, 2017).

Morrisson, Cécile (2002) "Byzantine Money: Its Production and Circulation", in Laiou, Angeliki (ed.) *The Economic History of Byzantium: From the Seventh through the Fifteenth Century*, Washington DC: Dumbarton Oaks Research Library and Collection: 909–966.

Müller, Wolfgang (1975) "Momente des bürgerlichen Staates in der griechischen Polis", *Probleme des Klassenkampfs*, No. 17/18: 1–25.

Nails, Debra (2002) *The People of Plato: A Prosopography of Plato and Other Socratics*, Indianapolis and Cambridge: Hackett Publishing Company.

Nicol, Donald M. (1988) *Byzantium and Venice: A Study in Diplomatic and Cultural Relations*, Cambridge: Cambridge University Press.

O'Connell, Monique (2009) *Men of Empire: Power and Negotiation in Venice's Maritime State*, Baltimore: The John Hopkins University Press.

Oliphant, Mrs. (1889) *The Makers of Venice. Doges, Conquerors, Painters, and Men of Letters*, London and New York: Macmillan and Co.

Papagianni, Eleutheria (2002) "Byzantine Legislation on Economic Activity Relative to Social Class", in Laiou, Angeliki (ed.) *The Economic History of Byzantium: From the Seventh through the Fifteenth Century*, Washington DC: Dumbarton Oaks Research Library and Collection: 1083–1093.

Pashukanis, Evgeny B. (1978) *Law and Marxism: A General Theory*, London: Pluto Press.

Peking Review (1969) Issue No. 38, September 19, www.marxists.org/subject/china/peking-review/1969/PR1969-38.pdf

Pellicani, Luciano (1994) *The Genesis of Capitalism and the Origins of Modernity*, New York: Telos Press.

Penna, Daphne (2012) *The Byzantine Imperial Acts to Venice, Pisa and Genoa, 10th–12th centuries, A Comparative Legal Study*, Groningen: Eleven International Publishing.

Perelman, Michael (2000) *The Invention of Capitalism: Classical Political Economy and the Secret History of Primitive Accumulation*, Durham: Duke University Press.

van der Pijl, Kees (2006) *Global Rivalries: From the Cold War to Iraq*, London: Pluto Press.

Pirenne, Henri (2014) *Medieval Cities: Their Origins and the Revival of Trade*, Princeton and Oxford: Princeton University Press.

Plekhanov, Georgi V. (1898) "On the Role of the Individual in History", www.marxists.org/archive/plekhanov/1898/xx/individual.html

Polanyi, Karl (1971) "Aristotle's Discourse on the Economy" in Polanyi, Karl, Conrad M. Arensberg and Harry W. Pearson (eds.), *Trade and Market in the Early Empires: Economies in History and Theory*, Chicago: Henry Regnery: 64–94.

Poulantzas, Nicos (1973) *Political Power and Social Classes*, London: New Left Books.

Poulantzas, Nicos (1975) *Classes in Contemporary Capitalism*, London: New Left Books.

Poulantzas, Nicos (1976) "The Capitalist State: A Reply to Miliband and Laclau", *New Left Review*, No. 95: 63–83.

Poulantzas, Nicos (1980) *State, Power, Socialism*, London and New York: Verso.

Pryor, John H. (1977) "The Origins of the Commenda Contract", *Speculum*, Vol. 52, No. 1: 5–37.

Pullan, Brian (2001) "Jewish Bankers and Monti di Pietà", in Davis, Robert C. and Benjamin Ravid (eds.), *The Jews of Early Modern Venice*, Baltimore and London: The John Hopkins University Press: 53–72.

Rachfahl, Felix (1906) *Wilhelm von Oranien und der niederlaendische Aufstand, Band I*, Halle: Verlag von Max Niemeyer.

Rachfahl, Felix (1907) *Wilhelm von Oranien und der niederlaendische Aufstand, Band II Abteilung I*, Halle: Verlag von Max Niemeyer.

Rachfahl, Felix (1908) *Wilhelm von Oranien und der niederlaendische Aufstand, Band II, Abteilung II*, Halle: Verlag von Max Niemeyer.

Rafie, Kaveh (2013) "The Philosophical Role of Cephalus in the Republic", www.academia.edu/3167386/The_Philosophical_Role_of_Cephalus_in_the_Republic

Read, Jason (2002) "Primitive Accumulation: The Aleatory Foundation of Capitalism", *Rethinking Marxism*, Vol. 14, No. 2: 24–49.

Rediker, Marcus (1989) "The Common Seaman in the Histories of Capitalism and the Working Class", *International Journal of Maritime History*, Vol. 1, No. 2: 337–357.

Resnick, Stephen and Richard Wolff (1979) "The Theory of Transition Conjunctures and the Transition from Feudalism to Capitalism in Western Europe", *Review of Radical Political Economics*, Vol. 11, No. 3 (Fall): 3–22.

Rey, Pierre-Philippe (1973) *Les Alliances de Classes*, Paris: Francois Maspero.

Richards, Alan (1986) *Development and Modes of Production in Marxian Economics: A Critical Evaluation*, London and New York: Harwood Academic Publishers.

Rosdolsky, Roman (1969) *Zur Entstehungsgeschichte des Marxschen "Kapital"*, Vol. II, Frankfurt/M.: EVA.

Rubin, Isaac I. (1979) *A History of Economic Thought*, London: Pluto Press.

Ruggiero Guido (1978) "Law and Punishment in Early Renaissance Venice", *Journal of Criminal Law and Criminology*, Vol. 69, No. 2: 243–256.

Sayers, Sean (1980) "Forces of Production and Relations of Production in Socialist Society", *Radical Philosophy*, No. 24, (Spring): 12–18.

Schaal, Hans (1931) *Vom Tauschhandel zum Welthandel. Bilder vom Handel und Verkehr der Vorgeschichte und des Altertums*, Leipzig und Berlin: Verlag und Druck von B.G. Teubner.

von Schmoller, Gustav (1903) "Werner Sombart, Der moderne Kapitalismus", *Schmollers Jahrbuch für Gesetzgebung, Verwaltung und Volkswirtschaft im Deutschen Reiche*, Vol. 51: 349–369.

Schumpeter, Joseph A. (September 1928) "The Instability of Capitalism", *The Economic Journal*, Vol. 38, No. 151: 361–386.

Semenova, Alla and L. Randall Wray (2015) "The Rise of Money and Class Society: The Contributions of John F. Henry", Levy Economics Institute of Bard College, Working Paper No. 832.

Senghaas, Dieter (ed.) (1982) *Von Europa lernen. Entwicklungsgeschichtliche Betrachtungen*, Frankfurt/M.: Suhrkamp.

Senior, Nassau (1951) *An Outline of the Science of Political Economy*, London: Allen & Unwin.

Sherrard, Philip (1966) *Byzantium*, New York: Time Incorporated.

Sieveking, Heinrich (1935) *Wirtschaftsgeschichte*, Berlin: Verlag Julius Springer.

Smith, Adam (2007) *An Inquiry into the Nature and Causes of the Wealth of Nations*, 2 vols., Indianapolis: Liberty Classics.

Sombart, Werner (1894) "Zur Kritik des ökonomischen Systems von Karl Marx", *Archiv für soziale Gesetzgebung und Statistik*, Vol. 7, No. 4: 555–594.

Sombart, Werner (1898) *Socialism and the Social Movement in the 19th Century, with an Introduction by John B. Clark*, London and New York: G. P. Putnam's Sons.

Sombart, Werner (1902) *Der moderne Kapitalismus. Erster Band. Die Genesis des Kapitalismus*, Leipzig: Verlag von Duncker & Humblot.

Sombart, Werner (1913) *Der Bourgeois. Zur Geistesgeschichte des modernen Kapitalismus*, München und Leipzig: Verlag von Duncker & Humblot.

Sombart, Werner (1915) *The Quintessence of Capitalism: A Study of the History and Psychology of the Modern Business Man*, London: T. Fisher Unwin, Ltd.

Sombart, Werner (1916a) *Der moderne Kapitalismus. Historisch-systematische Darstellung des gesamteuropäischen Wirtschaftslebens von seinen Anfängen bis zur Gegenwart. Erster Band. Einleitung – Die vorkapitalistische Wirtschaft – Die historischen Grundlagen des modernen Kapitalismus*, München und Leipzig: Verlag von Duncker & Humblot.

Sombart, Werner (1916b) *Der moderne Kapitalismus. Historisch-systematische Darstellung des gesamteuropäischen Wirtschaftslebens von seinen Anfängen bis zur Gegenwart. Zweiter Band. Das europäische Wirtschaftsleben im Zeitalter des Frühkapitalismus vornehmlich im 16., 17. und 18. Jahrhundert*, München und Leipzig: Verlag von Duncker & Humblot.

Sombart, Werner (1967) *Luxury and Capitalism*, Ann Arbor: University of Michigan Press.

Sombart, Werner (2001) *The Jews and Modern Capitalism*, Kitchener: Batoche Books.

Sophocles, Antigone [441 BC], Sir Richard Jebb (ed.), Perseus Digital Library, www.perseus.tufts.edu/hopper/

Sotiropoulos, Dimitris P., John Milios and Spyros Lapatsioras (2013) *A Political Economy of Contemporary Capitalism and its Crisis: Demystifying Finance*, London and New York: Routledge.

Spinoza, Baruch (2002) "Political Treatise", in Morgan, Michael L. (ed.), *The Complete Works*, Indianapolis: Hackett Publishing Company: 676–754.

Stalin, Joseph (1975) *Dialectical and Historical Materialism*, Calcutta: Mass Publications.

Stallsmith, Allaire B. (2007) "One Colony, Two Mother Cities: Cretan Agriculture under Venetian and Ottoman Rule", in Davies, Siriol and Jack L. Davis (eds.), *Between Venice and Istanbul: Colonial Landscapes in Early Modern Greece*, Athens: Hesperia Supplements, The American School of Classical Studies at Athens: 151–171.

Ste. Croix, G.E.M., de (1981) *The Class Struggle in the Ancient Greek World*, New York: Cornell University Press.

Ste. Croix, G.E.M., de (1984) "Class in Marx's Conception of History, Ancient and Modern." *New Left Review*, No. 146: 92–111.

Ste. Croix, G.E.M., de (2004) *Athenian Democratic Origins and Other Essays*, Oxford: Oxford University Press.

Sternberg, Fritz (1971). *Der Imperialismus*, Frankfurt/M.: Verlag Neue Kritik.

Strieder, Jakob (1968) *Zur Genesis des modernen Kapitalismus. Forschungen zur Entstehung der großen bürgerlichen Kapitalvermögen am Ausgange des Mittelalters und zu Beginn der Neuzeit, zunächst in Augsburg, Zweite, vermehrte Ausgabe*, New York: Burt Franklin.

Suchting, Wal (1982) "'Productive Forces' and 'Relations of Production' in Marx", *Analyse und Kritik*, No. 4: 159–181.

Sweezy, Paul (2006) "A Critique", in Hilton, Rodney (ed.) *The Transition from Feudalism to Capitalism*, Delhi: Aakar Books: 33–56.

Takahashi, Kohachiro (2006) "A Contribution to the Discussion", in Hilton, Rodney (ed.) *The Transition from Feudalism to Capitalism*, Delhi: Aakar Books: 68–97.

Tawney, Richard Henry (1963) *Religion and the Rise of Capitalism*, New York: Mentor Books.

Teschke, Benno (2003) *The Myth of 1648: Class, Geopolitics and the Making of Modern International Relations*, London and New York: Verso.

Teschke, Benno and Hannes Lacher (2007) "The Changing 'Logics' of Capitalist Competition", *Cambridge Review of International Affairs*, Vol. 20, No. 4: 565–580.

The National Archives (2017) "Getting the vote: Voting rights before 1832", www.nationalarchives.gov.uk/pathways/citizenship/struggle_democracy/getting_vote.htm (accessed October 2, 2017).

Udovitch, Abraham (1970) *Partnership and Profits in Medieval Islam*, Princeton: Princeton University Press.

Vasiliev, Alexander A. (1952) *History of the Byzantine Empire 324–1453*, Madison: The University of Wisconsin Press.

Wallerstein, Immanuel (1974) *The Modern World System*, New York: Academic Press.

Wallerstein, Immanuel (1979) "Aufstieg und künftiger Niedergang des kapitalistischen Weltsystems", in Senghaas, D. (ed.) *Kapitalistische Weltökonomie*, Frankfurt/M.: Suhrkamp Verlag.

Wallerstein, Immanuel (1980) *The Modern World System II*, New York: Academic Press.

Wallerstein, Immanuel (1996) "World System versus World-Systems: A Critique", in Frank, A. G. and B. K. Gills (eds.) *The World System: Five Hundred Years or Five Thousand?*, London and New York: Routledge.

Weber, Max (2001) *The Protestant Ethic and the Spirit of Capitalism*, London and New York: Routledge.

Whitfield, John Humphreys (1966) *Petrarch and the Renascence*, New York: Haskell House.

Wickham, Chris (2015) *Sleepwalking into a New World: The Emergence of Italian City Communes in the Twelfth Century*, Princeton and Oxford: Princeton University Press.

Wolf, Eric R. (1982) *Europe and the People Without History*, Berkeley and Los Angeles: University of California Press.

Wood, Ellen Meiksins (1991) *The Pristine Culture of Capitalism*, London: Verso.

Wood, Ellen Meiksins (2002) *The Origins of Capitalism: A Longer View*, London: Verso.

Wood, Ellen Meiksins (2003) *Empire of Capital*, London and New York: Verso.

Wray, L. Randall (1993) "The Origins of Money and the Development of the Modem Financial System", The Jerome Levy Economics Institute of Bard College and University of Denver, Working Paper No. 86, March.

Zolotas, Georgios I. (1924) *Istoria tis Chiou (History of Chios)*, Vol. B, Athens: Sakellariou.

Index

Printed in the United States
by Baker & Taylor Publisher Services